Instructor's Manual and Test Bank to Accompany

HOW TO DESIGN AND EVALUATE RESEARCH IN EDUCATION

THIRD EDITION

Carl P. Bahneman, Ph. D.

JACK R. FRAENKEL
San Francisco State University

NORMAN E. WALLEN
San Francisco State University

The McGraw-Hill Companies, Inc.

New York St. Louis San Francisco Auckland Bogotá
Caracas Lisbon London Madrid Mexico City Milan Montreal
New Delhi San Juan Singapore Sydney Tokyo Toronto

McGraw-Hill
A Division of The McGraw-Hill Companies

Instructor's Manual and Test Bank to Accompany
HOW TO DESIGN AND EVALUATE
RESEARCH IN EDUCATION Third Edition

ISBN 0-07-021775-0

1 2 3 4 5 6 7 8 9 0 BKM BKM 9 0 9 8 7 6 5

Table of Contents

I.	Introduction	1
II.	Suggested Objectives for a First Course in Educational Research	5
III.	A Sample Course Syllabus	6
IV.	General Suggestions for Teaching a First Course	11
V.	Chapter Tests and Teaching Suggestions	13
VI.	How to Use the Problem Sheets	155
VII.	Two Examples of a Completed Set of Problem Sheets	157
VIII.	Transparency Masters	210
IX.	Answer Key: Chapter Test Questions	241
X.	Two Additional Studies	251

Part One
Introduction

A. Purpose of this manual

This manual has been designed to accompany the textbook, *How to design and evaluate research in education*, by Jack R. Fraenkel and Norman E. Wallen. The text, in turn, has been designed for use in graduate or undergraduate courses in educational research.

B. Components

The manual is divided into nine parts presented in the following order:

Part I. Introduction. Part I identifies the purpose of the manual, briefly describes its contents, and presents an outline of the table of contents of the text. It also summarizes the important design features of the text.

Part II. Suggested Objectives for a First Course in Educational Research. Part II lists a number of objectives suitable for a first course in educational research. This list includes both content and skills objectives.

Part III. A *Sample Course Syllabus.* Part III presents a model syllabus that can either be used as is, or adapted by you to meet your particular instructional needs. A few suggestions are also made about the overall organization of the course.

Part IV. General Suggestions for Teaching the Course. Part IV suggests a number of in-class activities and assignments you can use to help students understand the basic concepts developed in the text.

Part V. Chapter Tests and Teaching Ideas. Part V restates the objectives for each chapter as stated in the textbook, and then identifies the important points to stress in each chapter, offers a few specific ideas for teaching the chapter, suggests some possible answers that might be given for each of the discussion questions found at the end of the chapter, and concludes with a chapter test designed to test students on their understanding and mastery of the chapter content. There are 19 separate tests, one for each chapter; each test begins and ends on a new page so that you can duplicate them if you so desire, or otherwise use them as you deem appropriate.

Part VI. Summary of the Problem Sheets. One of the unique features of the textbook is the use of problem sheets, so designed as to help students prepare a written research proposal. Each problem sheet has been designed to serve a particular purpose, and a summary of the contents of each is presented. When a student has filled out a full set of problem sheets, he or she will have essentially developed a complete research proposal.

Part VII. Two Sample Sets of Completed Problem Sheets. Part VII presents two examples of a completed set of these problem sheets as they were prepared by students in one of our classes.

Part VIII. Transparency Masters. Part VIII includes some 40 figures and tables that can be xeroxed and made into transparencies for use with an overhead projector during lectures or classroom discussions.

Part IX. Answer Key to Chapter Test Questions. Part IX includes the correct answers to each of the questions for the Chapter Tests.

Part X. Two Additonal Studies.

C. Textbook Table of Contents

PART ONE: INTRODUCTION TO RESEARCH
1. The Nature of Research

PART TWO: THE BASICS OF EDUCATIONAL RESEARCH
2. The Research Problem
3. Ethics and Research
4. Variables and Hypotheses
5. Reviewing the Literature
6. Sampling
7. Instrumentation
8. Validity and Reliability
9. Descriptive Statistics
10. Inferential Statistics
11. Statistics in Perspective
12. Internal Validity

PART THREE: RESEARCH METHODOLOGIES
13. Experimental Research
14. Correlational Research
15. Causal-Comparative Research
16. Survey Research
17. Content Analysis Research
18. Qualitative Research
19. Historical Research

PART FOUR: PREPARING RESEARCH PROPOSALS AND REPORTS
20. Writing Research Proposals and Reports

PART FIVE: RESEARCH BY PRACTITIONERS
21. Doing Research in Schools

APPENDICES
Appendix A: Table of random numbers
Appendix B: Normal curve table
Appendix C: Chi-square distribution
Appendix D: Illustration of the Statistical Procedures Described in Chapter Eleven

Glossary
Suggestions for Further Reading
Index

D. Design of the Text

The material in *How to Design and Evaluate Research in Education* is organized and presented in several ways. The presentation of information is accomplished through written, visual, and tabular means. Understanding of the information presented is enhanced through the use of a clear and direct writing style, the provision of many examples and figures to illustrate important ideas, the inclusion of discussion-type questions at the end of each chapter, and a summary of each chapter's main points.

Tables, graphs, charts, and other figures are presented when their use helps to convey information more concisely or more effectively than could be done in narrative form alone. We have made a deliberate effort to present information, whether in written, visual, or tabular form, as interestingly and appealingly as possible.

We have tried to use the many figures and tables as teaching devices. The various figures and tables have been interwoven with the textual material to enhance the attractiveness, interest, and appeal of the text. The illustrative material does more than that, however. It complements the text material and heightens students' understanding of what has been written. It also clarifies, illuminates or expands on an idea presented in the written material. All illustrations relate to some idea or concept that is being described in the text.

In addition to the many figures and tables to be found throughout the text, several learning aids have been provided within, and at the end of, individual chapters.

•*Overview.* Each chapter begins with an overview paragraph that introduces students to what the chapter is about.

•*Objectives.* Each chapter includes a set of enabling objectives which state, in behavioral terms, what students should be able to do after they have finished reading the chapter.

•*Main Points.* Each chapter concludes with a summary of the main ideas and concepts developed in the chapter.

•*Discussion Questions.* Each chapter includes a number of open-ended questions for students to discuss to enhance their understanding of the important concepts and ideas, as well as the nuances, of educational research.

•*Research Exercises/Problem Sheets.* At the end of each chapter can be found a "research exercise" for students to engage in as a way of checking their understanding of the chapter and preparing their own research proposal. Following the research exercise is a "problem sheet" that students can complete. When they have completed the entire set of problem sheets, they will have developed a research proposal of their own.

•*Sample Studies.* Chapters 13-19 include an example of a study that illustrates the kind of research described and discussed in the corresponding chapter.

•*Study Critiques.* Each of the studies in Chapters 13-19 is critiqued by the authors of the text in order to point out that all studies have both strengths and weaknesses, and to illustrate the process of critically evaluating research reports.

•*Student Proposal.* Chapter Twenty includes an example of a complete research proposal prepared by a student in one of our classes that illustrates what can be accomplished by students who use the text.

•*Research by Practitioners.* Examples of how small-scale research studies might be done in real-life classrooms are presented in Chapter Twenty-One.

•*Glossary.* A complete glossary of important terms discussed in the text can be found beginning on page 579.

E. Organization of Each Chapter

Each chapter, although dealing with different content, follows the same basic format:

•An introductory paragraph that sets the stage for the information contained in the chapter.

•A list of chapter objectives, which specify what the chapter intends to accomplish.

•A number of sections that make up the body of the chapter. Each section contains information related to the overall topic of the chapter.

•A list of "main points" which draw together and summarize the key ideas and concepts developed in the chapter.

•Several questions for students to discuss.

Part Two
Suggested Objectives for a First Course in Educational Research

A. Content Objectives

1. To understand and be able to explain briefly the fundamental concepts (e.g., hypothesis, sampling, replication, external validity) of educational research.

2. To understand and be able to explain the specific procedures (e.g., formulating a research problem, selecting a sample, designing a research instrument, making a scatterplot) involved in the conduct of educational research.

B. Skill Objectives

3. To be able to explain how to perform each of the following procedures (and, if asked, actually perform them):

- Formulate a research problem
- State a research hypothesis related to the research problem
- Identify variables in a hypothesis
- Write a justification for a hypothesis
- Define the terms of a hypothesis consitutively and operationally
- Conduct a review of the research literature on a given topic
- Locate or develop an instrument to test a hypothesis
- Perform a reliability and validity check on a research instrument
- Identify and seek to control threats to the internal and external validity of a research investigation
- Collect, summarize, and analyze research data using the appropriate instruments and tests
- Write up the findings of a research investigation
- Read a research report with understanding

This manual is designed to help you use the textbook effectively so that students can attain each of the content and skills objectives listed above to the maximum of their abilities.

Part Three
A Sample Course Syllabus

(Note to instructor): This syllabus is offered only as a sample for you to consider. It can be modified to suit your particular situation.

Course Number:_________ **Term:**_______________
Course Name:___________ **Room:**_______________
Professor:_______________ **Time:**_________________
Office hours:____________

SEMINAR IN EDUCATIONAL RESEARCH

Syllabus

This course is a graduate-level seminar, required as a part of all Master's programs in the School of Education. Emphasis in the course is on giving students a basic introduction to the fundamentals of educational research--what it involves, what types exist, and how to design and conduct such research. No prerequisites exist, other than graduate level standing.

I. Required Text.

Fraenkel, Jack R., & Wallen, Norman E. (1996). **How to design and evaluate research in education (3rd Ed).** New York: McGraw-Hill. Available for purchase in the bookstore.

II. Class Procedures and Activities.

Since this class is designated a seminar, it will be conducted so as to maximize discussion, not only between instructor and students, but also among students. To facilitate this intention, most class sessions will include one or more of the following:

-illustration, using visuals, of key research concepts developed through assigned readings;

-identification and discussion of these concepts in existing, published research studies;

-analysis and discussion of selected problems and puzzles involving these concepts;

-discussion of the design and development of individual student research proposals;

-analysis and critique of existing research.

Both large and small-group class sessions will be held. On some occasions, in order to promote a more in-depth analysis and discussion of selected problems and/or studies, students will work in small groups, and even, on occasion, in dyads. When information needs to be presented or discussed that is of value to the entire class, the class may meet as a whole, and then break into smaller groups for further discussion and application. Students also are encouraged to see the instructor during office hours, as listed above.

III. Topics Covered in the Course.

- Types of educational research
- Research questions and hypotheses
- Ethics in research
- Definitions of research terms
- The justification of research studies
- Variables in research
- Populations and samples
- Sampling procedures
- Research designs
- Types of instruments researchers use
- Instrument reliability and validity
- Internal validity
- External validity
- The writing of a research proposal
- Doing research in schools and other real-life settings

IV. Reading Assignments.

The reading for this course is basically of two types: (a) the reading of material in the textbook; and (b) the reading of handouts given out by the instructor. The handouts are of various kinds--studies taken from the research literature, interesting articles about new developments in research, puzzles, problems, or games on occasion, and other selections the instructor has found help to enrich the substance of the course and make it more enjoyable to students. The amount of reading to be done is not heavy; normally you will have one chapter per week to read in the textbook, plus one (short) study every other week during the latter part of the semester.

V. Overall Structure of the Course.

In the first part of the course, you will learn the basic concepts of educational research through reading about them in the textbook and discussing them in class. In the second part of the course, you will further your understanding of these concepts by reading some actual studies, and preparing a brief literature review. As an ongoing project, you will be completing an individual research proposal.

VI. Problem Sheets.

From time to time, you will be asked to complete various guideline sheets (called "problem sheets") to help you understand the fundamentals of research, and to apply them to your own work. A copy of the problem sheet that corresponds to a particular chapter can be found at the end of that chapter in the textbook. Usually, time will be allowed in class to work on these sheets, and to discuss them. They are quite short, and past classes have found them most helpful.

VII. **Class Meetings.**

The breakdown for the nature of the meetings of the class is as follows:

Week	Topic	Reading in text	Problem Sheet/Assignment (Hand in on date listed)
1	Orientation: Nature and types of research; Research problems and questions	Chapters 1-2	none
2	Ethics and research	Chapter 3:	Problem Sheets #1-2
3	Variables and Hypotheses	Chapter 4	Problem Sheets #3-4
4	The literature review	Chapter 5	Problem Sheet #5
5	Sampling	Chapter 6	Problem Sheet #6
6	Instrumentation	Chapter 7	Problem Sheet #7
7	Validity and reliability	Chapter 8	Problem Sheet #8
8	Descriptive statistics	Chapter 9	Problem Sheet #9
9	Inferential statistics and Statistics in perspective	Chapters 10-11	Problem Sheets #10 and 11
10	Internal validity	Chapter 12	Problem Sheet #12

11	Experimental research	Chapter 13	Problem Sheet #13 (Note: For Problem Sheets #13-19, you submit only the sheet that deals with the type of study that you are planning.)
12	Causal-comparative and correlational research	Chapters 14-15	Problem Sheet #14 or #15 (if planning one of these types of research)
13	Survey and content analysis research	Chapters 16-17	Problem Sheet #16 or #17 (if planning one of these types of research)
14	Qualitative and historical research	Chapters 18-19	Problem Sheet #18 or 19 (if planning one of these types of research)
15	Proposal and report writing	Chapter 20	**Proposal due**
16	Research in schools and other institutions	Chapter 21	--

VIII. Requirements.

•Completion of assigned reading. It is important to have read the assigned material by the date due, so that you can fully understand, and participate in, the class discussions.

•Participation in class discussions. Since the class is run as a seminar, we want, and need, everyone's input. Each student is expected to help in the development of other students' projects, and to be helped in return. Furthermore, much classwork is going to require that students work together and help each other.

•Attendance at all class meetings as scheduled. This is very important! You are expected to be in class. Much of the cause of difficulty which some students have experienced in the past has been due to the fact that they missed class. When a student misses class, he or she misses an opportunity to check understanding of the concepts being developed in the course, and to ask appropriate questions.

in Chapter 5. In essence, you locate, read, and summarize what research has already been done on a problem or topic, and hand it in for credit. We will talk about this more as the semester progresses.

•Critique a published study in your field. When you critique a study, you do more than just summarize it, you also identify the strengths and weaknesses in it. To be able to critique a study intelligently, however, you have to know something about research. Hence this assignment will not be due until we have completed the first part of the course which deals with the fundamentals of research. We shall talk more about the nature of this assignment later in the semester.

•Design a research proposal for a study. One of the best ways to learn about research is to think about doing it, and hence the major assignment in the course is to design a proposal for a research investigation that you would be able to conduct. (The best way to learn research is probably to actually do a small piece of research. Time constraints prevent this option, however, and hence you will be asked to do the next best thing--prepare a research **proposal for** such a study.) The research you design may be any one of several types, all of which will be discussed and explained early on in the course. Many students find this to be the most enjoyable and interesting part of the course. To help you prepare for this assignment, you will be given a number of **problem sheets** which will teach you how to design the proposal. Specific details and guidelines for doing this project will be handed out later in the semester.

Part Four
General Suggestions for Teaching a First Course

A course in educational research is one that students approach with considerable anxiety. Hence anything an instructor can do to help relieve that anxiety and instill confidence in students is well worthwhile. Partly this can be done by informing students of the course requirements and assignments at the very first meeting of the class, and making sure they are clear to all. In addition, however, we recommend that instructors engage students in a variety of activities in order to maximize involvement and understanding and minimize boredom. Accordingly, here are a number of possibilities for you to consider:

- ask students to prepare questions they would ask of other students to help them understand the basic ideas or key points developed in various chapters.

- discuss, in class, one or more of the questions to be found at the end of each of the chapters in the text.

- have students identify similarities and differences among the various ways of doing research described in Chapters 13-19 in the text.

- ask students to suggest alternative ways to investigate the same research problem, and then discuss with them which of the suggested ways they think would be most appropriate, and why.

- have students summarize the approach used by the authors of the research studies presented in Chapters 13-19.

- have students write a brief critique of a research study found in the literature.

- have individual students role-play the author of one of the studies in described in Chapters 13-19 in the text "justifying" the educational significance of his or her research to the rest of the class.

- answer student questions concerning material in the text and/or problems they have encountered in their preparation of the problem sheets.

- use any of the transparencies included in this manual to illustrate key concepts or ideas discussed in the text.

- present a lecture on recent developments in educational research to supplement the material in the text.

•have students work in small groups to discuss their progress in developing their own research proposals.

•have students describe problems (illustrating them using the chalkboard, if possible) they are having in developing their own research proposals, and ask the class as a whole to give feedback and suggestions as to how to alleviate these problems.

•have students locate and describe to the class an example of a research study they feel is particularly well done, and why.

Part Five
Chapter Tests and Teaching Suggestions

CHAPTER ONE
THE NATURE OF RESEARCH

Chapter Objectives

Reading this chapter should enable students to:

• *explain* what is meant by the term "educational research," and *give at least two examples* of the kinds of topics educational researchers might investigate.

• *explain* why a knowledge of scientific research methodology can be of value to educators.

• *name* and *give an example* of at least four ways of knowing other than the method used by scientists.

• *explain* what is meant by the term "scientific method."

• *give an example* of at least six different types of research methodologies used by educational researchers.

• *describe* briefly the basic components involved in the research process.

Points to Stress

1. Why educational research is important.
2. How the scientific method differs from other ways of knowing.
3. Different kinds of methodology used by educational researchers.
4. The features that all research methodologies have in common.

Teaching Suggestions

1. Hand out the course syllabus, explain how you intend to conduct the class, and answer any questions students have about course procedures or assignments.

2. Make a transparency of "Research Exercise One" (a master for this and other transparencies can be found in the section entitled "Transparency Masters" later in this manual) for display on an overhead projector. Explain that this is an example of what a problem sheet looks like, and that they will be asked to complete one after they have read each chapter. Point out that they will find them at the end of the chapters, and that by completing all of them, they will thereby prepare a complete research proposal by the end of the course.

3. Go over each section of the text, pointing out the distinguishing features (i.e., the overview, objectives, figures and tables, important points, and questions for discussions). Point out how each has been designed to help students learn the fundamental concepts of research.

4. Discuss your examination policy if you intend to give examinations, as well as any other assignments for the term you intend to have.

5. Make a transparency of the transparency master Figure 1.3, "The Research Process" (see the section entitled "Transparency Masters" later in

this manual) for display on an overhead projector. Point out to the class that although each of the steps shown are important ingredients in the research process, they do not always occur in the order shown (hence our drawing of the dotted lines in the figure). Ask students to suggest which steps they think might occur early and which later in the process, and why.

6. Make a chart on the board labeled "Similarities and Differnces in Research Methologies". Ask students to suggest any similarities and/or differences they notice after reading the section of research methodologies in the text) pages 8-13.

7. Have the class review the section on general Research Types, pages 13-14 in the text. Ask students if they can give an example of a descriptive, an associational, or an intervention-type study. Encourage them to start thinking about the kind of research study they intend to design.

Answers to Discussion Questions

(Note to Instructor: Many of these "Questions for Discussion" are open-ended in nature and have no right answer. Students should be encouraged to offer as many alternative answers as they think plausible, and to explain the reasons for the answers they give.)

1. Listed below are several research questions. What methodology do you think would be the most appropriate to investigate each?

a. What do students think are the least popular course in the high school curriculum, and why? *(survey)*

b. How do parents feel about the elementary school counseling program? *(interview or survey)*

c. How can Tom Adams be helped to learn to read? *(case study)*

d. Do students who have high scores on reading tests also have high scores on writing tests? *(correlational)*

e. Does team teaching help or hinder student learning? *(experiment or causal/comparative)*

f. What sorts of activities are of most interest to slow learners? *(qualitative)*

g. What effect does the gender of a counselor have on how he or she is received by counselees? *(causal-comparative)*

h. In what ways were the kinds of bills passed into law during the administrations of Richard Nixon and George Bush similar and different? *(historical)*

2. Can any of the above questions be investigated other than scientifically? Answer: *All of the questions could be investigated other than scientifically (e.g., through guessing, by asking uninformed or ignorant people, by haphazard, informal questioning, etc..), but the answers so obtained would probably not be very reliable.*

3. Can you think of some other ways of knowing besides those mentioned in this chapter? What are they? What, if any, are the limitations of these methods? Answer: *Revelation (that is, knowledge revealed to one by God) is a method of knowing that some people believe yields reliable knowledge. The*

limitation of such knowledge is that it is private in nature, and cannot be publicly substantiated.

4. What other questions, besides those mentioned in the text, can you suggest that would not lend themselves to scientific research? Answer: *Answers here will vary. Encourage all responses, but ask the students who propose the questions to explain why they think the question(s) cannot be researched scientifically.*

5. Many people seem to be uneasy about the idea of research, particularly research in schools. How would you explain this? Answer: *A fear of research has many causes: the fear of new ideas, the belief that some research procedures may be harmful or engender too great a degree of risk on the part of participants, a preference for other ways of knowing, the threat to established beliefs, etc.*

6. To what extent do you agree with the allegations raised by critical resarchers? Can you suggest any examples that might be used to support their position? Answer: *Examples might include: (a) the long term effects of comparing different ethnic, gender and age groups with respect to abilities, attitudes and beliefs; (b) selectivity in the characteristics studied as outcomes of schooling (e.g., algebra rather than altruism); (c) funding of research by government or private foundatations.*

TEST FOR CHAPTER ONE

1. A major difficulty with knowledge based on personal sensory experience is that it:
   (a) is difficult to obtain
   (b) is incomplete
   (c) requires training
   (d) is always distorted

2. Knowledge arrived at by consensus or majority agreement:
   (a) is the most trustworthy of all types of knowledge
   (b) is to be avoided
   (c) takes too long too obtain
   (d) is often in error

3. Knowledge that is based on expert opinion:
   (a) cannot be trusted
   (b) is the best we can get
   (c) is limited by the expert's experience
   (d) is scientific

4. Knowledge based on logical reasoning:
   (a) has specific prerequisites
   (b) does not apply to educational problems
   (c) is too difficult to be useful
   (d) is infallible

5. The essential characteristic of the scientific method is:
   (a) the testing of hypotheses
   (b) the identification of a problem
   (c) its public nature
   (d) the design of experiments

6. An investigator wishes to determine how much coverage current high school history texts give to the contributions of Black Americans to our history. She should conduct:
   (a) historical research
   (b) case studies
   (c) content analysis
   (d) experimental research

7-13. Which of the following types of research is the most appropriate for each of the research questions in items 7 through 13:

(a) experimental research
(b) correlational research
(c) causal-comparative research
(d) survey research:

_____ 7. Does alcoholism in a parent affect a child's self-esteem?

_____ 8. Do older college students have higher achievement?

_____ 9. Do teachers of high school biology courses discuss ethical issues as a part of the biology curriculum?

____ 10. Does a pre-operative visit from a speech therapist improve post-operative alaryngeal speech?

____ 11. Do ethnic minority college students view general education courses as useful?

____ 12. Do women with higher career satisfaction get along better with their fathers?

____ 13. Do relaxation techniques improve attention of learning handicapped students?

14-20. Which of the following research methodologies is most appropriate for each of the research questions in items 14-20?
(a) Correlational research
(b) Ethnographic research
(c) Historical research
(d) Survey research

____ 14. What are the characteristics of schools that have high morale?

____ 15. How do students with impaired vision feel about wearing glasses?

____ 16. What do gifted students do during study hall periods?

____ 17. Why is algebra taught in grade nine?

____ 18. Is counseling more successful if students like their counselor?

____ 19. How much do students know about the effects of particular drugs?

____ 20. Do anxious students do more poorly on tests than non-anxious students?

21-25. Which general research type best describes each of the questions asked in items 21 through 25?

(a) Descriptive
(b) Associational
(c) Intervention

21. Which subjects are best liked by American students?

22. Is the literature-based method effective in teaching reading?

23. Do first graders show more creativity if they like their teachers?

24. Does in-service training improve teaching?

25. What kind of students elect courses in ethnic studies?

CHAPTER TWO
THE RESEARCH PROBLEM

Chapter Objectives

Reading this chapter should enable students to:

- *give some examples* of potential research problems in education.
- *formulate* a research question.
- *distinguish* between researchable and non-researchable questions.
- *name* five characteristics which good research questions possess.
- *explain* what is meant, in research, by the term "relationship," and *give an example* of a research question which involves a relationship.
- *describe* three ways to clarify unclear research questions.
- *give an example* of an operational definition, and *explain* how such definitions differ from other kinds of definitions.

Points to Stress

1. How researchable questions differ from those that are non-researchable.
2. Why it is important, if possible, to look for possible relationships among data.
3. Different ways to define terms, and how operational definitions, in particular, are helpful in clarification.

Teaching Suggestions

1. Collect Problem Sheet #1 from the class. Ask students if they have any further questions about the problem sheets.

2. Many students are initially confused as to what makes a question researchable. We suggest you spend some time in class providing examples of researchable and non-researchable questions in order to clarify the distinction (see p. 26 in the text). As a further help in this regard, you might want to discuss question #1 on page 35 of the text with students in class.

3. Students often have trouble defining terms operationally. It may be helpful, therefore, to review the section on operational definitions in the text (pp. 29-30) in class, making sure that students understand which of the definitions on page 30 are operational and why. A helpful exercise here is to list a number of terms on the chalkboard and ask various students (either individually or working in small groups) to define them operationally.

4. Make a transparency of Figure 2.3 (a master for this and other transparencies can be found in the section entitled "Transparency Masters" later in this manual) for display on an overhead projector. Ask students to explain why Figure B depicts a relationship while Figure A does not. Explain to them why this is the case if they are not clear (see p. 34 in the text).

5. Break the class down into small groups to discuss and begin work on Problem Sheet #2.

Answers to Discussion Questions

(Note to Instructor: Many of these "Questions for Discussion" are open-ended in nature and have no right answer. Students should be encouraged to offer as many alternative answers as they think plausible, and to explain the reasons for the answers they give.)

1. Listed below are a series of questions. Think how a researcher could collect information (from friends, colleagues, students, or others) to help answer each question, at least in part. Could data be collected on all of these questions? If so, how? If not, why not?

a. Does client-centered or traditional therapy produce more satisfaction in clients? Answer: *Compare the satisfaction of two groups of counselees after a period of time (one group being exposed to client-centered and the other group being exposed to traditional therapy). The researcher would need to devise some way to measure "satisfaction," however, perhaps by having the members of each group simply say how satisfied they were with their therapy experience.*

b. How might staff morale be improved? Answer: *Send out a written questionnaire, or conduct personal interviews with the members of the staff with regard to the question.*

c. Should psychology be required of all students in graduate school? Answer: *This question, as stated, cannot be researched, since there is no way to collect data to answer the question. However, a researcher could ask people whether they think psychology should be required in graduate school.*

d. Do students learn more from a teacher of the same gender? Answer: *Compare the achievement of students who have been taught by a teacher of the same gender with students who have been taught by a teacher of the opposite gender. The researcher should do his or her best to keep as many other conditions and characteristics (e.g., grade level, age, ethnicity, etc. of students,;experience, age, ethnicity, etc. of teacher, and so forth) as similar as possible, however.*

2. What relationship (if there is one) is suggested in each of the above questions? Answer: *In 1a, the relationship suggested is between amount of satisfaction and type of therapy. No relationship is suggested in 1b and 1c. In 1d, the suggested relationship is between amount of learning and gender.*

3. Here are three examples of research questions. How would you rank them (1=highest) for clarity? for significance? Why?

a. How many students in the sophomore class signed up for a course in driver training this semester?

b. Why do so many students in the district say they dislike English?

c. Is inquiry or lecture more effective in teaching social studies?

Answer: *With regard to clarity, we would rank them a-c-b. With regard to significance, we would rank them c-b-a.*

TEST FOR CHAPTER TWO

1. Which of the following factors should not influence the decision when one is selecting a topic or problem for research?
   (a) Will solution of the problem advance knowledge in my field?
   (b) Will I be able to prove that my previously held beliefs are true?
   (c) Will the study lead to the development of other investigations?
   (d) Is the topic or problem amenable to research?

2. In conducting research, which of the following steps should generally be taken first?
   (a) Deciding on kinds of data to collect
   (b) Preparation of a summary of related research
   (c) Formulation of a working hypothesis
   (d) Formulation of the problem to be solved

3. Operational definitions are encouraged in research in order to:
   (a) conform to the requirement of statistical analysis
   (b) increase the probability that experiments will succeed
   (c) make terms used in a study as explicit as possible
   (d) make educational research more easily understood by laypersons

4. "In this study interest in science is represented by the sciences area score on the Occupational Interest Inventory, Grades 7 to Adult, McGraw-Hill, Inc., 1956." The preceding statement illustrates a(n):
   (a) operational definition
   (b) hypothesis
   (c) constitutive definition
   (d) research problem

5. Which of the following would be the least legitimate reason for conducting research on methods of teaching French?
   (a) You want to test certain deductions derived from a theory of language instruction.
   (b) Your school needs to evaluate its present French teaching methods.
   (c) You know in your own mind which method of teaching French is best, but lack empirical evidence of its superiority.
   (d) There are contradictions and inconsistencies in the results of previous research.

6. Which of the following is the most frequent error made by graduate students in education in formulating statements of the research problem?
   (a) Selecting a problem that is too broad
   (b) Selecting a problem that is trivial
   (c) Basing the problem statement on faulty assumptions
   (d) Stating a problem that has already been solved

7. Which of the following statements can be checked by means of scientific inquiry?
   (a) All high schools should teach driver education.
   (b) Driver education is more important than drug abuse education.
   (c) Driver education is an ideal subject for all students to take.
   (d) The accident rate of driver education graduates is lower than the accident rate of those who have not had driver education.

8. Which of the following definitions of the term "aggressive behavior" is operational?
   (a) Any act of hitting, shoving, or grabbing
   (b) Any behavior intended to cause injury to others
   (c) An "aggression" score on the XYZ behavior scale
   (d) Misbehavior resulting in removal from the classroom

9. A constitutive definition is one that:
   (a) uses other terms to explain meaning as concisely as possible
   (b) explains meaning by the use of examples
   (c) is obtained from a published dictionary
   (d) has previously been defined by another researcher or scholar

10. The authors argue that studies investigating relations are generally of more value because they:
   (a) make a greater contribution to knowledge
   (b) make it easier to clarify the study
   (c) are the starting place for all research
   (d) simplify data analysis

11. Justification for a study is generally based on the study's contribution:
   (a) to general knowledge
   (b) to professional practice
   (c) to theory
   (d) all of the above

12. Which of the following is an appropriate justification for a study describing drug use in high school?
   (a) This study will determine the extent to which specific drugs are being used by high school students.
   (b) The researcher believes that drug use is the most important problem facing the schools today.
   (c) This study will determine which drugs should be given priority in informational efforts.
   (d) Student dropout rates and poor achievement is a major concern in society today.

13. Which of the following fictitious diagrams shows a relationship between handedness and gender?

(a)

	left	right
	xx	xxx
male	xx	xxx
female	xx	xxx
	xx	xxx

(c)

	left	right
	xx	xxx
male	xx	xxx
female	xxx	xx
	xxx	xx

(b)

	left	right
	xx	xx
male	xx	xx
female	xxx	xxx
	xxx	xxx

(d)

	left	right
	xx	xx
male	xxx	xxx
female	xx	xx
	xxx	xxx

14. Which of the following is the most suitable as a statement of a research problem?

(a) What are the causes of the problems of high school dropouts in city schools?
(b) How do eight- to ten-year old Puerto Rican children in New York City respond to crises involving serious illness of other members of their families?
(c) How do young children express themselves?
(d) How can the problem of retardation in arithmetic be solved?

15. This research problem: "What is the vocabulary level of the history books, both text and reference sources, used in the secondary schools of the United States?" is:

(a) a good research problem for a beginner to use to get started in research
(b) far too broad
(c) much too narrow
(d) an area of concern for which no available research method is appropriate

16. Why is personal interest generally considered insufficient justification for a research study in education?

(a) Because the time and energy of other people is required
(b) Because the researcher's bias would make the study worthless
(c) Because such a study is likely to be trivial
(d) Because researchers must be disinterested in the topics they study

---

CHAPTER THREE
ETHICS AND RESEARCH

Chapter Objectives

Reading this chapter should enable students to:

- *Describe* briefly what is meant by "ethical" research.
- *Describe* briefly three important ethical principles recommended for researchers to follow.
- *State* the basic question with regard to ethics that researchers need to ask before beginning a study.
- *State* the three questions researchers need to address in order to protect participants in research from harm.
- *Describe* the procedures researchers must follow in order to ensure confidentiality of data collected in a research investigation.
- *Describe* when it might be appropriate to deceive participants in a research investigation and the researcher's responsibilities if such is the case in doing so.
- *Describe* the special considerations involved when doing research with children.

Points to Stress

1. The primary issue of "harm" to subjects.
2. The meaning and importance of confidentiality in research.
3. The meaning and importance of deception in research, and when it is justified.
4. The requirements for procedural review.
5. Special considerations when doing research with children.

Teaching Suggestions

1. Collect Problem Sheet #2 from the class and answer any questions students may have about it.

2. To help students become aware of the ethical dimensions in research, ask the class to comment about the ethical implications (if any) they see in each of the research ideas in question #1 on page 46 of the text. Follow this up with a discussion of question #2 on that page. The question of ethics is one that most students find fascinating, and one they are most interested in discussing.

3. Review each of the examples of research studies presented on pp. 41-43 of the text. Ask students if they agree with our assessment of the possible (a) harm; (b) confidentiality; and (c) deception involved in each, and/or if they see other possibilities that should be mentioned.

4. Let volunteers describe their potential research questions and what they have in mind at this point. See if other members of the class foresee any ethical problems.

5. Break the class down into small groups to discuss and begin work on Problem Sheet #3.

Answers to Discussion Questions

1. Here are three descriptions of ideas for research. Which (if any) might have some ethical problems? Why?

a. A researcher is interested in investigating the effects of diet on physical development. He designs a study in which two groups are to be compared. Both groups are composed of 11-year olds. One group is to be given an enriched diet, high in vitamins, that has been shown to have a strengthening effect on laboratory animals. A second group is not be be given this diet. The groups are to be selected from all the 11-year olds in an elementary school near the university where the researcher teaches. Answer: *The ethical problem here is that one group would be deprived of a possible helpful treatment.*

b. A researcher is interested in the effects of music on attention span. She designs an experimental study in which two similar high school government classes are to be compared. For a 5-week period, one class has classical music played softly in the background as the teacher lectures and holds class discussions on the Civil War (the period of history the class is studying during this time). The other class studies the same material and participates in the same activities as the first class, but does not have any music played during the 5 weeks. Answer: *There does not seem to be any ethical problem here, since the participants are not at risk, and the deception is minor.*

c. A researcher is interested in the effects of drugs on human beings. He asks for subjects from the warden of the local penitentiary to participate in an experiment. The warden assigns several prisoners to participate in the experiment, but does not tell them what it is about. The prisoners are injected with a number of drugs whose effects are unknown. Their reactions to the drug are then described in detail by the researcher. Answer: *This would appear to be unethical, as the possibility of serious harm to participants is likely, and they have not been informed of such.*

2. Which, if any, of the above studies would be exempt under the revised guidelines shown in Table 3.1? Answer: *We think study #2 would be exempt. Study #3 clearly would not be, and Study #1 probably would not be.*

3. Can you suggest a research study that would present ethical problems if done with children, but not if done with adults? Answer: *Studies inquiring into personal behavior, family relations, and/or religious or philosophical issues are much more questionable the younger the respondent.*

4. Are there any research questions that should *not* be investigated in schools? If so, why not? Answer: *In our opinion, only those that might bring either physical or psychological harm to students.*

TEST FOR CHAPTER THREE

1. A researcher who decides to deceive participants in a study should:
   (a) determine that the study cannot be done without deception
   (b) argue convincingly that the importance of the study justifies deception
   (c) undeceive participants as soon as possible
   (d) all of the above

2. The legal requirement that consent must be obtained:
   (a) applies to virtually all educational research
   (b) can be ignored in educational research
   (c) does not apply to most educational research
   (d) applies only to experimental studies in educational research

3. Whether or not a given study has the possibility of causing harm to participants:
   (a) can be determined by examining the pertinent legal documents
   (b) must be determined by a review board established by the sponsoring institution
   (c) depends on whether or not any experimentation is involved
   (d) depends on the researcher's definition of harm

4. Ethical behavior of educational researchers is guided primarily by:
   (a) laws governing research practices
   (b) rules established by local school districts or other local agencies
   (c) the nature of the research study
   (d) ethical standards established by the profession

5. Confidentiality requires that:
   (a) it be impossible to connect data to individuals
   (b) all data be collected anonymously
   (c) access to collected data be limited to research staff
   (d) participants not be asked for personal information

6. Which of the following groups are *not* protected by laws governing privileged communication?
   (a) Physicians
   (b) Attorneys
   (c) Clergy
   (d) Researchers

7. Informed consent to serve as a subject in research requires the signing of a document which states:
   (a) the purpose of the study
   (b) that the subject may end participation at any time
   (c) the probable risks involved
   (d) all of the above

8. Which of the following does not qualify as being "exempt" from risk?
   (a) Signed questionnaires describing financial status
   (b) Attitude scales pertaining to religion
   (c) Interviews regarding drug usage
   (d) Observation of anti-social behaviors

9. Research with minors presents special ethical concerns because:
   (a) they are less likely to cooperate
   (b) they are harder to get information from
   (c) they are less likely to understand what is being asked of them
   (d) they are more likely to be harmed

10. If a study involves risk to the participants, the researcher is *not* required to:
   (a) explain unknown risks
   (b) clarify all procedures to be used
   (c) remain available after participation should concerns arise
   (d) allow the participant to withdraw any time he or she wishes to do so

---

CHAPTER FOUR
VARIABLES AND HYPOTHESES

Chapter Objectives

Reading this chapter should enable students to:

•*explain* what is meant by the term "variable," and *state* at least five variables that might be investigated by educational researchers.

•*distinguish* between a quantitative and a categorical variable.

•*explain* how independent and dependent variables are related.

•*explain* how a variable differs from a constant.

•*explain* what a hypothesis is, and *formulate* at least two hypotheses that might be investigated in education.

•*name* at least two advantages and two disadvantages of stating research questions as hypotheses.

•*distinguish* between directional and non-directional hypotheses, and *give an example* of each.

Points to Stress

1. The difference between a variable and a constant.
2. The different kinds of variables that exist.
3. How a research hypothesis differs from a research question.
4. The difference between directional and non-directional hypotheses.

Teaching Suggestions

1. Collect Problem Sheet #3 from the class and answer any questions students may have about it.

2. Discuss with students the importance of studying relationships (see pp. 49-50 in the text). Have the class review the list of questions on page 49, pointing out that none of these questions involve relationships. You might ask some students to see if they can rephrase any of these questions so that they do involve relationships. You also might want to discuss question #1 on page 61 with the class at this point.

3. The concept of "variable" is of crucial importance in the study of research, yet it is one that many students have trouble with. Thus it is worth spending some time on the concept in class. You might want to review the material on pages 51-55 that deals with different types of variables. Of help in this regard is to go over discussion question #5 on page 61 of the text. Another possibility is to have a number of students name either a quantitative or categorical variable (e.g. "enthusiasm," "church preference," etc.) and ask other students to say what kind of variable it is.

4. List a number of research questions on the board (or ask that some students volunteer to do so). Have the class try to restate these questions as hypotheses.

5. To help students distinguish between directional and non-directional hypotheses, ask students to work together in small groups to try to complete discussion question #3 on page 61 of the text. Have each group pick a spokesperson to read some of the hypotheses they develop.

6. Break the class down into small groups to discuss and begin work on Problem Sheet #4.

Answers to Discussion Questions

(Note to Instructor: Many of these "Questions for Discussion" are open-ended in nature and have no right answer. Students should be encouraged to offer as many alternative answers as they think plausible, and to explain the reasons for the answers they give.)

1. Here are several research questions. Which ones suggest relationships?

a. How many students are enrolled in the sophomore class this year?

b. As the reading level of a text passage increases, does the number of errors students make in prounouning words in the passage increase?

c. Do individuals who see themselves as socially "attractive" expect their romantic partners also to be (as judged by others) socially attractive?

d. What does the faculty dislike about the new English curriculum?

e Who is the brightest student in the senior class?

f. Will students who score above the 90th percentile on a standardized reading test also score above the 90th percentile on a standardized writing test?

g. Which political party contains the most Protestants--the Democrats or the Republicans?

Answers: *(a) No ; (b) Yes ; (c) Yes ; (d) No ; (e) No ; (f) Yes; (g) Yes.*

2. What kinds of variables can you identify in each of the above questions?

Answer: *There are no variables in questions a and e. In d, reasons will probably vary, but there is no second variable. The variables in (b) are (1) the reading level of a text passage and (2) the number of errors made in pronouncing words. The variables in (c) are (1) the perception of one's own attractiveness and (2) the expectations one has that one's romantic partners be attractive. The variables in (f) are (1) the scores on a standardized reading test and (2) the scores on a standardized writing test. The variables in (g) are (1) the number of Protestants and (2) political party.*

3. See if you can restate each of the questions in #1 as (a) a directional hypothesis; (b) a non-directional hypothesis.

Answers: *(b) Directional: The number of errors students make in pronouncing words in a text passage increases (or decreases) as the reading level of the passage increases. Nondirectional: There will be a difference in the number of errors students make in pronouncing words in a text passage as the reading level of the passage increases.*

(c) Directional: Individuals who see themselves as socially "attractive" will (or will not) also expect their romantic partners to be (as judged by others) socially attractive. Nondirectional: There is a relationship between perception of attractiveness in oneself and in one's romantic partner.

(f) Directional: *Students who score above the 90th percentile on a standardized reading test will (or will not) also score above the 90th percentile on a standardized writing test.* Nondirectional: *Students who score above the 90th percentile on a standardized reading test will score differently on a standardized writing test from those scoring below the 90th percentile.*

(g) Directional: *The Democratic party has more (or less) Protestants than the Republican party.* Nondirectional: *There is a difference in the number of Protestants to be found in the Democratic and Republican parties.*

4. How would you rank each of the questions in #1 in terms of significance? Why? Answer: *Answers will vary here. Ask students to explain their rankings.*

5. Listed below are a number of variables. Which ones are quantitative and which ones are categorical?

a. Religious preference *(categorical)*
b. Neatness *(quantitative)*
c. Eye color *(categorical)*
d. Curiosity *(quantitative)*
e. Writing ability *(quantitative)*
f. Jumping ability *(quantitative)*
g. Fluency in Spanish *(quantitative)*
h. Test anxiety *(quantitative)*
i. Grade level *(categorical)*
j. Appreciation of classical music *(quantitative)*
k. Mathematics ability *(quantitative)*
l. Judged essay quality *(categorical, if using letter grades; quantitative, if using scoring system)*

6. What might cause a researcher to state a directional hypothesis rather than a non-directional hypothesis? What about the reverse? Answer: *Directional, if he or she expects a particular outcome. Nondirectional, if he or she thinks a relationship exists, but cannot predict its nature.*

7. Are there any variables that researchers should not study? Explain. Answer: *Possibilities include private opinions, preferences or attitudes, and family characteristics, such as cohesion and support. While we disagree, we respect the point of view that some things are "nobody's business."*

TEST FOR CHAPTER FOUR

1. "Students taught first aid by programmed instruction will achieve at a higher level than those taught first aid by the traditional method." The *independent variable* in this hypothesis is:
    (a) students
    (b) level of achievement
    (c) programmed instruction
    (d) method of instruction

2. In the example in item #1, the *dependent variable* is:
    (a) students
    (b) level of achievement
    (c) programmed instruction
    (d) method of instruction

3. Statements or predictions that are tested by collecting and analyzing objective evidence are called:
    (a) assumptions
    (b) indicators
    (c) hypotheses
    (d) premises

4. "Mentally retarded children who attend public school programs will show greater increases in social competence than will comparable children who attend institutional programs." This is an example of a(n):
    (a) directional research hypothesis
    (b) assumption
    (c) research question
    (d) nondirectional research hypothesis

5. Empirically testing an hypothesis is the process of determining:
    (a) whether it fits with previous knowledge
    (b) its logical consistency
    (c) if systematic observation confirms it
    (d) whether it is related to the problem at hand

6. A research report states that Group A was exposed to a new teaching method and Group B was exposed to a traditional method. At the end of a four-month period, each group was given the same achievement test. Group A had a mean score that was higher than the mean score for Group B. The dependent variable in this study was the:
(a) achievement scores of the students
(b) motivation of the students
(c) type of teaching
(d) length of the period of instruction

7. When a hypothesis is confirmed one should conclude that:
(a) it is consistent with existing theory
(b) the study was conducted properly
(c) the hypothesis is true
(d) the data provide evidence favorable to the belief that the hypothesis is true

8. If a researcher studies the effects of frustration on the frequency of aggressive behavior, degree of frustration should be regarded as a(n):
(a) dependent variable
(b) independent variable
(c) extraneous variable
(d) constant

9. Which of the following is likely to be of greatest value in formulating hypotheses for a scientific investigation?
(a) A high level of emotional involvement in the research problem
(b) A rigorous statistical design
(c) Clear indication of the variables involved
(d) A problem statement that is broad in scope

10. The *dependent variable* is so called because:
(a) scores on this variable are hypothesized to depend on, and vary with, the value of the independent variable
(b) the outcome of an experiment is hypothesized to depend on the effect that this variable has on the independent variable
(c) scores on this variable can be expected not to vary in an experiment
(d) scores on this variable depend on how they are manipulated by the researcher

11. Which of the following questions indicates a relationship?
(a) What are the effects of the new reading program?
(b) Do parents and teachers differ in expectations of achievement?
(c) To what extent is the new math curriculum being used by teachers?
(d) What do students expect to do after high school graduation?

12. Characteristics of persons or things that can assume different values are called:
    (a) distributions
    (b) observations
    (c) data
    (d) variables

13. In a research investigation, constants are:
    (a) to be avoided
    (b) variables that complicate interpretation
    (c) the treatments or methods being compared
    (d) none of the above

14. A *categorical variable* is one that varies in:
    (a) type but not amount
    (b) amount but not type
    (c) both type and amount
    (d) none of the above

15. Treating a variable such as "reading achievement" as a categorical variable:
    (a) is inconsistent with what is known about the variable
    (b) reduces the amount of information about the variable
    (c) both (a) and (b)
    (d) neither (a) nor (b)

16. An *outcome variable* is most similar to a(n:
    (a) independent variable
    (b) dependent variable
    (c) manipulated variable
    (d) extraneous variable

17. In a study comparing methods of improving critical thinking, what type of variable is "critical thinking?"
    (a) Dependent, outcome, quantitative
    (b) Dependent, manipulated, quantitative
    (c) Independent, manipulated, qualitative
    (d) Independent, outcome, quantitative

18. Which of the following is a quantitative variable?
    (a) Method of teaching mathematics
    (b) Self-esteem
    (c) Occupation
    (d) Country of birth

19. In the hypothesis, "Eleventh grade students will achieve more with teachers who are enthusiastic," which of the following is an extraneous variable?
    (a) Student achievement
    (b) Teacher enthusiasm
    (c) Eleventh grade students
    (d) Academic ability of students

20. A manipulated experimental variable is one that:
    (a) uses equipment
    (b) requires subjects to arrange materials
    (c) is arranged by the researcher
    (d) makes a study hard to interpret

21. Advantages of stating research questions as hypotheses include:
    (a) clarity
    (b) persuasiveness
    (c) efficiency
    (d) all of the above

22. Disadvantages of stating hypotheses include all of the following <u>except:</u>
    (a) enhancing unintentional researcher bias
    (b) overlooking other relationships
    (c) complicating the design of a study
    (d) enhancing the likelihood of researcher cheating

23. Which of the following is a non-directional hypothesis?
    (a) Students receiving peer tutoring will show greater mathematics gains than students not receiving peer tutoring.
    (b) Boys and girls will differ in their attitudes toward school.
    (c) "A" students have higher self-esteem than "C" students.
    (d) Science teachers ask more questions than social studies teachers.

CHAPTER FIVE
REVIEW OF THE LITERATURE

Chapter Objectives

Reading this chapter should enable students to:

•*describe* briefly why a literature review is of value.

•*name* the steps a researcher goes through in conducting a review of the literature.

•*describe* briefly the kinds of information contained in a general reference and *give an example* of such a source.

•*explain* the difference between a primary and a secondary source, and *give an example* of each type.

•*explain* what is meant by the phrase "search term" and how such terms are used in literature searches.

•*conduct* both a manual and a computer search of the literature on a topic of interest to them, and *write* a summary of their review.

Points to Stress

1. What constitutes a "review of the literature" and why it is of value to researchers.

2. The difference between general references, primary sources, and secondary sources.

3. What a "descriptor" is.

Teaching Suggestions

1. Collect Problem Sheet #4 from the class and answer any questions students may have about it.

2. Discuss with the class each of the types of sources for a literature search as discussed in the text. We have found it helpful to have the entire class look at each of the figures in the chapter that illustrate pages from these sources, answering any questions they may have about where to locate them in the library. You might want to have individual students write their research questions or hypotheses on the chalkboard, and have the rest of the class suggest what they think might be appropriate sources the individuals should consult for their literature review.

3. It might be a good idea to schedule some time for brief individual conferences with students who are having trouble getting "zeroed in" on their research question and/or hypothesis. The remainder of the class can break into small groups to discuss their approach to Problem Sheet #5.

4. If your library offers a tour of its resources and facilities, you might want to schedule one class meeting for this. We would suggest that you give students an assignment before the tour begins, however, to locate and describe three possible sources they intend to consult to help them "focus in" on the tour.

Answers to Discussion Questions

(Note to Instructor: Many of these "Questions for Discussion" are open-ended in nature and have no right answer. Students should be encouraged to offer as many alternative answers as they think plausible, and to explain the reasons for the answers they give.)

1. Why might it be unwise for a researcher not to do a review of the literature before planning a study? Answer: *The researcher might thereby unwittingly duplicate research that has already been done. Also, doing a survey of the literature might reveal dimensions the researcher had not previously considered, might suggest a different way or ways to proceed than originally planned, might suggest extraneous variables important to control, or modifications worth considering.*

2. Many published research articles include only a few references to related studies. How would you explain this? Is this justified? Answer: *Space limitations might prevent the listing of many references; authors might decide to use the space they are alloted to write a description of their procedures and findings; or in some cases the author(s) might have been unable to find very many related references. Laziness on the part of (a few) researchers could be a possibility, or there may not be much in the way of related literature to cite.*

3. Which do you think are more important to emphasize in a literature review-- the opinions of experts in the field, or related studies? Why? Answer: *Related studies. Experts often disagree, and some (alas!) are even wrong on occasion!*

4. Which of the secondary sources described in this chapter would be most appropriate to consult on the following topics?

a. Recent research on social studies education.

b. A brief overview on new developments in science teaching.

c. An extensive review of recent and past research on a particular research question.

d. A survey of recent research on homogeneous grouping.

Answers: *(a) Handbook of Research on Teaching; (b) Encyclopedia of Educational Research; (c) Review of Educational Research; (d) Review of Educational Research.*

5. One rarely finds books referred to in literature reviews. Why do you suppose this is so? Is it a good idea? Answer: *Usually because the material is too dated to be included in a review of current research. Other sources are more up-to-date in what they report. Original research is usually reported in journals.*

6. Which of the general references listed in this chapter would you consult on each of the following?

  a. Marriage and family counseling
  b. Elementary school administration
  c. Small group discussions
  d. Deaf children
  e. A master's thesis on client-centered therapy
  f. Archery instruction

Answers: *(a) Psychological Abstracts, Sociological Abstracts; (b) RIE, Education Index; (c) RIE, Education Index; (d) RIE, ECER; (e) Psychological Abstracts; (f) RIE, Education Index*

TEST FOR CHAPTER FIVE

1. Surveying related literature that has implications for the research question of an investigation should be done;
   - (a) before conducting a study
   - (b) while conducting a study
   - (c) after conducting a study
   - (d) only if a recent review is unavailable

2. Where should one look for a general summary of the research completed on "classroom learning?"
   - (a) *Journal of Educational Research*
   - (b) *Psychological Abstracts*
   - (c) *Encyclopedia of Educational Research*
   - (d) A current text on research methods

3. *Education Index* is most useful as a source of:
   - (a) research abstracts
   - (b) current research references
   - (c) names of research authorities
   - (d) names of institutions that conduct research

4. An advantage of *Current Index to Journals in Education* compared with *Education Index* is that CIJE:
   - (a) provides an evaluation of the quality of research in the projects reported
   - (b) includes lengthy abstracts of the most important articles
   - (c) has been published regularly for over 50 years
   - (d) provides brief abstracts for most articles

5. General references are most useful for:
   - (a) locating original reports of research
   - (b) reviewing the status of the research problem
   - (c) evaluating the adequacy of previous studies
   - (d) helping with methodological problems

6. The first step in conducting a literature search generally should be to refer to:
   - (a) general references
   - (b) primary sources
   - (c) secondary sources
   - (d) computer search sources

7. A common problem occurring at the beginning of a literature search is that:
   (a) the research problem is not specific enough
   (b) pertinent references cannot be obtained
   (c) primary sources are classified in so many ways
   (d) no mechanism exists for systematically organizing all the studies done

8. The term *database* in a computer search refers to the:
   (a) general reference programmed into the retrieval system
   (b) format the printout appears in
   (c) location of the central retrieval system
   (d) system of pricing a search

9. In locating primary sources, the starting place for most educational research is:
   (a) the *Encyclopedia of Educational Research*
   (b) *RIE* and *CIJE*
   (c) *Dissertation Abstracts*
   (d) *Education Index*

10. When starting to use a general reference, the first step is to:
    (a) read through the index
    (b) determine key terms and closely related terms
    (c) read through the listing of titles
    (d) locate one pertinent citation and examine the bibliography it contains

11. A journal article that is missing from local libraries can best be obtained from:
    (a) the author of the article
    (b) interlibrary loan
    (c) the publisher of the article
    (d) a secondary source

12. The main advantage of reports referenced in *RIE* as compared to journal articles is that they:
    (a) contain more recent work
    (b) are likely to contain more detail
    (c) contain material not found in journals
    (d) contain critical reviews

13. The recommended sequence for reading primary sources is:
    (a) the most recent first
    (b) the oldest first
    (c) begin about ten years back
    (d) group the last five years and begin anywhere among them

14. Common mistakes in preparing notes on primary sources include all of the following *except:*
    (a) incorrect citation
    (b) insufficient detail given on procedures
    (c) insufficient detail given on results
    (d) failure to verify the author's credentials

15. Which of the following is *not* an advantage of a computer search over a manual search?
    (a) Speed
    (b) Cost
    (c) Unwanted references
    (d) Thoroughness

16. In carrying out a computer search, which of the following is <u>not</u> required of the researcher?
    (a) Selecting the database
    (b) Deciding on the number of citations desired
    (c) Defining key terms
    (d) Selecting descriptors

17. What descriptor would you begin with to locate references on the following research question: "What effect does the use of word processors have on the grammatical skills of high school students?"
    (a) High school students
    (b) Word processors
    (c) Language skills
    (d) Computer-assisted instruction

18. Which of the following would <u>not</u> contain primary sources?
    (a) *Journal of Research in Mathematics Education*
    (b) *Journal of Experimental Education*
    (c) *Handbook of Research on Teaching*
    (d) *Child Development*

19. Which of the following is <u>least</u> likely to have a computer search capability?
    (a) A university library
    (b) A public library
    (c) A county office of education
    (d) A school district

20. A highly effective means of reducing the list of citations produced in a computer search is to:
    (a) reduce the number of descriptors used
    (b) instruct the computer to select only those fitting two or more descriptors
    (c) systematically delete by hand those that are inappropriate
    (d) use the Boolean operator "or"

CHAPTER SIX
SAMPLING

Chapter Objectives

Reading this chapter should enable students to:

- *distinguish* between a sample and a population.
- *explain* what is meant by the term "representative sample."
- *explain* how a target population differs from an accessible population.
- *explain* what is meant by "random" sampling, and *describe* briefly three ways of obtaining a random sample.
- *use* a table of random numbers to select a random sample from a population.
- *explain* what is meant by systematic sampling, convenience sampling, and purposive sampling.
- *explain* how the size of a sample can make a difference in terms of representativeness of the sample.
- *explain* what is meant by the term "external validity."
- *distinguish* between population generalizability and ecological generalizability, and *discuss* when it is, and when it is not, appropriate to generalize the results of a study.

Points to Stress

1. The difference between a sample and a population.
2. The difference between a random and a nonrandom sample.
3. How to obtain a random sample.
4. The difference between systematic, convenience, and purposive sampling.
5. How the size of a sample can make a difference with regard to external validity.
6. The difference between population and ecological generalizability.

Teaching Suggestions

1. Collect Problem Sheet #5 from the class and answer any questions students may have about it (you might want to delay the collection of this problem sheet in order to give students more time to search the literature).

2. To help students understand the difference between a sample and a population, make a transparency of Table 6.2, "A Hypothetical Population of 99 Students" (a master for this and other transparencies can be found in the section entitled "Transparency Masters" later in this manual) for display on an overhead projector. As you project the figure on the projector, have students look at the figure in their text (p. 104). Point out that any group of students selected from this population would constitute a sample. Then have the class look at the examples of samples and populations given on pages 92-93 of the text. Ask individual students to see if they can suggest a possible sample that might be obtained from each of the populations as well as vice-versa--a population from which one or more of the samples might have been taken.

3. To explore the concept of random sampling, make a transparency of Table 6.1, the table of random numbers (a master for this and other transparencies can be found in the section entitled "Transparency Masters" later in this manual) for display on an overhead projector. Review the selection of a random sample using this table as described on page 83 of the text. Then break the class down into small groups and have each group use the table to select another random sample to ensure that they understand how to use it.

4. Make transparencies of Figure 6.2, "Random Sampling Methods" and Figure 6.3, "Nonrandom Sampling Methods" (a master for this and other transparencies can be found in the section entitled "Transparency Masters" later in this manual) for display on an overhead projector. Ask students to describe how the two methods differ. Name a few populations (or use the ones listed on p. 92) and ask students to try to name a possible random and nonrandom sample that might be taken from each population.

5. Review the selection of different sized samples as described on pages 103-106. Have the class, working in small groups, repeat the exercise by drawing several random samples of their own from the population shown in Table 6.2 (page 104). Do their samples become more similar to the population as they increase in size? How would they explain the results they obtain?

6. Discuss with the class each of the questions on page 112 of the text.

7. Break the class down into small groups to discuss and begin work on Problem Sheet #6.

Answers to Discussion Questions

(Note to Instructor: Many of these "Questions for Discussion" are open-ended in nature and have no right answer. Students should be encouraged to offer as many alternative answers as they think plausible, and to explain the reasons for the answers they give.)

1. Listed below are three examples of sampling. One involves simple random sampling; one stratified sampling; and one cluster sampling. Which example involves which method?

a. Forty pennies are randomly selected from a large jar in which there is to be found $4.00 in pennies. Answer: *(Simple random sampling)*

b. A random sample of ten airports is surveyed by sending trained interviewers to solicit reactions about air safety from passengers disembarking from arriving airplanes. Answer: *(Cluster sampling)*

c. A community is found in which the total population consists of individuals with the following religious affiliations: Catholic, 25 per cent; Protestant, 50 per cent; Jewish, 15 per cent; nonaffiliated, 10 per cent. The researcher selects a random sample of 100 individuals, made up of 25 Catholics, 50 Protestants, 15 Jews, and 10 nonaffiliated. Answer: *(Stratified sampling)*

2. A team of researchers wants to determine the attitudes of students about the recreational services available in the Student Union on campus. The team stops the first 100 students they meet on a street in the middle of the campus, and asks questions about the Union to each of these students. What

are some possible ways that this sample might be biased? Answer: *Students who are majoring in certain subjects may not venture into the middle part of the campus. Further, depending on the time of day, the team may miss late afternoon or evening students.*

3. Suppose a researcher was interested in studying the effects of music on learning. She obtains permission from a nearby elementary school principal to use the two third grade classes in the school. The ability level of the two classes, as shown by standardized tests, grade point averages, and faculty opinion, is quite similar. In one class, the researcher plays classical music softly every day for a semester. In the other class, no music is played. At the end of the semester, she finds that the class in which the music was played has a markedly higher average in arithmetic than the other class, although they do not differ in any other respect. To what population (if any) might the results of this study be generalized? What, exactly, could the researcher say about the effects of music on learning? Answer: *The generalizability of this study is quite limited. The researcher would not be entitled to generalize beyond the classes in this particular school. Music appears to make a difference--at this school.*

4. When, if ever, might a researcher not be interested in generalizing the results of a study? Explain. Answer: *When the researcher cared only about the specific sample studied, as for example, when surveying faculty opinion in a particular school, or in evaluating a specific local program.*

5. "The larger a sample, the more justified a researcher is in generalizing from it to a population." Is this statement true? Why or why not? Answer: *Generally yes, but more important is the nature of the sample. Even very large samples can be unrepresentative. Randomness is the important thing.*

6. Some people have argued that no population can ever be studied in its entirety. Would you agree? Why or why not? Answer: *We would not agree. For example, all of the third graders in San Francisco could probably be studied with respect to certain variables, although it would be quite time consuming and expensive.*

TEST FOR CHAPTER SIX

1. The first step in selecting a sample should be to:
   (a) define the population
   (b) decide how to stratify the population
   (c) compile a list of the population
   (d) determine how to randomize

2. Generalizing research findings from a sample to the population is most likely to be justifiable when:
   (a) a small systematic sample is used
   (b) cluster sampling is used in a large, heterogeneous population
   (c) the null hypothesis is confirmed, regardless of the sampling procedures used
   (d) a large random sample is used

3. A research worker plans to evaluate high school students' reactions to a new policy on closed campus stations. He locates himself near the office of the Dean, where he interviews every fourth student who visits the Dean. He eventually secures data from 100 interviews and publishes his findings as the "Reactions of high school students to a new policy for a closed campus." What may be wrong with this approach?
   (a) Too small a sample
   (b) Inadequately defined problem
   (c) Inadequate techniques of analysis
   (d) Biased sample

4. A researcher drew a sample by selecting every tenth name in a telephone directory. Which of the following types of sampling did she use?
   (a) Simple random
   (b) Convenience
   (c) Stratified
   (d) Systematic

5. The most important consideration in selecting a sample is that the sample be
   (a) selected from the population by means of a table of random numbers
   (b) made up of a large number of subjects
   (c) representative of the population
   (d) selected from a large number of individuals or elements

6. In random sampling, it is necessarily true that:
   (a) a representative sample with a normal distribution will result
   (b) precisely similar samples will be obtained with each replication
   (c) each sampling unit has an equal probability of being selected
   (d) the sample will have low variability

7. The entire collection of people, elements, scores, or measurements to which conclusions are applied is:
   (a) an experimental design
   (b) an interval estimate
   (c) a population
   (d) a sample

8. The validity of generalizations based on a sample depends on the:
   (a) number of strata in the sample
   (b) representativeness of the sample
   (c) size of the population sampled
   (d) shape of the sampling distribution

9. The sample in a particular study is the:
   (a) group to which results are generalized
   (b) group that is selected
   (c) group on which data is obtained
   (d) group that agrees to participate

10. The accessible population in a study is the:
   (a) group from which one selects a sample
   (b) group to which one wishes to generalize results
   (c) group of persons selected in a study
   (d) group that participates in the study

11. In cluster random sampling:
   (a) individuals are selected randomly
   (b) individuals are randomly placed in groups
   (c) existing groups are randomly selected
   (d) available groups are used

12. The adequacy of cluster random sampling is most affected by the:
   (a) number of individuals in the population
   (b) number of individuals in the sample
   (c) number of individuals in each group
   (d) number of groups selected

13. The most important feature of a table of random numbers is that:
    (a) it contains a great many numbers
    (b) the numbers in the table are arranged in columns
    (c) there is no pattern to the numbers in the table
    (d) the numbers in the table have been produced by statisticians

14. Two stage cluster sampling refers to:
    (a) selecting groups and then individuals
    (b) selecting individuals and placing them in groups
    (c) selecting groups and then sub-groups
    (d) selecting a large number of individuals and then a sub-group

15. Random sampling is least effective when:
    (a) a convenience sample is used
    (b) a purposive sample is used
    (c) the population size is small
    (d) the sample size is very small

16. A purposive sample is used when:
    (a) the individuals to be chosen are believed to have the information desired
    (b) the researcher has a clear purpose for the study
    (c) the population cannot be specified
    (d) volunteers are desired

17. A stratified random sample is used when:
    (a) simple random sampling is not possible
    (b) the researcher wants to guarantee representativeness on specified variables
    (c) a simple random sample would be very large
    (d) the researcher wants to simplify data analysis

18. When a convenience sample is used, the researcher should not:
    (a) generalize to a specified population
    (b) describe it thoroughly
    (c) replicate the study
    (d) draw any conclusions

19. Recommended sample sizes are usually:
    (a) determined by mathematical formulas
    (b) determined by population size
    (c) based on the nature of the variables studied
    (d) based on professional experience

20. The term "external validity" includes:
    (a) population generalizability and ecological generalizability
    (b) population generalizability and instrument validity
    (c) internal validity and instrument validity
    (d) internal validity and ecological generalizability

21. Ecological generalizability includes the:
    (a) characteristics of the sample
    (b) characteristics of the population
    (c) characteristics of the environment
    (d) characteristics of the instruments

22. Which of the following is not true of replication?
    (a) The study is repeated with the same subjects
    (b) The study is repeated with very similar subjects
    (c) The study is repeated under the same conditions
    (d) The study is repeated under similar conditions

23. In using a table of random numbers:
    (a) the number of digits used is determined by the population size
    (b) the number of digits used is determined by the sample size
    (c) the number of digits used is determined by which table is used
    (d) the number of digits used is determined randomly

24. In reading a table of random numbers, the researcher begins:
    (a) with the top of the first column
    (b) with the top of any column
    (c) with the first row
    (d) with any number

25. The best way to obtain a representative sample is to:
    (a) use a purposive sample
    (b) use cluster random sampling--with five clusters
    (c) use a stratified random sample--with a total of 30
    (d) use a large simple random sample

26. Use of a volunteer sample is generally to be avoided because:
    (a) volunteers are hard to get
    (b) they are unlikely to be representative of the intended population
    (c) they are difficult to stratify
    (d) replication is difficult

CHAPTER SEVEN
INSTRUMENTATION

Chapter Objectives

Reading this chapter should enable students to:

•*explain* what is meant by the term "data."

•*explain* what is meant by the term "instrumentation."

•*name* three ways by which data can be collected by researchers.

•*explain* what is meant by the term "data-collection instrument."

•*describe* at least five types of researcher-administered instruments used in educational research.

•*describe* at least five types of subject-administered instruments used in educational research.

•*explain* what is meant by the term "unobtrusive measures," and *give at least two examples* of such measures.

•*name* at least four types of measurement scales, and *give an example* of each.

•*name* at least three different types of scores used in educational research, and *give an example* of each.

•*describe* briefly the difference between norm-referenced and criterion-referenced instruments.

•*describe* briefly how to score, tabulate, and code data for analysis.

Points to Stress

1. The meaning of the term "data."
2. The key questions that researchers must ask with regard to the instrumentation process (see pp. 115-116 in the text).
3. The distinction between researcher-administered, subject-administered, and informant-type instruments.
4. The fact that there are many ways to collect data.
5. Types of scores.
6. The distinction between norm-referenced and criterion-referenced instruments.
7. The four types of measurement scales.

Teaching Suggestions

1. Collect Problem Sheet #6 from the class and answer any questions students may have about it.

2. Go over the distinction between research, subject, and informant instruments presented on pages 117-118 of the text. Which of the three do they think would be the most frequently used? the easiest to use? the most difficult? Why? Then go over discussion question #4 on page 149 of the text with the class.

3. Review discussion question #1 on pages 148-149 of the text with the class.

4. Discuss the other questions on pages 148-149 with the class.

5. Make a small collection of commonly used instruments (specimen sets are usually available from publishers). Divide the class into 3-4 person groups to review a particular instrument and report back to the total class with whom they think the instrument might be used.

6. Break the class into small groups to discuss the most appropriate instrument(s) to use in their own (proposed) study.

7. Break the class down into small groups to discuss and begin work on Problem Sheet #7.

Answers to Discussion Questions

(Note to Instructor: Many of these "Questions for Discussion" are open-ended in nature and have no right answer. Students should be encouraged to offer as many alternative answers as they think plausible, and to explain the reasons for the answers they give.)

1. What type of instrument do you think would be best suited to obtain data about each of the following?

a. The free-throw shooting ability of a tenth-grade basketball team

b. How nurses feel about a new management policy recently instituted in their hospital

c. Parental reactions to a planned-for campaign to raise money for an addition to the school library

d. The "best-liked" boy and girl in the senior class

e. The "best" administrator in a particular school district

f. How well students in a food management class can prepare a balanced meal

g. Characteristics of all students who are biology majors at a midwestern university

h. How well students at one school compare to students at another school in mathematics ability

i. The potential of various high school seniors for college work

j. What the members of a kindergarten class like and dislike about school

Answers: *(a) Performance test; (b) Attitude scale; (c) Questionnaire; (d) Sociogram; (e) Behavior rating scale; (f) Performance test; (g) Questionnaire; (h) Achievement test; (i) Aptitude test; (j) Interview.*

2. Which of the following are examples of products and which are examples of procedures?

a. A class discussion

b. An outline for a term report

c. A poem

d. Attentiveness

e. Running a mile in 4:12 minutes

f. A chemical solution

Answers: *(a) Procedure; (b) Product; (c) Product; (d) Either; (e) Product; (f) Product.*

3. Would the following be measured most appropriately by an achievement test or a personality test?

a. Self-concept
b. Ability to compose a song
c. Ability to work with others on a research project
d. Ability to mix chemical solutions correctly
e. A student's feelings toward his or her classmates
f. Ability to use a dictionary

Answers: *(a) Personality; (b) Achievement; (c) Personality; (d) Achievement; (e) Personality; (f) Achievement.*

4. Who would be best equipped to fill out each of the following instruments--a researcher or the subjects of a study?

a. A checklist of the steps involved in tuning an automobile engine
b. A questionnaire asking for information about a person's previous work history
c. A rating scale evaluating performance in a basketball game
d. A tally sheet of questions asked by students in a biology class
e. An inventory of the supplies contained at a chemistry lab workstation
f. A record of monthly entries to and withdrawals from a payment book
g. A written description of an individual's behavior at a dance

Answers: *(a) Researcher; (b) Subjects; (c) Researcher; (d) Researcher; (e) Researcher; (f) Subjects; (g) Researcher.*

5. Of all the instruments we have presented in this chapter, which one(s) do you think would be the hardest to use? the easiest? Why? Which one(s) do you think would provide the most dependable information? Why?

Answers: *Hardest: Projective devices, due to difficulty in scoring; and performance checklists, due to the training required in their use. Easiest: rating scales. Dependability does not depend on instrument type, but generally those requiring judgments (e.g., rating scales) are more problematic.*

6. What type of scale -- nominal, ordinal, interval, or ratio -- would a researcher be most likely to use to measure each of the following?

a. Height of students in inches
b. Students ranked on aggressiveness of classroom behavior
c. Mechanical aptitude
d. Religious preference
e. Writing ability
g. Running speed
h. Weight gain or loss in pounds over a a three month period

Answers: *(a) ratio; (b) ordinal; (c) interval; (d) nominal; (e) interval; (f) ratio; g) ratio.*

7. Match each score in Column A with the best choice from Column B

A	B
1. standard score	a. poorest to use for research
2. raw score	b. score expressed as 10-2
3. age equivalent score	c. number of questions correct
4. percentile rank	d. preferred for research purposes

Answers: *1-d; 2-c; 3-b; 4-a*

8. "Any individual raw score, in and of itself, is meaningless." Would you agree? Explain. Answer: *This is correct. Students should realize that a raw score, in and of itself, means nothing unless it can be compared to the scores of others.*

9. "Derived scores give meaning to individual raw scores." Is this true? Explain. Answer: *Yes, it is true. They indicate how near or far away each score is from the mean of their group.*

10. It sometimes would not be fair to compare an individual's score on a test to the scores of other individuals taking the same test. Why? Answer: *Because some students may have previously had opportunities to acquire certain skills that others have not had, or had different experiences that enabled them to score better than others on the test. It depends on how the comparison is interpreted and used.*

TEST FOR CHAPTER SEVEN

1. Which of the following is most essential to skilled observation as a research technique applied in studying a student's behavior?
   (a) Recording primarily dramatic behavior
   (b) Recording primarily the "whys" of the behavior observed
   (c) Recording primarily the "whats" of the behavior observed
   (a) Using data obtained as bases for generalizations concerning the behaviors of other students

2. In which of the following would one be most likely to find a professional evaluation of a particular commercial standardized test?
   (a) *Journal of Educational Measurement*
   (b) *Encyclopedia of Educational Research*
   (c) *The Buros Mental Measurement Yearbook*
   (d) *Yearbook of Education*

3. The most serious limitation in the use of mailed questionnaires in research is in connection with:
   (a) deciding on the initial definition of the population
   (b) selecting the sample
   (c) obtaining responses
   (d) analyzing the data

4. Most widely used standardized achievement tests are useful because:
   (a) they indicate the full scope of what ought to be taught in schools
   (b) they are free of bias
   (c) they have been carefully prepared, tried out and refined through research
   (d) their scores are *not* influenced by curriculum variables, teacher effectiveness variables, or the child's home environment

5. One advantage that the interview has over the questionnaire is that it:
   (a) is more useful in probing for underlying feelings and attitudes
   (b) provides results with higher reliability
   (c) is less subject to errors in recording
   (d) costs less to use

6. Which of the following is most characteristic of skilled as opposed to unskilled observers in research?
   (a) Making generalized descriptions or evaluation rather than noting specific incidents
   (b) Interpreting behavior immediately on the basis of initial data so as to make confirmation by subsequent incidents unnecessary
   (c) Describing the subject's behavior rather than the personal reaction of the observer
   (d) Recording primarily dramatic or negative incidents

7. Rapport is most essential when which data gathering device is used?
   (a) Checklist
   (b) Interview
   (c) Observation
   (d) Rating scale

8. Interviews and questionnaires as a data collection method:
   (a) are more effective than observational techniques
   (b) reveal only information the subject is willing to report
   (c) cannot be considered to have validity
   (d) provide no information about past behavior

9. Which of the following are data?
   (a) Religious preferences
   (b) Political opinions
   (c) Test scores
   (d) All of the above

10. Which is an example of a researcher-completed instrument?
   (a) Questionnaire
   (b) Sociogram
   (c) Flow chart
   (d) Aptitude test

11. Which is an example of a subject-completed instrument?
   (a) Attitude scale
   (b) Performance checklist
   (c) Anecdotal record
   (d) Rating scale

12. How is "instrumentation" different from "instrument?"
   (a) Instrumentation includes the way in which the instrument was developed.
   (b) Instrumentation pertains only to certain types of instruments.
   (c) Instrumentation includes the way in which the instrument is used.
   (d) Instrumentation is not concerned with reliability and validity.

13. Which of the following is the best synonym for validity?
    (a) Consistency
    (b) Feasibility
    (c) Truthfulness
    (d) Economy

14. Which of the following is the best synonym for reliability?
    (a) Consistency
    (b) Usefulness
    (c) Truthfulness
    (d) Economy

15. Objectivity in research means:
    (a) the absence of judgment in instrumentation
    (b) minimizing personal bias
    (c) eliminating personal opinions as variables to be studied
    (d) eliminating emotions as variables to be studied

16. The use of previously developed instruments in a study is desirable because:
    (a) existing instruments will be more valid
    (b) existing instruments will be more reliable
    (c) instrument development leaads to biased results
    (d) instrument development is a complex undertaking

17. A previously existing instrument:
    (a) should always be used rather than one the researcher develops
    (b) will have adequate reliability
    (c) may be inadequate for purposes of the researcher
    (d) will lead to valid interpretations

18. A performance checklist:
    (a) minimizes observer judgment
    (b) requires the observer to rate behavior along a continuum
    (c) requires no prior knowledge on the observer's part
    (d) cannot be used to assess products

19. A good anecdotal record includes:
    (a) explanations for observed behavior
    (b) generalizations to typical behavior
    (c) concrete descriptive statements
    (d) evaluative statements

20. The primary difficulty with rating scales is:
    (a) the complexity of the format
    (b) the ambiguity of the points along the scale
    (c) the limits of what can be rated
    (d) that researchers tend not to like to use them

21. The distinguishing feature of projective techniques is that:
    (a) their interpretation is extremely complex
    (b) they are intentionally ambiguous
    (c) they are only used to assess attitudes
    (d) they use pictures

22. Aptitude tests differ from ability tests primarily in their:
    (a) purpose
    (b) format
    (c) content
    (d) difficulty

23. Which of the following consists of supply type items?
    (a) A multiple choice test
    (b) A matching test
    (c) An essay test
    (d) A true-false test

24. Which of these could be used as an aptitude test?
    (a) The semantic differential
    (b) A Likert scale
    (c) The Stanford Achievement Test
    (d) An observational checklist

25. Which of the following would be the least appropriate variable to assess with an observational tally sheet?
    (a) Off-task behavior
    (b) Question-asking
    (c) Interest in class activity
    (d) Critical thinking

CHAPTER EIGHT
VALIDITY AND RELIABILITY

Chapter Objectives

Reading this chapter should enable students to:

•*explain* what is meant by the term "validity" as it applies to the use of instruments in educational research.

•*name* three types of evidence of validity that can be obtained, and *give an example* of each type.

•*explain* what is meant by the term "correlation coefficient," and *describe* briefly the difference between positive and negative correlation coefficients.

•*explain* what is meant by the terms "validity coefficient" and "reliability coefficient."

•*explain* what is meant by the term "reliability" as it applies to the use of instruments in educational research.

•*explain* what is meant by the term "errors of measurement."

•*describe* briefly three ways to estimate the reliability of the scores or answers obtained using a particular instrument.

Points to Stress

1. The difference between validity and reliability.
2. The idea that validity and reliability refer to *evidence*, not to the instruments themselves.
3. What a correlation coefficient represents, and how validity and reliability coefficients are examples of such.
4. The different types of evidence pertaining to reliability and validity, and how each is obtained and evaluated.

Teaching Suggestions

1. Collect Problem Sheet #7 from the class and answer any questions students may have about it.

2. Stress the idea that the concept of validity refers to the amount of evidence there is to support inferences researchers want to make based on the data they collect, not to the instruments themselves. Students should understand that instruments do not have validity *per se*. Review the types of evidence a researcher might collect (see p. 154 in the text). Then go over discussion question #2 on pages 168-169 with students. It may be helpful to emphasize the essential (and older) idea that an instrument is valid if it measures what it is supposed to measure--in the specific context. This is often easier for students to grasp than the more recent interpretation.

3. Review the process of collecting content-related evidence described on pages 154-157 of the text. If students disagree that the questions measure the objective for which they were designed, ask them to suggest other possibilities. Another idea here is to list a few objectives on the board and have students, working in small groups, try to design questions or items to measure these objectives.

4. Review the examples of evidence that might be offered in support for a test of mathematical reasoning ability on pages 158-159 of the text. Have students rate these examples from strongest to weakest. Ask students to suggest other evidence that a researcher might collect for such a test.

5. Review discussion question #4 on page 169 with the class.

6. Ask students to have a few of their friends take the test shown in Figure 8.4 on page 165 of the text. They should reproduce and then record their scores using the worksheet shown in Figure 8.5 on that same page. This exercise will help them understand the concept of internal consistency.

7. Break the class down into small groups to discuss and begin work on Problem Sheet #8.

Answers to Discussion Questions

(Note to Instructor: Many of these "Questions for Discussion" are open-ended in nature and have no right answer. Students should be encouraged to offer as many alternative answers as they think plausible, and to explain the reasons for the answers they give.)

1. We point out in the chapter that scores from an instrument may be reliable but not valid, yet not the reverse. Why would this be so? Answer: *Because one can have consistency without truthfulness (e.g., a consistent liar). Without consistency, one has no idea which information to accept as potentially truthful.*

2. What type of evidence--content-related, criterion-related, or construct-related--would each of the following represent?

a. Ninety percent of the students who score high on a biology test receive A's as end-of-the-semester grades in Biology. *(criterion-related)*

b. A Professor of Ancient History at a large university looks over a test to measure student knowledge of Greek and Roman civilizations, and states that in his opinion, the test measures such knowledge. *(content-related)*

c. A researcher discovers that students who score high on a teacher-made test of writing ability also receive high marks in writing courses. She finds that they are also rated high in writing ability by their teachers, and that when they are asked to write a letter, they prepare one that two writing instructors independently judge to be clear and grammatically correct. *(construct-related)*

d. A typing instructor receives a letter from the local office of a large corporation stating that several of his recently hired students are "excellent typists" on the job. In checking his records, the instructor finds that all but one of these students scored high on his end-of-the-year typing test. *(criterion-related)*

3. If you calculated a correlation coefficient for two sets of scores and obtained a value of 3.7, you would have to say that:

a. a very positive relationship existed between the two sets of scores

b. students who scored highly on one of the instruments involved scored poorly on the other instrument

c. a negative relationship existed between the two sets of scores

d. something is wrong with the calculation of the coefficient

Answer: *(d) A correlation coefficient can never exceed ± 1.00*

4. What sorts of evidence might a researcher obtain to check on the validity of results from each of the following types of instruments?

a. A test designed to measure what ninth graders know about world geography

b. A performance test designed to measure an individual's ability to tune an automobile engine

c. A questionnaire designed to find out what people think will be the most pressing world problems in the next decade

d. A scale designed to measure the attitudes of people toward candidates running for political office in a given year

e. A participation flow chart designed to measure the amount of student participation in a class discussion

f. A performance checklist designed to measure how accurately and quickly soldiers can fieldstrip and clean a rifle

g. A scale designed to measure how students feel about their classmates

h. An essay examination designed to measure student ability to draw warranted conclusions from a historical document

i. A projective device designed to identify an individual's feelings of hostility should they exist

Answers: *(a) teacher ratings, work produced, a comparison with the course syllabus; (b) subsequent engine performance, supervisor ratings; (c) interviews, essays on the topic; (d) subsequent voting, scale given to spouse or close friend to fill out as the subject "would"; (e) video or audio taping, teacher ratings of each discussion; (f) supervisor ratings, peer ratings; (g) behavioral observations; (h) clinical interview, multiple-choice test, teacher ratings; (i) interviews with close friends, observation under frustrating conditions.*

5. What might be some examples of errors of measurement that could affect an individual's performance on a test? Answer: *Changes in lighting, physical condition at time of taking test, material to be typed, additional instructions just prior to taking the test.*

6. Which do you think is harder to obtain, validity or reliability? Why? Answer: *Validity. There are fewer ways to improve it, whereas reliability can be improved by adding or refining items.*

7. Might reliability ever be more important than validity? Explain. Answer: *No. Consistency is irrelevant to the researcher if interpretation is in error.*

8. How would you assess the QE Intelligence Test on p. 165 as a measure of validity? Explain. Answer: *It would depend on your definition of intelligence. The test logically appears to assess one's ability to see through attempts to mislead. Most definitions of intelligence do not explicitly include this characteristic, although it might well be considered as one aspect of current definitions.*

TEST FOR CHAPTER EIGHT

1. Validity can be assessed by finding the correlation between scores on:
   (a) a test and some independent, widely accepted measure of that variable
   (b) one form of a test and another form of that test
   (c) the even numbered items on a test and the odd numbered items on that test
   (d) two administrations of the same test

2. A common sense definition of validity refers to an instrument that:
   (a) yields consistent results on subsequent applications
   (b) has been adequately standardized and has norms available
   (c) measures what it is supposed to measure
   (d) discriminates adequately among high and low scorers

3. Reliability of measurement is concerned with:
   (a) systematic errors
   (b) relevance
   (c) consistency
   (d) proven value

4. An indispensable quality required for a good measuring instrument is that it produce evidence that is:
   (a) standardized
   (b) objective
   (c) valid
   (d) criterion referenced

5. The validity of scores on a teacher-made classroom achievement test should be appraised in terms of:
   (a) its usability and objectivity
   (b) its relation to the content and objectives of the course
   (c) the adequacy of its standardization
   (d) the discrimination and difficulty level of its items

6. The longer the time interval between a prediction and the event to be predicted, the:
   (a) smaller are the chances of making a good prediction
   (b) greater are the chances of making a successful prediction
   (c) fewer the variables there are to be considered
   (d) smaller the standard error

7. An arithmetic test is given twice within a few days to a student. The highest possible score is 40. He receives a score of 35 the first time and a score of 18 the second time. If similarly varying results are obtained with other students, the test is probably:
   (a) lacking in relevance
   (b) not sufficiently comprehensive
   (c) too difficult
   (d) unreliable

8. Which of the following statements is correct?
   (a) An instrument may or may not be valid.
   (b) Interpretations made from an instrument may or may not be valid.
   (c) Widely used instruments can be assumed to be valid.
   (d) Validity is secondary in importance to reliability.

9. Content-related evidence of validity would be provided by:
   (a) giving a math test on Monday and again on Friday
   (b) having experts review the test
   (c) obtaining scores on the even and odd-numbered items on the test
   (d) having two scorers independently score the test

10. Construct-related evidence of validity would be provided by:
   (a) favorable review by experts
   (b) correlations with other variables as predicted
   (c) demonstrating that scores are influenced by training
   (d) all of the above

11. Criterion-referenced evidence of validity would be provided by:
   (a) comparing scores on an instrument with scores on another instrument given to the same sample
   (b) giving the instrument again at a later time
   (c) comparing scores on the instrument with those obtained with another sample
   (d) giving a second instrument to a second sample

12. Which of the following is not a means of assessing internal consistency?
   (a) The split-half method
   (b) Test-retest method
   (c) The Kuder-Richardson method
   (d) The alpha method

13. Which of the following would be a way of assessing unreliability due to content and time?
    (a) Administering a reading test (Form X) on Monday and again on Friday
    (b) Administering a reading test (Form X) on Monday and calculating a split-half correlation
    (c) Administering a reading test (Form X) on Monday and Form Y on Friday
    (d) Administering a reading test (Form X) on Monday and calculating alpha

14. Which of the following is a way to assess the predictive validity of an algebra test?
    (a) Correlate test scores with teacher ratings in algebra
    (b) Correlate test scores with success as an engineer
    (c) Correlate test scores with algebra grades
    (d) Correlate test scores with scores on algebra homework assignments

15. Which of the following would be considered evidence of validity of observer ratings of social adjustment?
    (a) A correlation of .80 between two observers
    (b) A correlation of .50 with peer nominations for Class President
    (c) A correlation of .10 with a test of social adjustment
    (d) A correlation of .70 with a test of mechanical aptitude

16. Determining split-half reliability requires that:
    (a) each student's test be scored twice
    (b) some students be given half the items, others the remainder
    (c) half the students be given Form A, the rest Form B
    (d) each student be tested twice

17. Which of the following items logically measures "respect for differing cultures?"

(a) Asian-Americans should have to pay taxes	Agree	Disagree
(b) Asian-Americans contributed to building our railroads	Agree	Disagree
(c) Asian-Americans should be required to speak English only	Agree	Disagree
(d) Asian-Americans should be required to attend school	Agree	Disagree

18. Which of the following would be considered evidence of validity for a test of "hostility?"
    (a) A correlation of .10 with teacher ratings of hostile behavior
    (b) A much higher average score following a frustrating experience
    (c) A retest correlation of .50
    (d) A correlation of .70 with GPA

19. Criterion-related evidence of validity can be shown by:
    (a) the alpha coefficient
    (b) the expectancy table
    (c) the Spearman-Brown formula
    (d) all of the above

20. Errors of measurement are caused by:
    (a) changes in test items
    (b) changes in the people who take a test
    (c) changes in the administration of the instrument
    (d) all of the above

CHAPTER NINE
DESCRIPTIVE STATISTICS

Chapter Objectives

Reading this chapter should enable students to:

•*differentiate* between categorical and quantitative data, and *give an example* of each.

•*explain* the difference between a statistic and a parameter.

•*construct* a frequency polygon from data.

•*explain* what is meant by the terms "normal distribution" and "normal curve."

•*calculate* the mean, median, and mode of a frequency distribution of data.

•*calculate* the range and standard deviation for a frequency distribution of data.

•*explain* how any particular score in a normal distribution can be interpreted in standard deviation units.

•*explain* what a "z-score" is and *tell why* it is advantageous to be able to describe scores in z-score terms.

•*explain* how to interpret a normal distribution.

•*construct* and *interpret* a scatterplot.

•*explain* what a correlation coefficient is.

•*calculate* a Pearson correlation coefficient.

•*prepare* and *interpret* frequency tables, bar graphs, and pie charts.

•*prepare* and *interpret* a crossbreak table.

Points to Stress

1. The difference between quantitative and categorical data.
2. The difference between a statistic and a parameter.
3. How to construct a frequency polygon.
4. What a normal distribution looks like, why it is called such, and how to interpret such a distribution.
5. How any individual score in a normal distribution can be. interpreted in standard deviation units.
6. z-scores.
7. What a correlation coefficient represents.
8. How to construct and interpret a scatterplot.
9. How to prepare and interpret a crossbreak table.

Teaching Suggestions

1. Collect Problem Sheet #8 from the class and answer any questions students may have about it.

2. Make a transparency of Tables 9.1 and 9.2, the frequency distributions. Both are on the same transparency (a master for this and other transparencies can be found in the section entitled "Transparency Masters" later in this manual) for display on an overhead projector. Point out to the class that grouping frequencies has both advantages (condenses the distribution) and disadvantages (a loss of specific information concerning all of the scores in

the distribution). Then review the steps involved in the construction of a frequency polygon as described on pages 175-176 of the text. Have each student construct a frequency polygon from Table 9.2 and compare it with the one shown in Figure 9.1 on page 176 of the text. Their polygon should match the one shown in Figure 9.1 exactly.

3. Ask the class to look at Figure 9.4 on page 178 of the text. Point out that one of the major advantages of depicting data in frequency polygons is that doing so facilitates the comparison of two different frequency distributions. What can the class say about the distributions shown in Figure 9.4? Which group scored better than the other? How do they know?

4. To help students distinguish between the three measures of central tendency and the measures of variability, write some distributions of numbers on the chalkboard and ask the class to calculate the mean, median, and mode of each distribution. Do the same with the range and standard deviation. Ask students to "show" why the mean, median, and mode are considered measures of central tendency, and why the range and standard deviation are called "spreads."

5. Make a transparency of Figure 9.8, "The Normal Curve" (a master for this and other transparencies can be found in the section entitled "Transparency Masters" later in this manual) for display on an overhead projector. By referring to the curve, review those parts of the normal distribution that fall within and beyond a given standard deviation. Give them a few problems to solve, e.g.,

(a) If the mean of a normal distribution is 10 and the SD is 2, what percentage of the scores in the distribution would fall above a score of 12? (16%); Below a score of 6? (2.28%)

(b) If the mean of a normal distribution is 25 and the SD is 4, what score would lie at a point 1 SD above the mean? (29)

6. To help students understand the idea of z-scores, have the class compare Figure 9.9 on page 184 and Figure 9.11 on page 185 of the text. What similarities do they notice? Then have them compare Figure 9.9 with Figure 9.12. What can they say that would hold true of all of these figures?

7. To help students understand the concept of correlation, make a transparency of Figure 9.16, "Examples of Scatterplots" (a master for this and other transparencies can be found in the section entitled "Transparency Masters" later in this manual) for display on an overhead projector. Point out how the dots become more like a diagonal line of 45° as the correlation becomes stronger (and to notice that this is true regardless of the sign of the correlation). We have found it helpful if students actually place their pencil on each scatterplot so as to cover the maximum number of dots. Use Figure 9.17 to emphasize what a curvilinear relationship looks like. To illustrate how a scatterplot illustrates a correlation between two variables, have the class look at Table 9.7 and Figure 9.15 on page 190 of the text.

8. Discuss question #2 on page 201 of the text with the class.

9. Review with the class the section on crossbreak tables described in pages 196-198 of the text to help them understand the value of such tables, and how they can illustrate relationships between categorical variables.

10. Break the class down into small groups to discuss and begin work on Problem Sheet #9.

Answers to Discussion Questions

(Note to Instructor: Many of these "Questions for Discussion" are open-ended in nature and have no right answer. Students should be encouraged to offer as many alternative answers as they think plausible, and to explain the reasons for the answers they give.)

1. What would be the most appropriate average to use to answer each of the following questions?

a. What was the most frequent score in the class?
b. Which score had half of the scores in the class below it?
c. Which average uses all of the information available?

Answers: *(a) mode; (b) median; (c) mean.*

2. Would you expect the following correlations to be positive or negative? Why?

a. Bowling scores and golf scores
b. Reading scores and arithmetic scores
c. Age and weight
d. Life expectancy and daily use of cigarettes
e. Size and strength

Answers: *(a) negative--good bowlers will have high scores; good golfers will have low scores; (b) positive-both are related to general academic ability; better readers probably tend to do better in arithmetic; (c) positive for 5 year olds, since the smaller the child, the lower the weight; negative for over 50 year olds, since elderly people tend to lose weight; (d) negative, since the more one smokes, the lower the life expectancy; (e) positive, since bigger boys at this age will tend to be stronger.*

3. Match each item in Column A with the best choice from Column B

A	B
1. correlation coefficient	a. measure of central tendency
2. standard score	b. measure of variability
3. median	c. measure of relationship
4. standard deviation	d. measure of relative position

Answer: *1-c; 2-d; 3-a; 4-b.*

4. Why do you think so many people mistrust statistics? How might such mistrust be alleviated? Answer: *Many people do not understand statistics, and they are often misused (e.g., as in some advertising campaigns). The mistrust of statistics might be alleviated by helping more people to become familiar with some of the basic concepts involved.*

5. Could the range of a distribution ever be smaller than the standard deviation of that distribution? Why or why not? Answer: *No. The range encompasses 100% of a distribution, whereas standard deviation does not ($\pm$ 1 SD=only 68% of the cases).*

6. Would it be possible for two different distributions to have the same standard deviation but different means? What about the reverse? Explain. Answer: *Yes to both questions. See Figure 9.7 in this chapter.*
7. "The larger the standard deviation of a distribution, the more heterogeneous the scores in that distribution." Is this true? Explain. Answer: *Yes. The standard deviation is an indication of the variability of a distribution.*
8. "The most complete information about a distribution of scores is provided by a frequency polygon." Explain. Answer: *This is because all of the scores in the distribution and their relationship to each other are shown.*
9. Grouping scores in a frequency distribution has its advantages, but also its disadvantages. What might be some examples of each? Answer: *The advantage is that it provides a way to condense a lot of information, but the disadvantage is that in doing so, precision is lost since you lose distinctions within each interval.*
10. Any single raw score, in and of itself, tells us nothing. Would you agree? Explain. Answer: *This is generally true, since a single score is meaningless until it can be compared to other scores obtained using the same instrument. One has no idea, in looking at a score all by itself, whether it is a better or worse score than any other. (An exception is a score on a criterion-referenced test.)*
11. Why can a correlation coefficient never be larger than plus or minus 1.00? Answer: *Because all of the points fall on a straight line when r =1.00.*

TEST FOR CHAPTER NINE

1. The maximum possible correspondence or correlation between two variables is represented by a Pearson product-moment coefficient of:
   (a) -1.00
   (b) .00
   (c) .90
   (d) 2.00

2. Which of the following sets of scores has the largest standard deviation?
   (a) 312, 312, 312, 312, 312
   (b) 44, 45, 46, 46
   (c) 530, 531, 532, 533, 533
   (d) 6, 11, 38, 55, 68

3. Which one of these correlation coefficients has the least predictive value?
   (a) .87
   (b) .53
   (c) .19
   (d) -.28

4. The kind of graph on which one would determine the frequency of a given score by noting the height of the line is called a(n):
   (a) histogram
   (b) abscissa
   (c) frequency polygon
   (d) frequency table

5. Which of the following statements is correct?
   (a) The mean is a point in a distribution below which and above which 50% of the cases lie.
   (b) The mode is the least used measure of central tendency.
   (c) The median is equal to the sum of the scores divided by the number of scores.
   (d) The median is the same value as the 25th percentile.

6. If there are only a few very high scores and a large number of closely bunched low scores in a distribution:
   (a) the mean will be higher than the median
   (b) the median will be higher than the mean
   (c) the median and the mean will be the same
   (d) none of the above is correct

7. A test was given to two sections of a course. The results were:

Section I:	Mean	51
	Standard Deviation:	7
Section II:	Mean	51
	Standard deviation	13

Which of the following conclusions is correct?
(a) Section I did better on the test than Section II.
(b) Section I is more homogeneous than Section II.
(c) Section I has more bright students than Section II.
(d) The students in Section I performed less consistently than those in Section II.

8. When scores are grouped in constructing a frequency polygon or scatterplot:
(a) all intervals must be the same size
(b) individual scores (within intervals) are plotted
(c) there should be at least 30 intervals
(d) each interval should contain 5-10 scores

9. A z-score is obtained by:
(a) dividing the score by the standard deviation and subtracting from the mean
(b) adding the score to the standard deviation and dividing by the mean
(c) dividing the score by the mean and subtracting from the standard deviation
(d) subtracting the mean from the score and dividing by the standard deviation

10. In a normal distribution, ± 1 z-score includes about:
(a) 30% of the scores
(b) 50% of the scores
(c) 70% of the scores
(d) 90% of the scores

11. The median is equal to:
(a) the mean
(b) the mode
(c) the 25th percentile
(d) the 50th percentile

12. What is commonly known as the average is more correctly called the:
(a) median
(b) arithmetic mean
(c) geometric mean
(d) mode

13. The primary value of frequency polygons is that they:
    (a) are easy to construct
    (b) contain all the information in the original scores
    (c) are easy to interpret
    (d) can be used with categorical data

14. The standard deviation tells how:
    (a) much the scores in a distribution are spread out
    (b) one group compares in level of performance to another
    (c) highly one variable is related to another
    (d) an individual compares to a group

15. An advantage of **z**-scores is that:
    (a) persons will score higher on a **z**-score than on other scores
    (b) they are easier to obtain than percentile ranks
    (c) they have higher reliability than other types of scores
    (d) scores on different instruments can be compared

16. A correspondence exists between **z**-scores and percentile ranks if:
    (a) the calculations are done correctly
    (b) the mean equals the median
    (c) the scores are valid
    (d) the data approximate the normal distribution

17. In constructing a scatterplot:
    (a) the range of scores must be the same on each axis
    (b) each individual is plotted once
    (c) the X axis must be the dependent variable
    (d) the number of cases must be at least 50

18. Scatterplots are another way of showing the information given in:
    (a) means
    (b) standard deviations
    (c) correlation coefficients
    (d) crossbreak tables

19. A scatterplot can be used only when:
    (a) both variables are quantitative
    (b) both variables are categorical
    (c) one variable is categorical; the other is quantitative
    (d) any of the above

20. Whether a particular correlation coefficient is "good" depends on:
    (a) the situation to which it is applied
    (b) whether it exceeds .80
    (c) whether the sample to which it applies was randomly selected
    (d) the average on each variable to which it applies

21. A high correlation coefficient would be obtained from a scatterplot whose points:
    (a) can be described as encompassing a square
    (b) cluster around a horizontal line
    (c) cluster around a vertical line
    (d) cluster around a line drawn from upper left to lower right

22. Calculation of the Pearson Product-Moment Correlation Coefficient:
    (a) requires only the ability to add, subtract, multiply and divide
    (b) requires the ability to add, subtract, multiply, divide and take a square root
    (c) requires the ability to solve algebraic equations
    (a) requires the ability to perform simple calculus operations

23. Eta should be used when:
    (a) one variable is categorical
    (b) there are extreme scores on one (or both) variables
    (c) the relationship between variables is best described by a straight line
    (d) the relationship between variables is best described by a curve

24. Crossbreak tables are used when:
    (a) both variables are categorical
    (b) both variables are quantitative
    (c) one variable is categorical, the other is quantitative
    (d) all of the above

25. In a crossbreak table, expected frequency is:
    (a) the actual frequency in each cell
    (b) the value that is anticipated in each cell
    (c) the frequency in the margin of the dependent variable
    (d) none of the above

26. A relationship is shown in a crossbreak table by:
    (a) the size of expected frequencies
    (b) the number of categories on each variable
    (c) a large discrepancy between actual and expected frequencies
    (d) an increase in actual frequencies from lower left to upper right

27. The contingency coefficient:
    (a) is analogous to the correlation coefficient
    (b) is used only with crossbreak tables
    (c) can be less than 1.00
    (d) all of the above

CHAPTER TEN
INFERENTIAL STATISTICS

Chapter Objectives

Reading this chapter should enable students to:

- *explain* what is meant by the term "inferential statistics."
- *explain* the concept of sampling error.
- *describe* briefly how to calculate a confidence interval.
- *explain* the difference between a research hypothesis and a null hypothesis.
- *explain* briefly the logic underlying hypothesis testing.
- *explain* what is meant by the terms "significance level" and "statistically significant."
- *explain* the difference between a one- and two-tail test of significance.
- *explain* the difference between parametric and nonparametric tests of significance.
- *name* at least three examples of parametric tests that are used by educational researchers.
- *name* at least three examples of nonparametric tests that are used by educational researchers.
- *explain* the importance of random sampling.

Points to Stress

1. The difference between descriptive and inferential statistics.
2. The concept of sampling error.
3. How to calculate a confidence interval.
4. The meaning of statistical significance and how it differs from practical significance.
5. The difference between one and two-tailed tests of statistical significance.
6. Why random sampling is important with relation to inferential statistics.
7. The meaning of probability and how it is used in research studies.
8. Learning the names of commonly used statistical procedures and when they are appropriate.

Teaching Suggestions

1. Collect Problem Sheet #9 from the class and answer any questions students may have about it.

2. Make a transparency of Figure 10.3, "Distribution of Sample Means" (a master for this and other transparencies can be found in the section entitled "Transparency Masters" later in this manual) for display on an overhead projector. Have students compare this distribution with the one shown in Figure 9.9 on page 184 in Chapter Nine. What similarities do they notice? (This should help the class to realize that a sampling distribution of means with N>30 is a normal distribution.)

3. Make a transparency of Figure 10.4, "The 95% Confidence Interval" (a master for this and other transparencies can be found in the section entitled "Transparency Masters" later in this manual) for display on an overhead projector. Point out that the 95% C.I. encompasses an area $\pm$ 1.96 SEM from a sample mean. Ask students to calculate the 95% C.I. for different sample means and SEM's, e.g., (a) Mean=00, SEM=12 (76-48-123.52); (b) Mean=27, SEM=0.7 (25.628-28.372). Do the same for the 99% confidence interval.

4. Go over the problem presented in discussion question #1 on page 225 with the class.

5. Discuss question #2 on page 225 with the class.

6. Break the class down into small groups and begin work on Problem Sheet #10.

Answers to Discussion Questions

(Note to Instructor: Many of these "Questions for Discussion" are open-ended in nature and have no right answer. Students should be encouraged to offer as many alternative answers as they think plausible, and to explain the reasons for the answers they give.)

1. If your hypothesis is that the mean score on a test of critical thinking will be higher for women than men and you get the following data:

Mean for women=91.8
Mean for men=86.3
SEM=3

a. State the null hypothesis.

b. Would you use a one-tail or two-tail test of significance?

c. At the .05 level of significance, would you reject or not reject the null hypothesis?

d Would you say the research hypothesis is affirmed?

e. What is the 99% confidence interval for the difference between the populations (of men and women)?

f. What assumption is necessary in order for the answers to (a)-(e) to be precise?

Answers: *(a) There will be no difference between the mean score for women and the mean score for men on a test of critical thinking; (b) One-tailed-- because direction is stated (women higher than men); (c) Reject. 5.5/3=1.83 which gives .033 in one tail; (d) Yes, the null hypothesis is rejected; (e) 5.5$\pm$2.56 (3)=5.5 $\pm$ 7.68=-2.18 to 8.18; (f) that random samples of men and women were obtained.*

2. What is wrong with each of following statements?

a. Inferential statistics are used to summarize data.

b. A researcher wants to be very confident that the population mean falls within the 95% confidence interval, so she calculates (sample mean) ($\pm$1 SEM).

c. All inferential statistics require the assumption of nominal scales.

d. A researcher decides to make his research hypothesis and his null hypothesis identical.

e. It is sometimes easier to reject the null hypothesis with a two-tail than with a one-tail test.

f. Making inferences about samples is what inferential statistics is all about.

Answers: *(a) Inferential statistics are used when one is attempting to generalize to a population; it is descriptive statistics that are used to summarize data; (b) The 95% confidence interval = ±1.96 SEM, not 1 SEM; (c) Some require only nominal or ordinal; (d) This would be impossible, since the null hypothesis states that no relationship exists; (e) The probability is the same, but a smaller z is needed if the entire area of rejection is in only one tail; (f) The statement should read: "Making inferences from samples to populations is what inferential statistics is all about."*

3. What would you say to a researcher who decides to use a .20 level of significance? Why? Answer: *He or she is capitalizing a bit too much on chance, and will be wrong in rejecting the null hypothesis 1/5th or 20% of the time.*

4. "Hypotheses can never be proven, only supported." Is this true or not? Explain. Answer: *True--evidence is never totally complete.*

5. Is it possible for the results of a study to be of practical importance even though they are not statistically significant? Why or why not? Answer: *Yes, as when a researcher obtains a large difference with a small n. The researcher cannot be sure the difference does not also exist in the populaion, even if the probability is large (and precise).*

6. No two samples will be the same in all of their characteristics. Why won't they? Answer: *Because there are always too many characteristics on which the samples would have to match up.*

7. The standard error of the mean can never be larger than the standard deviation of the sample. Why? Answer: *Because* SEM = SD/ n-1.

8. How are z-scores related to the standard error of the mean? Answer: *The SEM is the standard deviation of a sampling distribution of means. A mean that is 2 SEM above the mean of the means equals a z-score of 2.00.*

TEST FOR CHAPTER TEN

1. Null hypotheses are used in statistics because:
   (a) use of other types of hypotheses shows that the researcher is biased
   (b) they are more easily understood than other types of hypotheses
   (c) they are required by the logic of tests of statistical significance
   (d) they simplify computations

2. A sample of 13 children has a mean IQ of 112 and a standard deviation of 15. Is it likely that this could be a random sample from a population whose mean is known to be 113.5?
   (a) Yes, it is likely that a random sample mean could deviate that much from a population mean.
   (b) No, a random sample mean could not deviate that much from a population mean.
   (c) No, the calculations are incorrect.
   (d) The question cannot be answered on the basis of the information given.

3. One type of null hypothesis is:
   (a) an experimental hypothesis that does not imply empirical testing
   (b) a statistical hypothesis that assumes there are differences of varying sizes among the effects of different treatments
   (c) an experimental hypothesis that has been found to be inconsistent with empirical data
   (d) a statistical hypothesis that states there are no differences among the effects of treatments

4. The purpose of inferential statistics is:
   (a) to describe the results of a study
   (b) to test whether results support the research hypothesis
   (c) to permit inferences from sample results to a population
   (d) to verify the accuracy of descriptive statistics

5. An assumption basic to all inferential statistics is:
   (a) the sample(s) must be randomly selected
   (b) measurements must be on an interval scale
   (c) sample size must be over 30
   (d) the null hypothesis is true

6. A sampling distribution is:
   (a) a distribution of scores in a sample
   (b) a frequency polygon made from sample values
   (c) a frequency distribution of population values
   (d) a frequency polygon based on all the scores in a population

7. The inference test used when both variables are categorical is:
   (a) the t test for r
   (b) the Mann-Whitney U test
   (c) Chi-Square
   (d) the Sign test

8. The determination of statistical significance of a mean makes use of:
   (a) the correspondence between **z**-scores and areas under the normal curve
   (b) the relationship between raw scores and percentile values
   (c) the calculation of the range of scores
   (d) the relationship between a frequency distribution and a frequency polygon

9. Establishing a 95% confidence interval enables a researcher to:
   (a) state the values that encompass all but 95% of the sample scores
   (b) state the values that encompass 95% of the sample scores
   (c) state the values that encompass 95% of the population parameters
   (d) state the values that encompass the population parameters in 95% of such instances

10. The standard deviation of a sampling distribution of means is called:
    (a) the standard error of the mean
    (b) the standard error of the difference in means
    (c) the standard error of measurement
    (d) a **z**-score

11. If p <.01, a researcher would:
    (a) accept the null hypothesis
    (b) reject the null hypothesis
    (c) reject the research hypothesis
    (d) none of the above

12. If p <.10, the researcher will be:
    (a) wrong in rejecting the null hypothesis 10 times in 100
    (b) wrong in accepting the null hypothesis 10 times in 100
    (a) right in rejecting the null hypothesis 10 times in 100
    (a) right in accepting the null hypothesis 10 times in 100

13. Calculation of the contingency coefficient requires:
    (a) calculation of the standard deviation
    (b) calculation of Chi-Square
    (c) calculation of the median
    (d) calculation of the standard error of the mean

14. A one-tailed test of statistical significance is appropriate when:
   (a) no research hypothesis was stated
   (b) a non-directional research hypothesis was stated
   (c) a directional research hypothesis was stated
   (d) the data show a skewed frequency polygon

15. A disadvantage of non-parametric inference tests is that they:
   (a) are less likely to show statistical significance than parametric tests
   (b) require more assumptions than parametric tests
   (c) require more valid data than parametric tests
   (d) are harder to calculate than parametric tests

16. A hypothesis which states that the experimental group mean will be higher than the control group mean should:
   (a) not use a test of statistical significance
   (b) use a one-tailed test of statistical significance
   (c) use a two-tailed test of statistical significance
   (d) use a Chi-Square test

17. The purpose of a confidence interval is to:
   (a) determine whether a relationship is of practical importance
   (b) assess the validity of scores
   (c) determine the range of sample scores
   (d) establish boundaries of population parameters

18. An advantage of non-parametric inference tests is that they:
   (a) are more sensitive than parametric tests
   (b) require the use of only a nominal scale
   (c) require a smaller sample than parametric tests
   (d) require fewer assumptions than parametric tests

19. The magnitude of sampling error of a mean depends on:
   (a) the size of the sample mean and the sample size
   (b) sample size and sample spread
   (c) sample spread and the magnitude of the mean
   (d) the size of the population mean and sample size

20. If the null hypothesis is rejected:
   (a) the research hypothesis is rejected
   (b) the research hypothesis is accepted
   (c) the research results cannot be interpreted
   (d) the research hypothesis is proven

21. The magnitude of Chi-Square depends on the:
    (a) number of degrees of freedom
    (b) size of the sample
    (c) total number of categories
    (d) differences between observed and expected frequencies

22. Which of the following inference tests is <u>not</u> appropriate for a comparison of two means in a causal comparative study?
    (a) The Mann-Whitney U test
    (b) ANOVA
    (c) Chi-square
    (d) A *t* test for independent means

23. Which of the following inference tests is appropriate for a comparison of rankings of two groups in a causal comparative study?
    (a) The Mann-Whitney U test
    (b) ANOVA
    (c) A *t* test for correlated means
    (d) A *t* test for independent means

24. Which of the following inference tests is appropriate for a comparison of means in an experiment in which each subject receives both treatments?
    (a) The Mann-Whitney U test
    (b) Chi-square
    (c) A *t* test for correlated means
    (d) A *t* test for independent means

25. Which of the following inference tests is appropriate for a comparison of means of four independent groups in an experimental study?
    (a) The Mann-Whitney U test
    (b) ANOVA
    (c) A *t* test for correlated means
    (d) A *t* test for independent means

CHAPTER ELEVEN
STATISTICS IN PERSPECTIVE

Chapter Objectives

Reading this chapter should enable students to:

- *state* at least two recommendations for comparing data obtained from two or more groups.
- *state* at least two recommendations for relating variables within a single group.
- *explain* what is meant by the term "effect size."
- *describe* briefly how to use frequency polygons, scatterplots, and crossbreak tables to interpret data.
- *differentiate* between statistically significant and practically significant research results.

Points to Stress

1. Why it is important to report effect size.
2. How frequency polygons, scatterplots, and crossbreak tables can be helpful in interpreting data.
3. The difference between statistically significant and practically significant research results.

Teaching Suggestions

1. Collect Problem Sheet #10 from the class and answer any questions students may have about it.
2. Discuss each of the recommendations presented in the chapter and summarized on page 237. Ask one or two students to select a study from the literature and tell how many of the recommendations were followed by the authors of the study. Since these recommendations are subject to debate, alternative views (e.g., when small relationships might be important) should be presented.
3. Discuss the difference between statistical significance and practical significance with the class. Ask students to give some examples of how the results of a study might be statistically, yet not educationally, significant.
4. Go over the calculations in Appendix D so that students realize they can perform the operations. If desired, provide new data, and have students (individually or in groups) carry out the calculations.
5. Break the class down into small groups to discuss and begin work on Problem Sheet #11.

Answers to Discussion Questions

(Note to Instructor: Many of these "Questions for Discussion" are open-ended in nature and have no right answer. Students should be encouraged to offer as many alternative answers as they think plausible, and to explain the reasons for the answers they give.)

1. Give some examples of how the results of a study might be significant statistically, yet unimportant educationally. Could the reverse be true?
Answer: *A difference between correlations of .50 and .52 might be statistically significant with a large enough sample, yet certainly would not be educationally important. The same could be true for a difference of 110 and 112 between the mean I.Q. scores of two groups. Also, a difference in means can be very small, but statistically significant if there is very small variability in each group. The reverse also could be true. A meaningful difference can be non-significant if one has a small n.*
2. How would you interpret the following fictitious results of a comparison of computer-based vs. no-computer mathematics classes on an end-of-semester examination?

	Computer Group	No-Computer Group
n	65	65
mean	63	60
range	20-85	18-90
SD	8.5	10.4

A t-test for independent means results in p<.05 (one-tailed test)

Answer: *The computer group is statistically significantly higher (if random samples were used). A three point mean difference is of questionable importance when the range of scores is 26-90 or 64. Effect size equals 3/10.4=.29 which is considerably below the recommended criterion of .50. The no-computer group appears to be more variable.*
3. How would you interpret the following fictitious results of a study correlating anxiety with task performance? What additional information would you want to have?

r =.20 (not significant at the .05 level)

Eta =.50 (significant at the .05 level)

Answer: *The relationship is best represented by a curve, not a straight line. You would want to see the scatterplot in order to interpret the relationship most accurately.*

4. How would you interpret the following fictitious data from a study relating gender and handedness? What additional information would you want to have?

	Male	Female	Total
Right-handed	100 (120)	170 (150)	270
Left-handed	60 (40)	30 (50)	90
Total	160	200	360

Answer: *Males are likely to be left-handed; females more likely to be right-handed (compare the actual and expected frequencies). But some questions to be asked would include: "Were random samples used?" "From what populations?" "Why are there fewer males than females?"*

5. Are there times when a slight difference in means (e.g., an effect size of less than .50) might be important? Explain your answer. Answer: *Yes, when they either support or refute theoretical preditions.*

TEST FOR CHAPTER ELEVEN

1. The first step in analyzing data in a comparison group study is to:
   (a) calculate averages
   (b) construct frequency polygons
   (c) calculate measures of variability
   (d) determine statistical significance

2. A useful means of evaluating obtained differences among averages is by:
   (a) comparison to averages of previously identified groups
   (b) examining the size of the groups
   (c) converting them to percentiles
   (d) calculating the magnitude of t

3. Which of the following is not a danger in using inferential statistics to evaluate differences in averages?
   (a) Important differences may be ignored
   (b) Resulting probabilities are likely to be in error
   (c) Complex calculations are likely to contain errors
   (d) Large samples can make trivial differences appear important

4. One commonly used index of effect size is obtained by:
   (a) dividing the difference between means by the standard error of measurement
   (b) dividing the difference between means by the standard error of the mean
   (c) dividing the difference between means by the standard deviation of the control group
   (d) none of the above

5. In a study comparing class size to mathematics achievement, the unit of analysis is:
   (a) the individual student
   (b) the class
   (c) the teacher
   (d) none of the above

6. It is generally recommended that an effect size (E.S.) be of what magnitude before concluding that a difference in means is important?
   (a) .25
   (b) .50
   (c) 1.00
   (d) 2.00

7. Scatterplots are recommended in addition to correlation coefficients because they:
   (a) can correct errors in calculating
   (b) provide a pictorial rather than a numerical assessment
   (c) indicate which average should be used
   (d) provide more information

8. Which of the following statements is correct?
   (a) More than one Pearson correlation coefficient can be calculated from the same scatterplot.
   (b) Only one Pearson correlation coefficient can be calculated from one scatterplot.
   (c) A scatterplot will show a higher relationship than the correlation coefficient calculated from it.
   (d) A scatterplot will show a lower relationship than the correlation coefficient calculated from it.

9. In practice, most useful correlations between different variables are between:
   (a) .00 and .30
   (b) .40 and .70
   (c) .70 and .90
   (d) over .90

10. If eta and *r* are in substantial disagreement:
   (a) eta should be used
   (b) *r* should be used
   (c) neither should be used
   (d) an error in calculation has been made

11. When in doubt as to whether parametric or nonparametric statistics are appropriate, a researcher should:
   (a) report only parametric statistics
   (b) report only nonparametric statistics
   (c) report both
   (d) use neither

12. The most appropriate indicator of the importance of a relationship between two categorical variables is:
   (a) the crossbreak table
   (b) Chi-Square
   (c) comparison of actual and expected frequencies
   (d) the contingency coefficient

13. In a study in which all subjects receive both treatments, the appropriate descriptive statistic to use is:
   (a) the Pearson correlation coefficient
   (b) the mean
   (c) the contingency coefficient
   (d) Chi-Square

14. The importance of a 15 point difference in means between two groups:
   (a) depends on the spread of scores in each group
   (b) depends on the shape of the frequency polygons
   (c) depends on the number of cases in each group
   (d) all of the above

15. Calculation of Pearson *r* is most justified when the points on a scatterplot:
   (a) approximate a triangular shape
   (b) contain a few points that do not fit the overall pattern
   (c) fall into two distinct groups
   (d) cluster around a diagonal line

16. Confidence intervals are recommended rather than significance tests because they:
   (a) provide more information
   (b) are easier to calculate
   (c) require fewer mathematical assumptions
   (d) do not require as large a sample

17. When random sampling was not used, probabilities obtained from inferential statistical procedures should:
   (a) not be reported
   (b) be treated only as crude indices
   (c) be reported only if less than .01
   (d) be used as the primary index of the importance of results

18. If inferential statistics are calculated, they should be obtained:
   (a) as the first step in data analysis
   (b) as part of a comprehensive assessment of results
   (c) only after demonstration that the magnitude of the obtained relationship is worthy of attention
   (d) as part of the determination of effect size

19. In a comparison group study using two randomly selected groups, effect size=.24, and p<.01. This means the:
    (a) difference in means is small and probably due to sampling error
    (b) difference in means is small but probably is not due to sampling error
    (c) difference in means is large enough to be important, but may well be due to sampling error
    (d) difference in means is large and probably not due to sampling error

20. A researcher discussing the information in item #19 could be criticized for:
    (a) making too much of a trivial relationship
    (b) incorrect use of inferential statistics
    (c) an error in computation
    (d) all of the above

CHAPTER TWELVE
INTERNAL VALIDITY

Chapter Objectives

Reading this chapter should enable students to:

•*explain* what is meant by the term "internal validity."

•*explain* what is meant by a "subject characteristics" threat to internal validity, and *give an example* of such a threat.

•*explain* what is meant by a "mortality" threat to internal validity, and *give an example* of such a threat.

•*explain* what is meant by a "location" threat to internal validity, and *give an example* of such a threat.

•*explain* what is meant by an "instrumentation" threat to internal validity, and *give an example* of such a threat.

•*explain* what is meant by a "testing" threat to internal validity, and *give an example* of such a threat.

•*explain* what is meant by a "history" threat to internal validity, and *give an example* of such a threat.

•*explain* what is meant by a "maturation" threat to internal validity, and *give an example* of such a threat.

•*explain* what is meant by a "subject attitude" threat to internal validity, and *give an example* of such a threat.

•*explain* what is meant by a "regression" threat to internal validity, and *give an example* of such a threat.

•*explain* what is meant by an "implementer" threat to internal validity, and *give an example* of such a threat.

•*identify* various threats to internal validity in published research articles.

•*suggest* possible remedies for specific examples of the various threats to internal validity.

Points to Stress

1. Why it is important to control for internal validity
2. The various threats to internal validity discussed in the chapter

Teaching Suggestions

1. Collect Problem Sheet #11 from the class and answer any questions students may have about it.

2. Xerox a few published research studies from the literature and bring them to class. Break the class down into small groups to search for any threats to internal validity they can find in these studies. Assign one student from each group to report on what they find.

3. Ask students to suggest additional examples for each of the threats to internal validity besides those given in the chapter.

4. Review discussion question #4 on page 257 in the text with the class.

5. Hold a class discussion on question #6 on page 258 with the class.

6. Break the class down into small groups to discuss and begin work on Problem Sheet #12.

Answers to Discussion Questions

(Note to Instructor: Many of these "Questions for Discussion" are open-ended in nature and have no right answer. Students should be encouraged to offer as many alternative answers as they think plausible, and to explain the reasons for the answers they give.)

1. Can a researcher prove conclusively that a study has internal validity? Explain. Answer: *No. One can never rule out all of the possible alternative explanations for the results of a study.*
2. In Chapter Six, we discussed the concept of "external validity." In what ways, if any, are internal and external validity related? Can a study have internal validity, but not external validity? If so, how? What about the reverse? Answer: *Both internal and external validity affect the interpretation of the results of a study. Both can be weak and thus limit conclusions. A study can have internal validity, but no external validity if there is good control of possible threats even though a convenience sample was used. The reverse is also possible if a random sample was used, even though there was poor control over possible threats.*
3. Many students often confuse the concept of "internal" validity with the idea of "instrument" validity. How would you explain the difference between the two? Answer: *Internal validity has to do with the possibility of alternative explanations for study results due to the effect of extraneous factors. Instrument validity has to do with the adequacy of the measurement process.*
4. What threat (or threats) to internal validity might exist in each of the following:

a. A researcher decides to try out a new mathematics curriculum in a nearby elementary school and compare student achievement in math with that of students in another elementary school using the regular curriculum. The researcher is not aware, however, that each of the students in the "new curriculum" school have computers to use in their classrooms

b. A researcher wishes to compare two different kinds of textbooks in two high school chemistry classes over a semester. She finds that 20 percent of one group, and ten percent of the other group are absent during the administration of unit tests.

c. In a study investigating the possible relationship between marital status and perceived changes during the last five years in the women's liberation movement, men and women interviewers get different reactions from female respondents to the same questions.

d. Teachers of an experimental English curriculum as well as teachers of the regular curriculum administer both pre- and post-tests to their own students.

e. Eighth grade students who volunteer to tutor third graders in reading show greater improvement in their own reading scores than a comparison group which does not participate in tutoring.

f. A researcher compares the effects of weekly individual and group counseling on the improvement of study habits. Each week, the students counseled as a group fill out questionnaires on their progress at the end of their meetings. The students counseled individually, however, fill out the questionnaires at home.

g. Those students who score in the bottom ten percent academically in a school in an economically depressed area are selected for a special program of enrichment. The program includes special games, extra materials, special "snacks," specially colored materials to use, new books, etc. The students score substantially higher on achievement tests six months after the program is instituted.

h. A group of elderly people is asked to fill out a questionnaire designed to investigate the possible relationship between "activity level" and "sense of life satisfaction."

i. In the same high school, two mathematics teachers succeed in getting personal computers for their students to use in class. The achievement scores of their classes are subsequently compared to the achievement scores of other classes which do not have computers.

Answers: *(a) history; (b) loss of subjects (also called mortality); (c) data collector characteristics; (d) data collector bias and testing; (e) subject characteristics; (f) location; (g) regression; (h) testing; (i) subject characteristics.*

5. How could you determine whether the threats you identified in each of the situations in #4 actually exist? Answers: *(a) Obtain the necessary information; (b) Find out why subjects were absent; (c) See if "reactions" are related to "marital status;" (d) Observe testing by teachers and interview subjects regarding possible "testing" threat; (e) Compare volunteers to the comparison group on variables related to reading improvement; (f) Observe some students in both settings; interview students in both groups regarding how they responded to the questionnaire; (g) Collect data on a comparison group selected in the same way; (h) Interview subjects on their perceptions of the study.*

6. Which of the threats we have discussed in this chapter do you think is the most important for a researcher to consider? Why? Which do you think would be the most difficult to control? Explain. Answer: *Most important: subject characteristics threat (groups likely to differ unless one employs random assignment and has a large n. Data collector bias may influence data; implementation can affect how treatments are administered. Most difficult to control: history (never can know all the events affecting subjects), implementation (implementers can never be totally neutral); loss of subjects (cannot prevent loss of subjects, and there is no way to adjust for unequal loss).*

TEST FOR CHAPTER TWELVE

1. Which of the following is the best way to control for the unwanted influence of maturation processes in an experiment?
   - (a) Increase the sample size for the experiment
   - (b) Use a pretest as well as a posttest
   - (c) Use a control group
   - (d) Use subjects who have stabilized with regard to maturational level

2. Students with low, average, and high scores on a commercial reading achievement test were used in a study designed to determine the effectiveness of a new method of teaching fifth grade reading. There were no other control or comparison groups. It was found that the low group made the greatest gain over a six month period. Concluding that the new method was most effective with the low group fails to consider some of the possible factors or influences, the most significant of which is:
   - (a) reactive effects of the experimental procedures
   - (b) contemporary history
   - (c) pretesting procedures
   - (d) statistical regression

3. Referring to the study in item #2 again, for what additional reason might the conclusion be unjustified?
   - (a) There was too small a number of experimental variables being studied to permit an adequate analysis of relationships.
   - (b) There was no adjustment for maturational processes.
   - (c) The classes using the new method were all from one school, which would allow the operation of extraneous variables.
   - (d) There was no comparison group.

4. Which of the following is a question of <u>internal</u> validity in experimental research?
   - (a) How widely can the results of the experiment be generalized?
   - (b) Was the sample representative of the population?
   - (c) Has maturation influenced the dependent variable?
   - (d) Did the instruments permit valid interpretations?

5. Subjects performing well merely because they are being observed (and not necessarily because of any effect of treatment) are considered to be under the influence of:
   - (a) the Hawthorne effect
   - (b) the novelty effect
   - (c) the halo effect
   - (d) none of the above

6. Internal validity often receives little attention in research proposals, perhaps because:
   (a) it is not very important
   (b) there is no agreement as to what it means
   (c) there is no way to handle problems of internal validity
   (d) a study can be carried out without considering it

7. The threat of "subject characteristics" refers to differences among subjects on:
   (a) a dependent variable
   (b) an independent variable
   (c) an extraneous variable
   (d a treatment variable

8. A threat to internal validity is the same as:
   (a) bias on the part of the researcher
   (b) an alternative explanation of results
   (c) a limitation on the generalizability of results
   (d) poor internal consistency of scores

9. Loss of subjects is a threat to internal validity because:
   (a) it reduces the size of the sample
   (b) those "lost" may differ on the dependent variable from the remainder
   (c) it reduces the power of statistical tests of significance
   (d) it means that results of the study are less generalizable

10. Which of the following is <u>not</u> an example of a possible location threat?
   (a) Experimental and control groups are in different schools.
   (b) Experimental classes are smaller than control group classes.
   (c) All tests are given in a noisy gymnasium.
   (d) Some parents are interviewed at home, others at school.

11. Instrument decay refers to the possibility that:
   (a) test content becomes "dated" during the course of a study
   (b) data collectors are lost during a study
   (c) records of data are lost during a study
   (d) the instrument is systematically altered during the course of a study

12. Loss of subjects is a serious threat to internal validity in an experimental study if:
   (a) the sample was too small to begin with
   (b) the loss is the same for all groups
   (c) more are lost from one group
   (d) losses are due to dislike of the researcher

13. Data collector characteristics may be a threat to internal validity if:
   (a) they are related to measurement of the dependent variable
   (b) they are related to the independent variable
   (c) more than one person collects the data in a study
   (d) all of the above

14. Which is the least effective means of controlling data collector bias?
   (a) Extensive training of the data collectors
   (b) Using norm-referenced instruments
   (c) Preventing data collectors from knowing the purpose or hypothesis of the study
   (d) Using a large sample

15. Loss of subjects in a study can best be handled by:
   (a) random replacement of subjects who are lost
   (b) providing demographic data on those who are "lost"
   (c) making statistical adjustments to the data
   (d) making every effort not to lose subjects

16. Which of the following might be a possible testing threat to the internal validity of a study?
   (a) A data collector allows some students additional time on a test.
   (b) Students are tested before and after a film on prejudice.
   (c) Experimental and control groups are given different instruments.
   (d) Some students mark answers on the test booklets.

17. A history threat to internal validity refers to the possibility that:
   (a) the dependent variable is affected by past experiences of the subjects
   (b) historical events are incorrectly reported
   (c) unknown events occurring during the study may affect the dependent variable
   (d) the prior history of the researcher may lead to unconscious bias

18. An implementer threat to internal validity in a study comparing two methods is best controlled by:
   (a) allowing teachers to select the method they will use
   (b) insisting that each teacher use the assigned method
   (c) making sure that all teachers are equal in ability
   (d) using many teachers with each method

19. When the same questionnaire is scored for opinions on two or more topics, a threat to internal validity may exist because:
   (a) respondents may psych out the researcher's hypothesis
   (b) the questionnaire becomes too long
   (c) some items may be similar to other items
   (d) reliability of both scores is likely to be reduced

20. In an experimental study, a subject characteristics threat may be present if:
    (a) experimental and control groups differ in size
    (b) age is related to the dependent variable
    (c) age is the independent variable
    (d) both (a) and (b) above are correct

21. In which of the following is a history threat least likely to occur?
    (a) Experimental and control groups are in the same classroom.
    (b) Experimental and control groups are different classes in the same school.
    (c) Experimental and control groups are in different schools.
    (d) Experimental and control groups are limited only to females.

22. With which of the following findings would a maturation threat be of most concern?
    (a) "Skills in long division showed marked improvement after three weeks of instruction in computer use."
    (b) "Third grade reading scores demonstrated substantial gains after six months of perceptual training."
    (c) "Knowledge of history improved greatly after a year of inquiry training."
    (d) "Foreign language usage was greatly enhanced by two years study in a language laboratory."

23. Which of the following illustrates an attitudinal threat to internal validity?
    (a) Teachers resented having to try a new curriculum approach.
    (b) The new curriculum was too difficult for the grade level in which it was used.
    (c) Students resented not receiving the new curriculum.
    (d) Test questions did not validly assess the new curriculum.

24. A regression threat to internal validity refers to the fact that:
    (a) groups selected at extremes will score closer to the average on retesting
    (b) students often forget what they learned during an intervention
    (c) a relationship is likely to be smaller when a study is replicated
    (d) data collectors can influence scores by their behavior

25. Which threat would not apply to a correlational study?
    (a) Subject characteristics
    (b) Data collector bias
    (c) History
    (d) Testing

CHAPTER THIRTEEN
EXPERIMENTAL RESEARCH

Chapter Objectives

Reading this chapter should enable students to:

•*describe* briefly the purpose of experimental research.

•*name* the basic steps involved in conducting an experiment.

•*describe* two ways in which experimental research differs from other forms of educational research.

•*explain* the difference between random assignment and random selection, and the importance of each.

•*explain* what is meant by the phrase "manipulation of variables", and *describe* at least three ways in which such manipulation can occur.

•*distinguish* between examples of weak and strong experimental designs, and *draw diagrams* of such designs.

•*identify* various threats to internal validity associated with different experimental designs.

•*explain* at least three ways in which various threats to internal validity in experimental research can be controlled.

•*explain* how matching can be used to equate groups in experimental studies.

•*describe* briefly the purpose of factorial and counterbalanced designs, and *draw diagrams* of such designs.

•*describe* briefly the purpose of a time-series design, and *draw a diagram* of this design.

•*describe* briefly the purpose of single-subject designs, and *draw diagrams* of at least two such designs.

•*explain* briefly why it is important to replicate single-subject designs.

•*describe* briefly how to assess probable threats to internal validity in an experimental study.

•*recognize* an experimental study when they come across one in the literature.

Points to Stress

1. How experimental research differs from other types of research.
2. The difference between random selection and random assignment.
3. What it means to "manipulate" a variable.
4. The difference between strong and weak experimental designs.
5. Why experimental research is considered important to do.
6. How to evaluate (and control) threats to internal validity.

Teaching Suggestions

1. Collect Problem Sheet #12 from the class and answer any questions students may have about it.

2. Go over each of the research designs described in pages 267-284 of the text with the class to be sure the class understands them. Answer any questions students may have about particular designs.

3. Make a transparency of Figure 13.4, "Example of a Randomized Posttest-Only Control Group Design," and Figure 13.5, "Example of a

Randomized Pretest-Posttest Control Group Design." Both are on the same transparency. Then prepare a transparency of Figure 13.6, "Example of a Randomized Solomon Four-Group Design" (the masters for these transparencies can be found in the section entitled "Transparency Masters" later in this manual) for display on an overhead projector. Showing students these three designs closely following one another should help them understand the various components of an experimental design.

4. To help students understand the difference between a design that uses matched subjects and one that does not, make a transparency of Figure 13.7, "Example of a Randomized Posttest-Only Control Group Design, Using Matched Subjects" (a master for this and other transparencies can be found in the section entitled "Transparency Masters" later in this manual) for display on an overhead projector. Have students compare it with Figure 13.4.

5. To help students understand how an independent variable can *interact* with one or more dependent variables make a transparency of Figure 13.11, "Illustration of Interaction and No Interaction in a 2 by 2 Factorial Design" (a master can be found in the section entitled "Transparency Masters" later in this manual) for display on an overhead projector. Ask one student to explain why it is that (b) represents an example of interaction while (a) does not (see text pp. 279-280).

6. Make transparencies of the Single-Subject and Multiple-Baseline Designs, and of Figure 13.16, "Illustration of Multiple Baseline Design" (masters can be found in the section entitled "Transparency Masters" later in this manual), for display on an overhead projector. Ask the class to describe what differences they notice between these designs and the other experimental designs described in the chapter.

7. Make a transparency of Table 13.1, "Effectiveness of Experimental Designs in Controlling Threats to Internal Validity" (a master can be found in the section entitled "Transparency Masters" later in this manual) for display on an overhead projector. You may disagree with our assessment of some designs. If so, discuss your views with the class. Ask the class if any of them disagree with our assessment of the designs, and if so, why.

8. Go over the three steps for evaluating the likelihood of a threat to internal validity occurring in an experimental study that we suggest on page 286 of the text. Ask the class to try using the steps themselves with a study they find in the literature. Have a few students report their results to the class.

9. Discuss the article entitled "The Effects of Word Processing on Written Composition" on pages 292-300 of this chapter. Ask students to suggest any additional strengths or weaknesses in the article besides those we identify in our analysis on pages 301-304. You might want the class (eventually) to give their opinions as to which of the articles we have analyzed in Chapters 13-19 they think is the strongest and the weakest, and why.

10. Go over discussion questions #4 and #5 with the class.

Answers to Discussion Questions

(Note to Instructor: Many of these "Questions for Discussion" are open-ended in nature and have no right answer. Students should be encouraged to offer as many alternative answers as they think plausible, and to explain the reasons for the answers they give.)

1. An occasional criticism of experimental research is that it is very difficult to conduct in schools. Would you agree? Why or why not? Answer: *We would agree. Many classroom teachers are not eager to try new methods, since they are busy people with stressful jobs, and they hesitate to engage in activities that may take time away from what they see to be their primary focus--teaching. Further, it is often very difficult to control extraneous variables in schools, to standardize implementation, or to ensure random assignment of subjects to treatment and comparison groups.*

2. Are there any cause-and-effect statements that you can make that you believe would be true in most schools? Would you say, for example, that a sympathetic teacher "causes" elementary school students to like school more? Answer: *Answers will vary here. Be sure to ask students to explain the reasoning behind the answers they give.*

3. Are there any advantages to having more than one independent variable in an experimental design? If so, what are they? What about more than one dependent variable? Answer: *The advantage of having more than one independent variable in an experimental design is that the researcher can thereby explore the possibility of a greater number of "causes." Likewise for more than one dependent variable--more than one "effect" can be looked for. Also, interactions, which are often important, can be studied.*

4. What designs could be used in each of the following studies? (Note: More than one design is possible in each instance.)

a. A comparison of two different ways of teaching spelling to first graders.

b. The effectiveness of weekly tutoring sessions on the reading ability of third graders.

c. A comparison of a third period high school English class taught by the discussion method with a third period (same high school) English class taught by the lecture method.

d. The effectiveness of reinforcement on decreasing stuttering in a student with this speech defect.

e. The effects of a year long weight-training program on a group of high school athletes.

f. The possible effects of age, gender, and method on student liking for history.

Answers: *(a) a posttest-only control group, or a pretest-posttest control group design; (b) a time series design; (c) a matching only control group design; (d) a single subject, either ABAB or multiple baseline, design; (e) a randomized control group design; (f) a factorial design.*

5. What flaw can you find in each of the following studies?

a. A teacher tries out a new mathematics textbook with her class for a semester. At the end of the semester, she reports that the interest of the class in mathematics is markedly higher than she has ever seen it in the past with other classes using another text.

b. A teacher divides her class into two subgroups, with each subgroup being taught spelling by a different method. Each group listens to the teacher instruct the other group while they wait their turn.

c. A researcher calls for eighth grade students to volunteer to tutor third grade students who are having difficulty in reading. She gives those who volunteer a pre-test designed to measure their "willingness to be a tutor." She compares their effectivenss as tutors with a control group not given the pre-test. They have a much higher mean effectiveness score.

d. A teacher decides to try out a new textbook in one of her social studies classes. She uses it for four weeks, and then compares the scores on a unit test of this class with the scores of her other classes. All classes are studying the same material. During the unit test, however, a fire drill occurs, and the class loses about ten minutes of the time allotted for the test.

e. An interviewer goes door to door in an ethically mixed neighborhood to ask the residents questions concerning their feelings about living in this area. She has a list of forty questions she tries to ask each resident. One of the questions which some people refuse to answer is "Why do you like to live in this neighborhood?"

f. Two groups of third graders are compared with regard to running ability. One group is tested during physical education class in the school gymnasium, while the other is tested after school on the football field.

g. A researcher compares a third-period English class with a fifth-period Chemistry class in terms of their interest in the subject taught. The English class is taught by the discussion method, while the Chemistry class is taught by the lecture method.

Answers: *(a) This is a one-shot case study, and the higher interest perceived by the teacher at the end of the semester could be due to a number of other factors besides the new text. (b) Here we have multiple-treatment interference. Each group knows what is happening to the other group, and hence their performance may be affected accordingly. (c) The teacher has (unwittingly, we assume) created a pretest effect. Also the use of volunteers may produce a subject characteristics bias. (d) The fire drill represents a history threat. (e) The locations are different. (f) Time of day is different.*

TEST FOR CHAPTER THIRTEEN

1. Why are control groups necessary in certain experiments?
   (a) To make sure that the experimenter is honest
   (b) To make it easier to estimate the influence of the independent variable
   (c) To enable the researcher to repeat the experiment
   (d) To enable the researcher to identify the dependent variable

2. One difference between the experimental and other methods in research has to do with the:
   (a) number of subjects
   (b) control of variables
   (c) recording of data
   (d) time span of the study

3. In a large high school, the 25 students who scored highest on an English pretest were placed in a special class. At the end of one semester, they were given another English achievement test. The mean grade level equivalents were compared for the two tests. This is an example of a:
   (a) one-group pretest-posttest design
   (b) randomized control group pretest-posttest design
   (c) time series design
   (d) static group comparison design

4. The feature that best characterizes experimental research is the:
   (a) repetition of observations
   (b) systematic variation of conditions
   (c) making of exact measurements
   (d) concept of correlation

5. Which of the following is a probable independent variable in an experiment?
   (a) Self-esteem
   (b) Reading achievement
   (c) Teacher friendliness
   (d) Aggressive behavior

6. Experimental research is the most powerful research method for:
   (a) identifying important dependent variables
   (b) determining cause and effect
   (c) identifying possible relationships
   (d) generalizing the results of a study

7. In order to do an experimental study of the effects of TV viewing, a researcher must:
   (a) determine how much TV is watched by each subject
   (b) locate groups that differ in amount of TV viewed
   (c) arrange for some subjects to view more TV than others
   (d) ask subjects a series of questions about the effects of TV viewing

8. Which of the following can be present in an experimental study?
   (a) Random assignment and random selection
   (b) Random assignment without random selection
   (c) Random selection without random assignment
   (d) All of the above

9. The primary defect of the one-shot case study is:
   (a) there is no way to tell whether the treatment had any effect
   (b) poor control over the subjects characteristics threat
   (c) poor control of researcher bias
   (d) inability to control for maturation

10. In order to be a threat to the internal validity of an experimental study an extraneous variable such as age must:
   (a) be related to the dependent variable
   (b) differ among treatment groups
   (c) both (a) and (b)
   (d) neither (a) nor (b)

11. Loss of subjects in a given experiment constitutes a probable threat to the internal validity of the study if:
   (a) those lost are representative of their original groups
   (b) a greater number are lost from one group than from the other(s)
   (c) losses are not randomly replaced
   (d) statistical adjustments are not made

12. A major problem with experimental research in education is that:
   (a) there is no way to control a "history" threat
   (b) there is no way to control the subject characteristics threat
   (c) the researcher may not have sufficient control over treatments
   (d) there is no way to control data collector bias

13. Which is <u>not</u> a serious threat in a one group pretest-posttest design?
   (a) Maturation
   (b) Characteristics of subjects
   (c) History
   (d) Statistical regression

14. Which is likely to be the most serious threat in a static-group comparison design?
    (a) Maturation
    (b) History
    (c) Testing
    (d) Characteristics of subjects

15. An important difference between experimental and non-experimental research is that the independent variable in experimental research is:
    (a) quantitative
    (b) randomly assigned
    (c) constant
    (d) manipulated

16. The randomized posttest only control group design is least effective in controlling:
    (a) maturation
    (b) subject characteristics
    (c) implementer effect
    (d) history

17. The randomized pretest-posttest control group design requires the researcher to decide whether:
    (a) subject characteristics need to be controlled
    (b) information on the pretest is worth the possible bias
    (c) to randomize before or after the pretest is given
    (d) administration of the pretest is worth the effort required

18. A researcher would be likely to use matching in a randomized posttest control group design:
    (a) only if he or she misunderstood randomization
    (b) in order to control for a possible history threat to internal validity
    (c) in order to control for loss of subjects
    (d) if the number in each treatment group is small

19. An advantage of statistical matching over mechanical matching is that:
    (a) no subjects are lost due to matching
    (b) the data are easier to analyze
    (c) less reliable measures can be used
    (d) it provides better control of a possible testing threat

20. A researcher would use matching rather than random assignment when:
    (a) the sample is large
    (b) better control is needed
    (c) random assignment is impossible
    (d) data on matching variables is easily obtained

21. The counterbalanced design is subject to a(n):
    (a) subject characteristics threat
    (b) multiple treatment interference threat
    (c) attitude of subjects threat
    (d) maturation threat

22. The purpose of the Solomon Four-Group design is to:
    (a) control for effects of pretesting
    (b) avoid having to assign subjects randomly to groups
    (c) permit use of a smaller sample
    (d) control for loss of subjects

23. The time-series design is seldom used because:
    (a) data collection is so time consuming
    (b) data are likely to be unreliable
    (c) it provides poor control for a subject characteristics threat
    (d) it provides poor control for maturation

24. A factorial design can be used to:
    (a) study the combined effect of two or more variables
    (b) control the subject characteristics threat
    (c) assess the effect of several independent variables
    (d) all of the above

25. During the second baseline in ABA and ABAB designs, the researcher hopes to see:
    (a) the curve flatten out parallel to the X axis
    (b) the curve continue the trend shown in "B"
    (c) the curve reverse the trend shown in "B"
    (d) none of the above

26. Use of a multiple baseline design requires that:
    (a) the behaviors observed be distinctly different from one another
    (b) baseline data on all behaviors be obtained during the same time span
    (c) the same treatment be used with all behaviors
    (d) all of the above

27. The primary limitation of single-subject designs is:
    (a) unreliability of measures
    (b) poor control of a maturation threat
    (c) limited generalizability
    (d) poor control of a history threat

28. Which of the following threats are not controlled by any of the designs discussed in Chapter Thirteen?

  (a) Subject characteristics and maturation
  (b) Testing and history
  (c) Implementer and data collector bias
  (d) Data collector characteristics and loss of subjects

CHAPTER FOURTEEN
CORRELATIONAL RESEARCH

Chapter Objectives

Reading this chapter should enable students to:

•*describe* briefly what is meant by associational research.
•*state* the two major purposes of correlational studies.
•*distinguish* between predictor and criterion variables.
•*explain* the role of correlational studies in exploring causation.
•*explain* how a scatterplot can be used to predict an outcome.
•*describe* what is meant by a prediction equation.
•*explain* briefly the ideas underlying multiple correlation, factor analysis, and path analysis.
•*identify* and *describe briefly* the steps involved in conducting a correlational study.
•*describe* the procedures followed in correlation studies.
•*interpret* correlation coefficients of different magnitudes.
•*explain* the rationale for partial correlation.
•*describe* some of the threats to internal validity that exist in correlation studies, and *explain* how to identify them.
•*discuss* how to control for these threats.
•*recognize* a correlational study when they come across one in the educational research literature.

Points to Stress

1. The difference between correlation and causation.
2. How a scatterplot can be used to predict an outcome.
3. What a correlation coefficient represents.
4. How to evaluate (and control) threats to internal validity.

Teaching Suggestions

1. Hold individual conferences to discuss Problem Sheet #13 with those students who are designing an experimental study and want to discuss their progress.

2. Review the concept of correlation by making a transparency of Figure 14.1, "Scatterplot Illustrating a Correlation of +1.00" (a master can be found in the section entitled "Transparency Masters" later in this manual) for display on an overhead projector. Point out that all of the dots fall on a diagonal line, and hence the correlation is a perfect positive correlation. Ask a student to draw on the chalkboard what a perfect negative correlation (-1.00) would look like. Project a transparency of Table 14.1 using an overhead projector, covering up the headings, and ask students to identify which of the three distributions the scatterplot in Figure 14.1 represents (it represents distribution A).

3. Make a transparency of Figure 14.2, "Prediction of Relationship between Variables Using a Scatterplot" (a master can be found in the section

entitled "Transparency Masters" later in this manual) for display on an overhead projector. Have them look at Table 14.2 in the text to realize that the scatterplot in Figure 14.2 represents the data in Table 14.2. To further help students see the relationship between frequency distributions and scatterplots, you might want to have students make scatterplots of a number of distributions.

4. Use Figure 14.2 to illustrate how a score can be predicted from a scatterplot. Give some hypothetical "Teacher Expectation of Failure" scores, and ask students to say what the predicted "Disruptive Behavior" score would accordingly be.

5. To illustrate how two variables can be related to each other, but not to a third variable, make a transparency of Figure 14.6, "Circle Diagrams Illustrating Relationships Among Variables" (a master can be found in the section entitled "Transparency Masters" later in this manual) for display on an overhead projector.

6. Discuss any of the questions on page 337 of the text with the class.

7. Discuss the article entitled "Moral Development and Empathy in Counseling" on pages 327-332 of this chapter. Ask students to suggest any additional strengths or weaknesses in the article besides those we identify in our analysis on pages 333-335. You might (eventually) want the class to give their opinions as to which of the articles we have analyzed in Chapters 13-19 they think is the strongest and the weakest, and why.

8. Go over the three steps for evaluating the likelihood of a threat to internal validity occurring in a correlational study that we suggest on page 323 of the text. Ask the class to try using the steps themselves with a correlational study they find in the literature. Have a few students report to the class their results.

9. We have found that most students are able to follow the rationale for partial correlation (see p. 320). If necessary, however, you may want to have the class look at Figure 14.4 in the text as you go over the steps in class.

Answers to Discussion Questions

(Note to Instructor: Many of these "Questions for Discussion" are open-ended in nature and have no right answer. Students should be encouraged to offer as many alternative answers as they think plausible, and to explain the reasons for the answers they give.)

1. A researcher finds a correlation of .43 between the scores on a test of writing ability and a test of speaking ability for a group of high school sophomores. On the basis of this correlation, which of the following conclusions, if any, would be justified?

a. Students who write well will also speak well.

b. Students who speak poorly will also write poorly.

c. No relationship exists between writing and speaking ability.

Answer: *Both (a) and (b) would be justified, since the correlation is positive, although there would be a number of exceptions.*

2. What is wrong with the following statements?

a. If each of two variables are highly correlated with a third variable, then they will also be highly correlated with each other.

b. A correlation of +.51 is better than a correlation of -.51.

c. On the whole, a researcher would generally be more pleased if the results of a study revealed a strongly positive correlation between two variables than if they revealed a strongly negative one.

Answers: *(a) The statement could be true, but it is not necessarily true. "A" might be correlated with "B" and "B" with "C," but this does not mean that "A" must be correlated with "C". See Figure 14.6 on page 326 in this chapter. (b) Both indicate the same degree of relationship. One is a negative correlation, the other is a postive correlation. (c) The answer here is the same as in (b). Both indicate the same degree of relationship--the same amount of strength.*

3. What is the difference between an effect and a relationship? Answer: *An effect inplies some degree of causation, a time sequence (effects are produced by causes). A relationship means only that two variables are connected in some way, but neither necessarily has to have been caused by the other (a third variable may be the culprit!).*

4. Suppose a researcher finds that a particular student's high school GPA is 2.75. Use the prediction equation on page--to predict the student's GPA (assume that a=.23 and b=.69). Answer: *.23 + .69(2.75)=2.13.*

5. Why are samples smaller than 30 likely to give an inaccurate estimate of the degree of relationship that exists between two variables? Answer: *Because r will fluctuate considerably based on what particular individuals happen to be in the sample. The sampling error is large.*

6. What is the difference, if any, between the sign of a correlation and the strength of a correlation? Answer: *The sign of a correlation indicates the nature of the relationship between the two variables. A positive sign (positive correlation) means that as one variable increases, the other also increases. A negative sign (negative correlation) means that as one variable increases, the other decreases. The strength of a correlation refers to the degree or intensity of the relationship; the higher the correlation, the stronger it is, regardless of sign.*

7. Which correlation is more indicative of a strong relationship: r=-.78 or r=+53? Answer: *r=-.78.*

8. Are there any types of instruments that could not be used in a correlational study? If so, why? Answer: *Those that yield categorical data only, e.g., questionnaire data on ethnicity, political preferences, etc.*

9. Would it be possible for a correlation to be statistically significant, yet educationally insignificant? If so, give an example. Answer: *Yes. A correlation of .05 might be statistically significant, if the n was large enough, yet would be educationally meaningless.*

10. Why do you suppose people often interpret correlational results as proving causation? Answer: *They think that "A" causes "B" based on prior experience with one (or a few) instances, or because it is consistent with their own "theories."*

TEST FOR CHAPTER FOURTEEN

1. When the correlation between two variables is high, we know that:
   (a) one variable has at least a small amount of causal influence on the other
   (b) both variables are the result of a common influence
   (c) the variables are independent
   (d) none of the above is necessarily true

2. A correlation coefficient of -0.79 between time spent in typing practice and the number of typing errors means that:
   (a) there is a positive correlation between the number of hours spent in typing practice and the number of typing errors
   (b) there is a cause-and-effect relationship between typing practice and typing errors
   (c) as time spent in practice increased, errors tended to decrease
   (d) the correlation coefficient has no meaning because it is negative

3. In which of the following would one be most likely to find a correlation coefficient of zero or close to zero?
   (a) Shoe sizes of adult males correlated with their salaries.
   (b) Age correlated with the cost of life insurance.
   (c) Age of car correlated with trade-in value.
   (d) Intelligence correlated with grades in arithmetic.

4. Which of the following procedures would yield the most appropriate data for studying the relationship between intelligence and achievement?
   (a) Administering an achievement test and an intelligence test to one sample of subjects
   (b) Administering an achievement test to one sample of subjects and an intelligence test to another sample of subjects
   (c) Administering an achievement test to one sample of subjects, all of whom have an I.Q. of 100
   (d) Administering an achievement test to two samples of subjects and an intelligence test to two different samples of subjects

5. A researcher studied the relationship between the use of alcohol and grades in college. She found that a larger proportion of drinkers received low grades than did teetotalers. She should conclude that:
   (a) bad grades drive students to drink
   (b) drinking causes bad grades
   (c) drinking habits and grades are related
   (d) drinking habits and grades are unrelated

6. Correlational research differs from experimental research in that:
   (a) there is no manipulation of variables
   (b) random sampling is not used
   (c) there is no concern regarding internal validity
   (d) researcher bias is not a problem

7. Correlational research is used to:
   (a) explore possible cause and effect sequences
   (b) predict future behavior
   (c) suggest experimental studies
   (d) all of the above

8. A regression line is used to:
   (a) estimate the score on one variable from the score on another variable
   (b) correct data for the regression threat to internal validity
   (c) estimate the extent to which material has been forgotten
   (d) connect the points in a scatterplot

9. Multiple regression is a technique for:
   (a) eliminating the effect of extraneous variables in a correlational study
   (b) adjusting scores for a data collector threat
   (c) predicting a criterion from two or more predictors in combination
   (d) reviving childhood memories

10. Discriminant function analysis is used to:
    (a) reduce the number of variables to a more manageable level
    (b) simplify the calculation of a multiple correlation coefficient
    (c) predict group membership from two or more quantitative variables
    (d) describe the relationships among several categorical variables

11. Path analysis is a technique for:
    (a) exploring theoretical cause-effect relationships
    (b) determining a regression line
    (c) estimating the amount of error associated with a predicted score
    (d) reducing the effects of an extraneous variable

12. Factor analysis has as its primary goal:
    (a) generalization
    (b) prediction
    (c) simplification
    (d) replication

13. What do multiple regression, path analysis and factor analysis all have in common?
    (a) They all result in a prediction equation.
    (b) They all are techniques for controlling threats to internal validity.
    (c) They all use the same basic equation.
    (d) They all begin with the correlations among all pairs of variables.

14. Partial correlation is a procedure for:
    (a) simplifying the determination of a regression line
    (b) reducing the nuimber of variables to a more manageable level
    (c) controlling a subject characteristics threat
    (d) exploring theoretical cause-effect relationships

15. Which is a probable threat to the internal validity of a correlational study?
    (a) History
    (b) Maturation
    (c) Instrument decay
    (d) Implementation

16. The rationale on which partial correlation is based includes:
    (a) determining the correlation between each original variable and the extraneous variable
    (b) adjusting each original variable by using its correlation with the extraneous variable
    (c) determining the correlation between the adjusted scores of each subject
    (d) all of the above

17. A correlation coefficient of .50 is considered satisfactory for:
    (a) test-restest reliability
    (b) observer agreement
    (c) validity
    (d) individual prediction

18. Which is <u>not</u> a likely threat to the internal validity of a correlational study?
    (a) Regression
    (b) Subject characteristics
    (c) Data collector bias
    (d) Location

19. In order to eliminate age as an explanation for a .55 correlation between oral vocabulary and reading proficiency, a researcher must determine:
    (a) the age of each subject
    (b) the correlation between age and oral vocabulary
    (d) the correlation between age and reading proficiency
    (d) all of the above

20. Socio-economic status would be considered an alternative explanation for a correlation of .60 betwen interest and achievement if:
    (a) the correlations between socio-economic status and the other variables were .10 and .20
    (b) the correlations between socio-economic status and the other variables were .90 and .10
    (c) the correlations between socio-economic status and the other variables were .50 and .40
    (d) the correlations between socio-economic status and the other variables were .10 and .80

CHAPTER FIFTEEN
CAUSAL-COMPARATIVE RESEARCH

Chapter Objectives

Reading this chapter should enable students to:

•*explain* what is meant by the term causal-comparative research.

•*describe* briefly how causal-comparative research is both similar to, yet different from, both correlational and experimental research.

•*identify* and *describe* briefly the steps involved in conducting a causal-comparative study.

•*draw* a diagram of a design for a causal-comparative study.

•*describe* how data are collected in causal-comparative research.

•*describe* some of the threats to internal validity that exist in causal-comparative studies.

•*discuss* how to control for these threats.

•*recognize* a causal-comparative study when they come across one in the educational research literature.

Points to Stress

1. Similarities and differences between causal-comparative and experimental research.
2. The three types of causal-comparative study.
3. The value of causal-comparative research for certain kinds of research questions.
4. How to evaluate (and control) threats to internal validity.

Teaching Suggestions

1. Hold individual conferences to discuss Problem Sheet #14 with those students who are designing a correlational study.

2. Make transparencies of the illustration on p. 345 (Basic Causal-Comparative Designs,), and Figure 15.1, "Example of the Basic Causal-Comparative Design" (masters can be found in the section entitled "Transparency Masters" later in this manual) for display on an overhead projector. Have them compare these designs with some of the experimental designs in Chapter Thirteen. What differences do they notice? Similarities?

3. Discuss the article entitled "Some Effects of Training on the Competence of Beginning Teachers" on pages 351-359 of this chapter. Ask students to suggest any additional strengths or weaknesses in the article besides those we identify in our analysis on pages 359-362. You might (eventually) want the class to give their opinions as to which of the articles we have analyzed in Chapters 13-19 they think is the strongest and the weakest, and why.

4. Go over the three steps for evaluating the likelihood of a threat to internal validity occurring in a causal-comparative study that we suggest on

page 323 of the text. Ask a volunteer to see if he or she can find a causal-comparative study in the literature to use the steps with, and report to the class their results.

5. Discuss any of the questions on pages 339-340 of the text with the class.

6. Review the similarities and differences between causal-comparative, correlational, and experimental research listed on page 319 of the text. Ask the class if they can suggest any additional similarities and/or differences than those listed here.

7. Ask students to suggest some research questions that can only be studied using a causal-comparative methodology.

Answers to Discussion Questions

(Note to Instructor: Many of these "Questions for Discussion" are open-ended in nature and have no right answer. Students should be encouraged to offer as many alternative answers as they think plausible, and to explain the reasons for the answers they give.)

1. Suppose a researcher was interested in finding out what factors cause delinquent behavior in teenagers. What might be a suitable comparison group for the researcher to use in investigating this question? Answer: *The same age group without a history of delinquency.*
2. Are there any types of instruments that could not be used in a causal-comparative study? If so, why? Answer: *Yes. For example, the questioning behavior of boys and girls could be observed in a second (or any) grade classroom.*
3. Can you suggest any other threats to internal validity besides those we mention in this chapter that might endanger a causal-comparative study? Answer: *Time of day at which the treatment is given or the data are collected in intervention (type 3) studies.*
4. When, if ever, might a researcher prefer to conduct a causal-comparative study rather than an experimental study? Suggest an example. Answer: *When an experiment is very costly to conduct, when comparing methods already in place (e.g., computer vs. non-computer classes), or when ethical issues preclude manipulation of the independent variable.*
5. What sorts of questions, if any, might lend themselves better to causal-comparative research than to experimental research? Why? Answer: *Those involving non-manipulable variables.*
6. Which do you think would be easier to do, causal-comparative or experimental research? Why? Answer: *Causal-comparative, since it primarily involves locating the relevant groups to be compared, whereas experimental research always involves some arrangement of the experimental treatment and conditions.*
7. Is random assignment possible in causal-comparative research? What about random selection? Explain. Answer: *No, it is impossible to use random assignment since the subjects are already formed into groups. Random selection, however, is possible, since a researcher could identify the populations to be compared and select randomly from each.*

8. Suppose a researcher was interested in the effects of team teaching on student attitudes toward history. Could such a topic be studied by means of causal-comparative research? If so, how? Answer: *Yes, by locating examples of groups who already have been exposed to a team teaching situation and compare them with similar groups not so exposed.*
9. What sorts of variables might it be wise for a researcher to think about controlling for in a causal-comparative study? What sorts of variables, if any, might be irrelevant? Answer: *Subject characteristics, location and instrumentation; also Implementer, history and maturation in Type 3 studies. The latter are generally irrelevant in type 1 and type 2 studies.*
10. Might a researcher ever study the exact same variables in an experimental study that he or she studied in a causal-comparative study? If so, why? Answer: *Yes, but in type 3 studies only. Both treatment and outcomes could be the same. The experiment permits stronger inferences about causation.*
11. We state in the text that, in general, quantitative variables should not be collapsed into categorical variables because (a) the decision to do so is almost always an arbitrary one, and (b) too much information is lost by doing so. Can you suggest any quantitative variables that, for these reasons, should not be collapsed into categorical variables? Answer: *Some examples of quantitative variables that should not be collapsed into categorical variables would include reading achievement, critical thinking ability, attitudes toward busing, and self-esteem*. Can you suggest some quantitative variables that could justifiably be treated as categorical variables? Answer: *Some quantitative variables that might justifiably be collapsed would be (a) aggressive behavior: a researcher might compare a group of students whose behavior was so extreme as to result in expulsion from school with a group whose aggressive behavior was "tolerable;" (b) depression: a researcher might compare a group of students whose depression resulted in an inability to function in school or on a job with a group of students still able to function successfully.*
12. Suppose a researcher reports a higher incidence of childhood sexual abuse in adult women who have eating disorders than in a comparison group of women without eating disorders. Which variable is more likely to be the cause of the other? What other variables could be alternative or contributing causes? Answer: *Sexual abuse* is more likely to be the cause, due to time sequence. Other variables that might be a cause would include *age of puberty, number of siblings, presence of mother in the home, physical attractiveness,* and *self-image.*
13. Are there any research questions that cannot be studied by the causal-comparative method? Answer: *Only questions involving a "new" treatment or method (one that is not already in existence) and which therefore must be created by the researcher--an experimental study.*
14. A professor at a private women's college wishes to assess the degree of alienation present in undergraduates as compared to graduates at her

institution, using an instrument that she developed. (a) Which method, causal-comparative or experimental, would you recommend she use in her inquiry? Why? Answer: *It must be causal-comparative since the researcher cannot manipulate the independent variable.* (b) Would the fact that she plans to use an instrument that she herself developed make any difference in your recommendations? Answer: *No.*

TEST FOR CHAPTER FIFTEEN

1. Which of the following is not possible in causal-comparative research?
   (a) Use of comparison groups
   (b) Random assignment to treatment or comparison groups
   (c) Measurement
   (d) Observation

2. One way of providing some control in a causal-comparative research design is to:
   (a) match the subjects in the groups to be compared on as many extraneous variables as possible
   (b) list all of the subjects from the population under study and randomly assign them to experimental and control groups
   (c) do a pilot study before carrying out the main research
   (d) obtain measurements on an additional dependent variable

3. Causal-comparative research is so named because:
   (a) it is a way of exploring cause-effect relationships
   (b) it is the most effective method of determining cause and effect
   (c) it is intended only to explain reasons for group membership
   (d) it systematically alters causes in order to study their effects

4. Most causal-comparative studies begin with:
   (a) measurement of the dependent variable
   (b) assignment of subjects to treatment groups
   (c) known differences among two or more groups
   (d) measurement of the independent variable

5. Causal-comparative studies are conducted when experimentation is:
   (a) too expensive
   (b) impossible
   (c) unethical
   (d) all of the above

6. The causal-comparative and experimental methods are similar in that both:
   (a) require random selection of subjects
   (b) require random assignment of subjects
   (c) involve at least one categorical variable
   (d) require repeated measurement of subjects

7. The causal-comparative and correlational methods differ in that the causal-comparative method:
   (a) requires at least one categorical variable
   (b) attempts to explore causation
   (c) requires more reliable scores
   (d) requires a larger sample

8. The appropriate statistical procedure when all variables are categorical is the:
   (a) scatterplot
   (b) crossbreak table
   (c) frequency polygon
   (d) correlation coefficient

9. In a causal-comparative study, groups should be compared on:
   (a) only the variable of primary interest
   (b) all variables that are easily measured
   (c) those variables suggested by the researcher's rationale
   (d) only quantitative variables

10. A pitfall in much causal-comparative research is:
   (a) failure to define comparison groups carefully enough
   (b) using groups that are too homogeneous
   (c) matching on too many variables
   (d) use of inappropriate descriptive statistics

11. Matching to control a subject characteristics threat is often inappropriate for:
   (a) studies exploring causes of group membership
   (b) studies exploring consequences of group membership
   (c) studies exploring consequences of an intervention
   (d) all of the above

12. The most threats to the internal validity of a causal-comparative study occur in:
   (a) studies exploring causes of group membership
   (b) studies exploring consequences of group membership
   (c) studies exploring consequences of an intervention
   (d) studies comparing biologically determined groups

13. A researcher wishes to assess the effects of a new teaching technique on student performance in two sections of a high school mathematics course. She plans to control relevant variables by matching the subjects in the two sections. The relevant variables that she considers to be important are age, sex, amount of high school education, level of aspiration, and intelligence. She will arrange to have one section taught by the new technique and the other by a conventional technique. If she attempts to match on all of the variables listed, what problem is she likely to encounter?

(a) An excessive range of mental ability
(b) Excessive overlap among the dependent variables selected
(c) A lack of statistical techniques for analyzing results of this kind
(d) An insufficient number of cases for some of the classifications

14. Evaluating specific threats to internal validity in a causal-comparative study involves all of the following <u>except:</u>

(a) identifying factors related to the variable(s) on which groups are compared
(b) determining whether each factor is controlled by random assignment
(c) judging whether comparison groups are likely to differ on these factors
(d) prioritizing the seriousness of identified threats

15. In a causal-comparative study, comparison groups:

(a) are set up by the researcher
(b) are already in existence
(c) are obtained by random assignment
(d) cannot exceed three in number

16. Which of the following hypotheses can only be studied by using the causal-comparative method?

(a) Participation in a values clarification program will improve self-esteem.
(b) Girls have higher self-esteem than boys.
(c) Students high in self-esteem achieve higher grades when they attend college.
(d) Self-esteem decreases between ages 8 and 18.

17. Causal-comparative studies wherein all variables are categorical:
    (a) are impossible
    (b) are of little value
    (c) require a large number of variables
    (d) are relatively infrequent in education

18. A comparison of delinquents vs. non-delinquents might be made in order to:
    (a) determine probable factors leading to delinquency
    (b) predict future behavior of delinquents
    (c) test a theory on the development of delinquency
    (d) all of the above

19. When a quantitative variable is divided into categories:
    (a) precision is reduced
    (b) the basis for dividing is usually hard to defend
    (c) both (a) and (b)
    (d) neither (a) nor (b)

20. The major threat to internal validity in a causal-comparative study is:
    (a) location
    (b) subject characteristics
    (c) data collector bias
    (d) instrument decay

CHAPTER SIXTEEN
SURVEY RESEARCH

Chapter Objectives

Reading this chapter should enable students to:

- *explain* what a survey is.
- *name* three types of surveys conducted in educational research.
- *explain* the purpose of surveys.
- *explain* the difference between a cross-sectional and a longitudinal survey.
- *describe* how survey research differs from other types of research.
- *describe* briefly how a survey is conducted.
- *describe* briefly how mail surveys, telephone surveys, and face-to-face interviews differ, and *state* at least two advantages and disadvantages of each type.
- *describe* the most common pitfalls in developing survey questions.
- *explain* the difference between a closed-ended and an open-ended question, *give an example* of each, and *discuss* at least two advantages and disadvantages of each type.
- *explain* why nonresponse is a problem in survey research, and *name* at least two ways to improve the rate of response in surveys.
- *name* at least two threats to validity that can affect the results of a survey, and *explain* how such threats can be controlled.
- *recognize* an example of survey research when they come across one in the educational literature.

Points to Stress

1. How surveys provide useful information.
2. The difference between surveys and other types of research.
3. Limitations of surveys.
4. The distinction between closed-ended and open-ended questions.
5. Why nonresponse is a problem in survey research, and what to do about it.

Teaching Suggestions

1. Hold individual conferences to discuss Problem Sheet #15 with any students who are designing a causal-comparative study.
2. Make a transparency of Table 16.1,"Advantages and Disadvantages of Survey Data Collection Methods" (a master can be found in the section entitled "Transparency Masters" later in this manual) for display on an overhead projector. Ask students if they can suggest any additional advantages or disadvantages besides those listed in the table.
3. Discuss question #3 on page 400 with the class.
4. Write some examples of possible answers to discussion question #3 on page 400 of the text (see suggestions below) on the chalkboard. Ask volunteers to suggest other possibilities and have other members of the class critique them.

5. Make a transparency of Figure 16.1, "Example of Several Contingency Questions in an Interview Schedule" (a master can be found in the section entitled "Transparency Masters" later in this manual) for display on an overhead projector. Answer any questions students may have about the contingency format, and then break the class into two to three person groups to write contingency questions of their own.

6. Discuss the article entitled "Essay vs. Multiple-Choice Type Classroom Exams: The Student's Perspective" on pages 384-396 of this chapter. Ask students to suggest any additional strengths or weaknesses in the article besides those we identify in our analysis on pages 396-398. You might want the class to give their opinions as to which of the articles we have analyzed in Chapters 13-19 they think is the strongest and the weakest, and why.

7. Have the class work in small groups to construct questions on a specified topic. Have each group then present their questions to the total class for (a) responses, and (b) suggested improvements.

Answers to Discussion Questions

(Note to Instructor: Many of these "Questions for Discussion" are open-ended in nature and have no right answer. Students should be encouraged to offer as many alternative answers as they think plausible, and to explain the reasons for the answers they give.)

1. For what kinds of topics might a personal interview be superior to a mail or telephone survey? Give an example. Answer: *Those requiring detailed explanation or clarification of particular questions; those requiring the establishment of personal rapport with the individuals in the sample; those requiring probing or followup of particular questions.*

2. When, if ever, might a telephone survey be preferable to a mail survey? to a personal interview? Answer: *(a) When clarification or probing is required; (b) When subjects are asked to describe possibly embarrassing activities or behavior, such as recalling childhood events; or when anonymity is called for (e.g., when personal or sensitive questions will be asked).*

3. Give an example of a question a researcher might use to assess each of the following about members of a teachers group:

a. their income
b. their teaching style
c. their biggest worry
d. their knowledge of teaching methods
e. their opinions about homogeneous grouping of students

Answers: *Some examples might be:*

(a) In which of the following income brackets do you fall? (Various income brackets would then be listed, e.g., below $15,000; $15,001 to $25,000, etc.)

(b) How would you describe your teaching style, that is, the manner in which you teach your classes?

(c) What is your biggest worry in life?

(d) Which of the following teaching methods do you know the least about? (1) lecture; (2) small group discussions; (3) case studies; (4) inquiry teaching.

(e) Are you in favor, against, or neutral with regard to the homogeneous grouping of students?

4. Suppose a researcher is interested in finding out how elementary school administrators feel about elementary school counseling. Write a series of three contingency questions that could be used in a personal interview, and be prepared to discuss them. Answer: *The questions students prepare in response to this question will vary. Be sure, however, that they do write contingency questions (see pages 377-378 in the text).*

5. Which mode of data collection --mail, telephone, or personal interview-- would be best for each of the following surveys?

a. The reasons why some students drop out of college before they graduate

b. The feelings of high school teachers about special classes for the gifted

c. The attitudes of people about raising taxes to pay for the construction of new schools

d. The duties of secondary school superintendents in a midwestern state

e. The reasons why individuals of differing ethnicity did or did not decide to enter the teaching profession

f. The opinions of teachers toward the idea of minimum competency testing before permanent tenure would be granted

g. The opinions of parents of students in a private school toward the elimination of certain subjects from the curriculum

Answers: *Our opinion would be: (a) personal interview; (b) mail or personal interview; (c) telephone or mail; (d) personal interview; (e) personal interview or mail; (f) mail; (g) telephone or mail.*

6. Listed below are some definitions of target populations from which a sample is to be selected and surveyed. See if you can improve (make more precise) the definitions of each:

a. "All of the counselors in the school"

b. "All of the parents of the students in our school"

c. "All of the administrators in the school district"

d. "All chemistry students"

e. "All of the teachers of the gifted"

Answers: *Possible definitions that students might offer are many. Expect considerable variation in what students offer. Here are some examples to present in case students have difficulty making the definitions more precise: (a) all persons identified as counselors by the Principal of Jefferson School; (b) all of the persons having custodial responsibility for the students in Jefferson School; (c) all of the elementary and secondary school principals in the district; (d) all chemistry majors; (e) all of the teachers of students with IQ scores above 135.*

7. Look at each of the open-enaded questions on page 374 in the text. See if you can restate these in a closed-ended form. Answer: *Again, answers will vary. Here are some possibilities:*

(1) Rate the importance of each of the following characteristics as one a good administrator should possess:

	Unimportant			*Extremely important*	
patience	*1*	*2*	*3*	*4*	*5*
creativity	*1*	*2*	*3*	*4*	*5*
honesty	*1*	*2*	*3*	*4*	*5*
initiative	*1*	*2*	*3*	*4*	*5*
tact	*1*	*2*	*3*	*4*	*5*

(2) Which of the following is the most important problem facing public school teachers today?

a. Lack of discipline of students
b. Poor pay
c. Inadequate resources
d. Lack of administrative support
e. Class size

(3) In the list below, circle what you think are the three most useful activities for a classroom teacher to use:

a. student reports
b. homework
c. small group discussions
d. lectures
e. weekly tests
f. field trips

8. Try to restate any one of the closed-ended questionson page 374 of the text in a contingency format. Answer (Question 1C): *Have you taken a science class during the past semester?*

Yes ____ *No* ____

If yes, did you enjoy it?

Yes ____ *No* ____

9. What suggestions can you offer, beyond those given in this chapter, for improving the rate of response in surveys? Answer: *Replies will vary. Encourage students to explain the reasons behind their responses.*

TEST FOR CHAPTER SIXTEEN

1. Survey research is concerned primarily with:
   (a) explaning phenomena
   (b) determining relationships among variables
   (c) reporting existing conditions
   (d) statistical inference

2. Is it important to follow-up those persons in a survey who did not return questionnaires mailed to them?
   (a) No, because high precision is not needed in questionnaire surveys
   (b) No, because such delayed returns would be of doubtful value
   (c) Yes, because the sample that has already returned the questionnaire may be biased
   (d) Yes, because descriptive statistics require a large sample

3. The longitudinal method in developmental studies has the advantage of:
   (a) more extensive data on individual subjects
   (b) data for different age groups at the same point in time
   (c) prompt data gathering
   (d) no sampling errors

4. The purpose of most surveys is to:
   (a) explore cause and effect
   (b) obtain information from a sample
   (c) test hypotheses
   (d) describe the characteristics of a population

5. Items used in survey research can include:
   (a) test questions
   (b) questions of belief
   (c) factual questions
   (d) all of the above

6. In a panel study, the researcher obtains information from:
   (a) the same sample at different points in time
   (b) different samples at different times
   (c) different samples at the same time
   (d) an entire population at different points in time

7. The difference between a trend study and a cohort study is that a cohort study obtains data from:
   (a) the same sample at different points in time
   (b) different samples from the same specific population
   (c) different samples from a population whose members change somewhat
   (d) an entire population at different points in time

8. Which method cannot be used in conjunction with the survey method?
   (a) The experimental method
   (b) The causal-comparative method
   (c) The correlational method
   (d) All can be used

9. The major problem with mail surveys is the:
   (a) low response rate
   (b) cost
   (c) time required
   (d) training required

10. The primary advantages of the interview are:
   (a) high response rate and opportunity for clarification of questions
   (b) cost and training required
   (c) anonymity and cost
   (d) time required and response rate

11. An advantage of multiple-choice questions as compared to open-ended questions is that they:
   (a) are easier to construct
   (b) are easier to score
   (c) require more questions to cover a given topic
   (d) are easier to administer

12. An advantage of open-ended questions as compared to multiple-choice questions is that they:
   (a) are easier to score
   (b) are preferred by respondents
   (c) are less subject to misinterpretation
   (d) provide more variety of responses

13. Which of the following is the best question?
    (a) Do you favor tuition tax credits as a way of alleviating educational problems?
    (b) Do you support tuition tax credits?
    (c) Do you believe tuition tax credits would, on the whole, have more desirable than undesirable consequences?
    (d) Do you agree that tuition tax credits would not have negative effects?

14. A contingency question is one that:
    (a) is contingent upon the use of specialized vocabulary
    (b) depends on the answer to a prior question
    (c) provides at least three response questions
    (d) is only given to predetermined respondents

15. A cover letter should accomplish all of the following except:
    (a) ensuring cooperation of the respondent
    (b) assuring confidentiality
    (c) clarifying the researcher's hypotheses
    (d) facilitating a reply

16. Interviewers should be trained to do all of the following except:
    (a) establish a friendly relationship with the respondent
    (b) show their own views regarding the study
    (c) follow-up on ambiguous answers
    (d) ask questions in a standard manner

17. Which of the following is not likely to distort the results of a survey?
    (a) The location where data is obtained
    (b) The format of the questionnaire
    (c) The characteristics of the data collector
    (d) Statistical regression

18. Which of the following questions is most appropriately studied by means of a survey?
    (a) What are the effects of higher level questioning?
    (b) Are there differences between boys and girls in initiating social interaction?
    (c) What do university graduates view as strengths and weaknesses in their education?
    (d) What are the causes of high school school dropout?

19. Which of the following is an example of a cross-sectional survey?
    (a) An attitude scale is given to samples of 8, 10 and 12 year olds.
    (b) An opinionnaire is mailed to the same sample of graduates every year.
    (c) A group of gifted children is assessed every other year until adulthood.
    (d) None of the above.

20. Which of the following is a way researchers attempt to reduce non-response in survey studies?
    (a) Selecting inoffensive interviewers
    (b) Making cash payments to respondents
    (c) Having the study endorsed by prestigious individuals
    (d) All of the above

CHAPTER SEVENTEEN
CONTENT ANALYSIS RESEARCH

Chapter Objectives

Objectives. Reading this chapter should enable you to:

- *Explain* what a content analysis is
- *Explain* the purpose of content analysis
- *Name* three or four ways content analysis can be used in educational research
- *Explain* why a researcher might want to do a content analysis
- *Summarize* an example of content analysis
- *Describe* the steps involved in doing a content analysis
- *Describe* the kinds of sampling that can be done in content analysis
- *Describe* two advantages and two disadvantages of content analysis research
- *Recognize* an example of content analysis research when you come across it in the educational literature

Points to Stress

1. How content analysis research differs from the other types of research discussed in the text.
2. How content analysis can be used in educational research.
3. Steps involved in content analysis research.
4. The difference between manifest and latent content.
5. Some of the advantages and disadvantages of content analysis research compared to other kinds of educational research

Teaching Suggestions

1. Hold individual conferences to discuss Problem Sheet #17 with those students who are designing a content analysis study.

2. Review with the class the advantages and disadvantages of content analysis research described on pages 416-417 of the text. Ask students if they can suggest any in addition to what is listed here.

3. Review some of the applications of content analysis research described on pages 406-407 of the text to ensure students are clear about some of the possible uses of this type of research in education.

4. Review the steps involved in content analysis research as described on pages 407-413 of the text.

5. Discuss the differences between manifest and latent conten as described on pages 411-412 of the text, and ask students to give another example of each.

4. Discuss the example of content analysis research presented on pages 417-433 of this chapter. Ask students to suggest any additional strengths or weaknesses in the article besides those we identify in our analysis on pages 435-436. You might want the class to give their opinions (eventually) as to

which of the articles we have analyzed in Chapters 13-19 they think is the strongest and the weakest, and why.

5. Discuss any of the questions on pages 437-438 with the class.

6. If you have time, you might bring in a sample document of some type (an editorial, a magazine article, a short excerpt from a novel, a textbook, etc., and have the class suggest what sort of content analysis might be done on the document (oractually try to do a content analysis on the document, and then discuss the difficulties, if any, they encounter).

Answers to Discussion Questions

(Note to Instructor: Many of these "Questions for Discussion" are open-ended in nature and have no right answer. Students should be encouraged to offer as many alternative answers as they think plausible, and to explain the reasons for the answers they give.)

1. When, if ever, might it be more appropriate to do a content analysis than to use some other kind of methodology? Answer: *When it is important to be unobtrusive (e.g., a study of records of domestic violence; when it provides the most direct information (e.g., an analysis of bias in the media rather than obtaining opinions about bias); or when the study requires analysis of existing information, especially when large amounts of such information must be analyzed (e.g., an analysis of textbooks).*

2. When might it be inappropriate to use content analysis? Answer: *When more direct information is available (e.g., a direct observation of events is preferable to an analysis of the written accounts of events). When the study requires an intervention rather than an anlysis of existing information, although content analysis may be helpful in analyzing information.*

3. Give an example of some cataegaories a researcher might use to tabulate data in each of the following content analyses:

a. To investigate the amount and types of humor on television

b. To find out whether women are portrayed differently in novels today as compared to those of 30 years ago

c. To investigate the social implications of impressionistic paintings

d. To investigate whether civil or ciminal law makes the most distinctions between men and women

e. To describe the assumptions made in elementary school science programs

Answers: *(a) 1. visual/auditory/both. 2. Object of humor: self/family/friend/authority figure.*

(b) 1. optimistic/pesimistic/disappointed. 2. Past/present/future.

(c) 1. Supports social institutions/critical of social institutions/attacks social institutions. 2. optimistic/pessimistic/neither.

(d) Analysis of typescripts of court proceedings:

	Men		*Women*	
	Civil	*Criminal*	*Civil*	*Criminal*
Number of Cases				
Percent convictions				
Length of sentence				
<1 year				
2-5 years				
5-15 years				
>15 years				

(e) active learner/passive learner; equipped lab/homemade equipment; no math required/arithmetic required/ math beyond arithmetic required (e.g., sets, probability).

4. Which of the following proposed studies might lend themselves well to content analysis?

a. Finding out how teachers and students in an inner-city high school view the implementation of a new counseling program

b. Finding out whether women are portrayed differently in novels today as compared to those of 30 years ago

c. Finding out whether a new spelling book is more effective in helping students learn to spell than one that has previously been used

d. Finding out if the playing of classical music in writing classes helps students produce more original stories

e. Finding out if vocabulary level is related to speaking ability

g. Finding out how well kindergartners play with each other in the sandbox during recess

h. Finding out what courses were required to graduate from high school in the year 1890

Answers: *(a) Interview or questionnaire preferable. Content analysis may be useful in analysis. (b) Requires a content analysis of novels published during each time period. (c) An experimental or causal/comparative study in indicated. (d) Requires a content analysis of stories produced. (e) A correlational analysis of measures of each ability is indicated. Content analysis would probably be useful in analyzing examples of speaking ability. (f) Content analysis of written material may be useful. A content analysis of transcribed behavior during public and/or private reading may be helpful. The latter would probably be supplemented with some form of interviewing. (g) Direct observation is indicated. A content analysis may be useful in analyzing observational data. (h) A historical study is required. Content analysis probably would not be useful since the information obtained is straightforward.*

5. Which do you think would be more difficult to code--the manifest or the latent content of a movie? Why?Answer: *Latent since it requires judgments as to intentions, relationships, and the like. Manifest content could include*

tabulations within such categories as acts of physical violence, touching, verbal expression of affection, anger, and so forth.

6. "Never code only the latent content of a document without also coding at least some of the manifest content." Would you agree with this statement? Why or why not? Answer: *No. While coding of manifest content is generally recommended, there are times when it makes no sense (e.g., an analysis of moods created by various kinds of music. Since moods are so subjective, manifest content such as smiles or grimaces may lack validity).*

7. In terms of difficulty, how would you compare a content analysis approach to the study of social bias on television with a survey approach? In terms of useful information? Answer: *Content analysis is more difficult since an analysis of a large sample of programs would be necessary. It would, however, provide more direct information and checking the validity (manifest vs. latent) of the content is probably more persuasive than attempting to check the validity of the survey--unless, of course, the question were addressed to people's opinions about bias (but this is a different question).*

TEST FOR CHAPTER SEVENTEEN

1. Which of the following would be suitable for a content analysis study?
(a) a play
(b) rap music
(c) dinosaur bones
(d) all of the above

2. Which of the following would be best studied by means of a content analysis study?
(a) aggressive behavior males compared to females
(b) effects of a particular drug on aggressive behavior
(c) changes in attitudes toward aggressive behavior over the past 100 years
(d) the effect of age on aggressive behavior

3. The Whiting and Child study of child rearing illustrates the use of content analysis in conjunction with:
(a) experimental research
(b) ethnographic research
(c) historical research
(d) all of the above

4. A primary advantage of content analysis is:
(a) its' unobtrusive nature
(b) its' power to determine cause and effect
(c) its' use of statistical analysis
(d) the simplicity of analysis

5. Content analysis is a means of studying:
(a) written material
(b) communications
(c) visual images
(d)historical artifacts

6. Sampling methods used in content analysis studies include:
(a) stratified random sampling
(b) purposive sampling
(c) convenience sampling
(d) all of the above

7. The important difference between latent and manifest content is that latent content:
   - (a) is more valuable
   - (b) is easier to use
   - (c) requires more judgment
   - (d) all of the above

8. Appropriate procedures for checking reliability in content analysis include:
   - (a) coder/scorer agreement
   - (b) test-retest
   - (c) split-half
   - (d) all of the above

9. Appropriate procedures for checking validity in content analysis include:
   - (a) latent vs. manifest content
   - (b) comparison with other instruments
   - (c) both (a) and (b) above
   - (d) none of the above

10. The essential element of a content analysis is:
    - (a) a random sample of units
    - (b) establishing unambiguous categories
    - (c) determining relationships among categories
    - (d) obtaining enough units in each category

11. Content analysis can be used to:
    - (a) avoid sampling problems
    - (b) test hypotheses
    - (c) avoid problems of internal validity
    - (d) simplify problems of analysis

12. Advantages of content analysis include all of the following <u>except</u>:
    - (a) relative ease of data collection
    - (b) clear validity of findings
    - (c) permits study of the past
    - (d) relative ease of replication

13. The connection between purpose and choice of content in a content analysis study:
    - (a) is obvious
    - (b) is of little consequence
    - (c) must be made clear
    - (d) must be based on theory

14. In a content analysis study, the categories may come:
    (a) from in initial definitions of the researcher
    (b) from theory
    (c) inductively, from reviewing content
    (d) all of the above

15. The issue of validity in content analysis:
    (a) is a major limitation
    (b) is easily satisfied
    (c) applies only to cause and effect
    (d) is unimportant

16. The most common means of data analysis in content analysis studies is:
    (a) determining frequencies in categories
    (b) calculating means and standard deviations
    (c) calculating inferential statistics
    (d) preparing frequency polygons

17. Clarification of categories in content analysis can be done by:
    (a) constitutive definitions
    (b) unambiguous examples
    (c) explaining connections to theory
    (d) all of the above

18. The Gerbner study of violence on television illustrates:
    (a) the use of multiple categories
    (b) the use of frequencies to obtain scores
    (c) the use of frequency polygons in content analysis
    (d) all of the above

19. In content analysis, the crucial definitions are those which:
    (a) describe the categories or scores
    (b) are theoretical
    (c) describe data analysis procedures
    (d) describe the sample

20. Content analysis is most likely to be used with:
    (a) experimental research
    (b) correlational research
    (c) historical research
    (d) causal/comparative research

CHAPTER EIGHTEEN
QUALITATIVE RESEARCH

Chapter Objectives

Reading this chapter should enable students to:

•*explain* what is meant by the term "qualitative research."

•*describe* at least four general characteristics that most qualitative studies have in common.

•*describe* briefly the steps involved in qualitative research.

•*name* three types of qualitative research conducted in education.

•*name* four types of inteviews conducted by qualitative researchers.

•*give an example* of the six types of questions an interviewer might ask in a qualitative study.

•*explain* what is meant by the term "key actor."

•*explain* what is meant by the term "participant observation."

•*explain* what is meant by the term "nonparticipant observation," and *describe* at least three different forms of nonparticipant observation studies that are conducted in education.

•*describe* briefly at least four roles that an observer can take in a qualitative study.

•*explain* what is meant by the term "ethnographic research," and *give an example* of a research question that might be investigated in an ethnographic study.

•*name* one advantage and disadvantage of ethnographic research.

•*explain* what is meant by the term "fieldnotes," and how they differ from field jottings, a field diary, and a field log.

•*explain* the difference between descriptive and reflective fieldnotes.

•*describe* briefly at least three techniques researchers use to check on the validity and reliability of their perceptions.

•*Explain* how generalizing differs in qualitative and quantitative research.

•*recognize* an example of a qualitative study when they come across one in the educational research literature.

Points to Stress

1. How qualitative research differs from the other types of research discussed in the text (i.e., its naturalistic emphasis).
2. The place of objectivity in qualitative research.
3. The concept of triangulation, and its use in qualitative research.
4. The value of replicating qualitative studies.
5. The difficulties involved in generalizing from qualitative studies.

Teaching Suggestions

1. Hold individual conferences to discuss Problem Sheet #17 with those students who are designing a survey study.

2. Review with the class the advantages and disadvantages of ethnographic research described on pages 454-455 of the text. Ask students if they can suggest any in addition to what is listed here.

3. Make a transparency of Figure 18.1, "Roles of an Observer in Qualitative Research" (a master can be found in the section entitled

"Transparency Masters" later in this manual) for display on an overhead projector. Ask students if they can suggest examples of situations that would illustrate an observer in each of these roles.

4. Discuss the article entitled "Becoming an Elementary Social Studies Teacher: A Study of Perspectives" on pages 466-486 of this chapter. Ask students to suggest any additional strengths or weaknesses in the article besides those we identify in our analysis on pages 486-489. You might want the class to give their opinions (eventually) as to which of the articles we have analyzed in Chapters 13-19 they think is the strongest and the weakest, and why.

5. Discuss any of the questions on page 4441 with the class.

6. Have students work in small groups for 20 minutes to prepare field notes on the activities of their fellow students (during the same class time). Ask each group to examine results for similarities and differences. Then have some of the groups report their "findings" to the total class.

Answers to Discussion Questions

(Note to Instructor: Many of these "Questions for Discussion" are open-ended in nature and have no right answer. Students should be encouraged to offer as many alternative answers as they think plausible, and to explain the reasons for the answers they give.)

1. What do you see as the greatest strength of qualitative research? the biggest weakness? Answer: *Strength: richness of detail. Weakness: possibility of researcher bias; poor generalizability.*

2. Are there any topics or questions that could not be studied using a qualitative approach? If so, give an example. Is there any type of information that qualitative research cannot provide? If so, what might it be? Answer: *Any topics that require the manipulation of variables. Strictly speaking, there is no information that cannot be provided through qualitative research. However, there may be information such as people's opinions that can only be obtained from respondents and they may be unwilling to provide it. Information regarding the effects of a particular treatment is not usually obtained through qualitative investigations.*

3. A major criticism of qualitative (especially ethnographic) research is that there is no way for the researcher to be totally objective about what he or she observes. Would you agree? What might an ethnographer say to rebut this charge? Answer: *This is true. However (as an ethnographer might say in rebuttal), this is true of any type of research. Ethnographers can try to clarify their own biases.*

4. Supporters of qualitative research say that it can do something that no other type of research can do. If true, what might this be? Answer: *Obtain a more wholistic picture of what happens.*

5. Are there any kinds of information that other types of research can provide better than qualitative research? If so, what might they be? Answer: *Yes. Experimental studies can better provide more information about the nature of cause and effect relationships; correlational studies can provide more*

precise predictions; survey studies can provide more information from a greater number of people at one time; quantitative studies typically provide better data of a quantitative nature.

6. How would you compare qualitative research to the other types of research we have discussed in this book in terms of difficulty? Explain your reasoning. Answer: *It is the hardest to do well because it requires so much of the researcher with regard to attentiveness to so many things and trying to eliminate the researcher's own bias. The procedural controls present in other research designs are not applicable to qualitative research.*

7. "Observing people without their knowledge and/or recording their comments without their permission is unethical." Would you agree? Explain your reasoning. Answer: *This would depend on what is being observed and under what conditions. Observing the behavior of pedestrians at a crosswalk is hardly unethical; observing a teacher's actions in a classroom might be unethical; observing a counseling interview after a counselor has promised a student that his comments would be confidential definitely would be unethical.*

TEST FOR CHAPTER EIGHTEEN

1. Which of the following procedures is not typical of school applications of the case study method?
   (a) Interviews with parents
   (b) Interviews with the individual being studied
   (c) Observations of the individual in a variety of situations
   (d) Collecting data from a large number of subjects

2. In qualitative research:
   (a) reliability and validity of instrumentation are relatively unimportant
   (b) researchers attempt to structure situations to facilitate observation
   (c) random sampling is common
   (d) an attempt is made to understand complex phenomena in their entirety

3. In qualitative research, the role of the researcher is to:
   (a) reduce information to numerical form
   (b) become highly familiar with the context of the study
   (c) develop instruments for data collection
   (d) carry out statistical analyses

4. Which of the following is more likely to be found in a qualitative study compared to other methods?
   (a) A description of the patterns of interaction among the members of a group
   (b) A description of the skills of the members of a group
   (c) An analysis of group productivity
   (d) A description of group attitudes toward various issues

5. Hypotheses in qualitative research usually:
   (a) emerge as the study progresses
   (b) are stated at the outset
   (c) are irrelevant
   (d) are non-directional

6. In qualitative research, "process" is seen as:
   (a) too nebulous to study
   (b) secondary to "products"
   (c) an important aspect to be investigated
   (d) an unavoidable part of data collection

7. The unique perceptions of individuals are most likely to be viewed by qualitative researchers as:
   (a) undesirable and unreliable sources of data
   (b) useful for illustrating the results of a study
   (c) irrelevant to the purposes of the study
   (d) an essential part of an investigation

8. Data analysis in qualitative studies, compared to quantitative studies, is:
   (a) inductive rather than deductive
   (b) deductive rather than inductive
   (c) theoretical rather than applied
   (d) applied rather than theoretical

9. The main difference between participant and non-participant observation is that:
   (a) participant observation is more objective
   (b) participant observation is less difficult
   (c) participant observation is more obvious
   (d) participant observation is less detached

10. Which of the following is an example of participant observation?
   (a) A teacher decides to observe her students on the playground
   (b) A researcher becomes a member of a street gang
   (c) A researcher records student behavior in the lunchroom
   (d) A researcher teaches an observation method to a graduate student

11. The main limitation of simulations is:
   (a) the difficulty of arranging them
   (b) individuals do not like to participate in them
   (c) poor generalizability
   (d) participants may be poor actors

12. Advantages of audio and videotapings include all of the following except:
   (a) improved reliability of scoring
   (b) direct recording of actual behavior
   (c) clarity of visual and auditory content
   (d) availability for re-analysis

13. "Triangulation" refers to:
   (a) a method for selecting participants in a qualitative study
   (b) checking validity with multiple instruments
   (c) checking reliability with multiple forms
   (d) checking representativeness of situations

14. "Observer effect" includes all of the following except:
 (a) lack of agreement among observers
 (b) distracting those observed from the task at hand
 (c) causing those observed to try to please the observer
 (d) prior expectations on the part of the observer

15. Sampling in an observation study includes:
 (a) selecting individuals
 (b) selecting contexts
 (c) selecting behaviors
 (d) all of the above

16. Researchers using ethnographic research most frequently use which methods of data collection?
 (a) Questionnaires and interviews
 (b) Testing and observation
 (c) Observation and interviews
 (d) Observation and unobtrusive measures

17. Which question is most specifically appropriate for an ethnographic study?
 (a) What are the causes of school dropout?
 (b) What are the effects of computer assisted instruction?
 (c) What are the important factors affecting school morale?
 (d) How does self-esteem affect school success?

18. Which of the following would not be appropriate to use in an ethnographic study?
 (a) Video tapes
 (b) Projective techniques
 (c) Student products
 (d) All are appropriate

19. The primary advantage of ethnographic research is the:
 (a) comprehensiveness of perspective
 (b) precision of observation
 (c) generalizability of results
 (d) efficiency of data collection

20. The primary limitation of ethnographic research is:
 (a) limited instrumentation
 (b) researcher bias
 (c) biased sampling of respondents
 (d) lack of hypotheses

21. The issue of validity of instrumentation in ethnographic research is:
    (a) irrelevant
    (b) basically the same as in other methods
    (c) solved by triangulation
    (d) less important than in other methods

22. Which of the following statements would be likely to appear in a researcher's field notes?
    (a) Mrs Jones told James to go to the office.
    (b) Mrs Jones punished James.
    (c) Mrs. Jones made me feel irritable.
    (d) Mrs. Jones should be asked why she sent James to the office.

23. Which of the examples in item #22 would be found in a researcher's "field jottings?"
    (a) Mrs Jones told James to go to the office.
    (b) Mrs Jones punished James.
    (c) Mrs. Jones made me feel irritable.
    (d) Mrs. Jones should be asked why she sent James to the office.

24. Which of the examples in item #22 would be found in a researcher's field diary?
    (a) Mrs Jones told James to go to the office.
    (b) Mrs Jones punished James.
    (c) Mrs. Jones made me feel irritable.
    (d) Mrs. Jones should be asked why she sent James to the office.

25. The main limitation of the structured interview is:
    (a) responses are hard to analyze
    (b) responses must fit predetermined categories
    (c) respondents often dislike this format
    (d) the training required of the interviewer

26. The main limitation of the informal interview is:
    (a) the difficulty of getting comparable information
    (b) respondents may be uncomfortable
    (c) the time required
    (d) the variety of topics covered

27. A "key actor" is most similar to:
    (a) a skilled craftsman
    (b) a trained soldier
    (c) a research scientist
    (d) a village elder

CHAPTER NINETEEN
HISTORICAL RESEARCH

Chapter Objectives

Reading this chapter should enable students to:

- *describe* briefly what historical research involves.
- *state* at least three purposes of historical research.
- *give some examples* of the kinds of questions investigated in historical research.
- *name* and *describe* briefly the major steps involved in historical research.
- *give some examples* of historical sources.
- *distinguish* between primary and secondary sources.
- *distinguish* between external and internal criticism.
- *discuss* when generalization in historical research is appropriate.
- *locate* examples of published historical studies, and *critique* (at least some of) the strengths and weaknesses of these studies.
- *recognize* an example of a historical study when they come across one in the literature.

Points to Stress

1. The uniqueness of historical research in that it focuses on past events and occurrences.
2. The difference between a primary and a secondary source.
3. The distinction between external and internal criticism.
4. Limitations on generalizing the results of a historical study.

Teaching Suggestions

1. Hold individual conferences to discuss Problem Sheet #18 with those students who are designing a qualitative study.
2. Review the list of historical research questions on page 496 in the text. Ask students to suggest some additional topics and/or questions that might be pursued through historical research.
3. Review the examples of primary and secondary sources on pages 498-499. Check to ensure that students are clear about the distinction between these two types of historical sources. Ask students to give some additional examples of each type of source.
4. Discuss questions #2 and #3 on page 521 of the text with the class.
5. Review the distinction between external and internal criticism given on pages 500-501 of the text. Which form of criticism would students judge to be more important? Why?
6. Discuss the article entitled "The Social Studies Component of the Southern Literacy Campaign: 1915-1930" on pages 504-518 of this chapter. Ask students to suggest any additional strengths or weaknesses in the article besides those we identify in our analysis on pages 518-520. You might at this time (if you have not before) want the class to give their opinions as to which

of the articles we have analyzed in Chapters 13-19 they think is the strongest and the weakest, and why.

7. Ask students to identify a research question on a topic involving recent events on campus and discuss specific information sources that would be appropriate to consult for more information.

Answers to Discussion Questions

(Note to Instructor: Many of these "Questions for Discussion" are open-ended in nature and have no right answer. Students should be encouraged to offer as many alternative answers as they think plausible, and to explain the reasons for the answers they give.)

1. A researcher wishes to investigate changes in graduation requirements since 1900. Pose a possible hypothesis the researcher might investigate. What sources might he or she consult? Answer: *Here is one possibility, although students might suggest others: "High school graduation requirements were less extensive in 1900 than they are today." Sources the researcher might consult would include school district records of the time, newspaper articles published in 1900 or shortly before, and articles on the period published in historical journals.*

2. Which of the following would constitute examples of a primary historical source (assume they are genuine)?

a. An article on intelligence testing written by a school psychologist
b. The Encyclopedia of Educational Research
c. A final examination booklet
d. A spelling primer used in a midwestern school in 1840
e. A bulletin from a school principal
f. An eighteenth-century school desk
g. A 1969 newspaper announcing the landing of men on the moon
h. A menu from a school cafeteria

Answer: *(c), (d), (e) ,(f) and (h); (a) might qualify if it contained original research.*

3. Why might a researcher be cautious or suspicious about each of the following sources?

a. A typewriter imprinted with the name "Christopher Columbus"
b. A letter from Franklin D. Roosevelt endorsing John F. Kennedy for the presidency of the United States
c. A "Letter to the Editor" from an eighth-grade student complaining about the inadequacy of the school's advanced mathematics program
d. A typed report of an oral interview with a recently fired teacher describing the teacher's complaints against the school district
e. A 1920 high school diploma indicating a student had graduated from the tenth grade
f. A high school teacher's attendance book indicating no absences by any member of her class during the entire year of 1942
g. A photograph of an elementary school classroom in 1800

Answers: *(a) the typewriter was not yet invented; (b) FDR died in 1945; (c) It would be unlikely to find an advanced math program in many eighth grades;*

also most eighth graders would not have sufficient knowledge (or probably the interest) to be able to judge the adequacy of such a program; (d) Such a teacher would likely be biased against the district; (e) Students graduated from the twelfth, not the tenth, grade in high schools; (f) It is highly unlikely that there would be no absences for an entire year; also this was during World War II, and it is probable, if it were a twelfth grade class, that some students might have left school to join the service; (g) Cameras were not yet available for picture taking.

TEST FOR CHAPTER NINETEEN

1. Which of the following presents the greatest difficulty in forming definitive conclusions in historical research?
   (a) The obtainable evidence pertaining to historical events is often incomplete.
   (b) The scientific method does not fit historical problems.
   (c) The most readily available evidence for historical studies is usually primary data only.
   (d) The type of reasoning involved in historical research makes it impossible to use hypotheses.

2. Which of the following is an appropriate step to take in the external criticism of an original document used in historical research?
   (a) Determining who actually wrote the document
   (b) Establishing the author's competence
   (c) Making a study to determine the author's meaning
   (d) Analyzing the author's possible bias

3. For which of the following problems would historical research be most appropriate?
   (a) Trends in patterns of financing Nebraska public schools
   (b) Current concepts of "faculty motivation" of public high school principals in Texas
   (c) Effects of "social acceptance" on tendencies to "withdraw"
   (d) The developmental needs of eighth graders in San Francisco, California

4. A researcher is studying a speech known to have been delivered by Vice President Spiro Agnew in 1971. She is attempting to establish whether those parts of the speech that referred to American education truly represent the state of education in the U.S. at that time. She is doing:
   (a) content analysis
   (b) causal analysis
   (c) internal criticism
   (d) external criticism

5. Historical research is usually limited in terms of:
   (a) researcher bias
   (b) little or no control over sampling
   (c) lack of control of threats to internal validity
   (d) all of the above

6. In external criticism, one asks:
   (a) Is the document authentic?
   (b) Is the document telling the truth?
   (c) Does the document agree with other contemporary sources?
   (d) Does the document yield information that agrees with one's hypothesis?

7. Which of the following questions is the least appropriate for historical research?
   (a) To what extent do tuition tax credits perpetuate segregation?
   (b) Why is school compulsory in the United States?
   (c) Which computer software program is most effective in teaching algebra?
   (d) To what extent does additional funding of schools improve student achievement?

8. A problem of particular importance in designing a historical study is selecting:
   (a) too broad a topic
   (b) a topic on which there is no information
   (c) a topic that cannot be quantified
   (d) a topic that requires the consent of participants

9. Which of the following is a source of data for a historical study?
   (a) Oral statements
   (b) Written documents
   (c) Relics
   (d) All of the above

10. Which of the following is a primary source?
   (a) A poem expressing the writer's feelings after a strike
   (b) An observer's description of a school teachers strike
   (c) A magazine article based on interviews with striking teachers
   (d) A film using videotapes made during the strike

11. Which of the following questions does not apply to external criticism?
   (a) What was the intent of the document?
   (b) Was the author emotionally involved in the events described?
   (c) Under what conditions was the document written?
   (d) When was the document written?

12. Which of the following questions does not apply to internal criticism?
   (a) Did the author have a biased point of view?
   (b) Could the event(s) have taken place as described?
   (c) Where was the document written?
   (d) Would people have behaved as described?

13. Which of the following is a secondary source?
    (a) A teacher's description of misbehavior in the school cafeteria
    (b) A principal's summary of actions taken by the school board
    (c) A student's report card
    (d) A school record of absences

14. The main advantage of the historical method is that it is:
    (a) the only way to investigate certain questions
    (b) less intrusive than other methods
    (c) easier to use than other methods
    (d) inexpensive

15. Which of the following is unique to historical research?
    (a) Information of questionable validity
    (b) Researcher bias
    (c) Inevitable loss of data
    (d) Reliance on written information

16. Which of the following is not an essential step in historical research?
    (a) Limiting the problem to be studied
    (b) Defining terms
    (c) Checking validity
    (d) Statistical analysis

17. Presentism means:
    (a) assuming that earlier people had the same historical perspective that we do
    (b) attributing current behavior patterns to people who lived at an earlier time
    (c) making sure that a witness to an event was present at the time
    (d) the ability to accurately forecast future events based on current data

18. Which is not a common purpose of historical research?
    (a) To test hypotheses
    (b) To determine cause-effect relationships
    (c) To aid in prediction
    (d) To avoid unnecessary repetition

19. An educator wishing to do a historical study should:
    (a) design methodological controls for threats to internal validity
    (b) be highly skilled in instrument development
    (c) work under the guidance of an experienced historian
    (d) be prepared to do random sampling

20. Which threat to internal validity is most serious in historical studies?
    (a) Data collector bias
    (b) Subject characteristics
    (c) History
    (d) Maturation

CHAPTER TWENTY
WRITING RESEARCH PROPOSALS AND REPORTS

Chapter Objectives

Reading this chapter should enable students to:

- *describe* briefly the main sections of a research proposal and a research report.
- *describe* the major difference between a research proposal and a research report.
- *write* a research proposal.

Points to Stress

1. The difference between a research proposal and a research report.
2. The importance of having all sections of a proposal and/or report clearly related to one another.
3. The questions to ask concerning one's progress in proposal development that are presented throughout the chapter.

Teaching Suggestions

1. Hold individual conferences to discuss Problem Sheet #19 with those students who are designing an historical study.
2. Answer any final questions students have about the preparation of their research proposal.
3. Go over the sample student proposal presented on pages 537-547 of the text with the class. Answer any questions they may have about it. Encourage students to identify other strengths and weaknesses of the study besides the ones we have identified.
4. You might want at this time to hold a discussion with the class about their perceptions of the strengths and weaknesses of the course, and ask for their suggestions as to how it might be improved.

Answers to Discussion Questions

(Note to Instructor: Many of these "Questions for Discussion" are open-ended in nature and have no right answer. Students should be encouraged to offer as many alternative answers as they think plausible, and to explain the reasons for the answers they give.)

1. To what extent should a researcher allow his or her personal writing style to influence the headings and organizational sequence in a research proposal (assuming that there is no mandatory format prescribed by, for example, a funding agency)? Answer: *To the extent it maximizes clarity and communicates the researcher's intent.*
2. To what common function do: (a) the problem statement; (b) the research question; and (c) the hypotheses all contribute? In what ways are they different? Answer: *All contribute to an indication of the researcher's purpose in conducting the study. The problem statement and research question indicate overall direction; the hypothesis is more specific.*

3. When instructors in introductory research courses evaluate research proposals of students, they sometimes find logical inconsistencies among the various parts. What do you think are the most commonly found inconsistencies? Answer: *Between purpose and hypotheses; definitions and instruments to be used; instrumentation process and sample involved; sample selection and control for internal validity; and appropriateness of the data analysis techniques and the nature of the hypothesis.*
4. Why is it especially important in a study involving a convenience sample to provide a detailed description of the characteristics of the sample in the research report? Would this be true for a random sample as well? Explain. Answer: *Because doing so provides the only possible way for a reader to judge the generalizability of such a study to his or her own situation. This would not be true for a random sample, since the use of such permits generalization to the identified population.*
5. Why is it important for a researcher to discuss threats to internal validity in: a) a research proposal? b) a research report? Answer: *(a) to take steps to try and control these threats; (b) to report what was done to control the threats and to acknowledge the limitations of the study.*

TEST FOR CHAPTER TWENTY

1. In writing the justification for a proposed study, the author should assume that:
    - (a) readers are familiar with related studies
    - (b) the importance of the problem is self evident
    - (c) interest in the question is sufficient
    - (d) none of the above

2. Stating a research hypothesis is generally considered to be:
    - (a) essential
    - (b) desirable
    - (c) undesirable
    - (d) unnecessary

3 The goal of the "definitions" section of a proposal is to:
- (a) eliminate all ambiguity in terms used
- (b) reduce ambiguity as much as possible
- (c) state terms as they are commonly used
- (d) define each word in the research hypothesis

4. The "sample" section of a research proposal must state:
    - (a) a detailed plan for obtaining subjects
    - (b) the final number of subjects in a study
    - (c) the size of the population to which generalization is intended
    - (d) how the sample will be stratified

5. In planning a study, a researcher should, in general:
    - (a) plan to develop his or her own instruments
    - (b) use instruments that are widely known and used
    - (c) use only instruments with proven evidence of validity
    - (d) plan to use existing instruments if appropriate

6. When using existing instruments, a researcher should:
    - (a) rely on accompanying manuals for evaluation of reliability and validity
    - (b) plan to check reliability and validity as part of the study
    - (c) consider positive reviews in Mental Measurements Yearbooks as sufficient
    - (d) assume instruments sold commercially are adequate as regards evidence of reliability and validity

7. Using a second instrument to check validity is usually:
   (a) impossible
   (b) unnecessary
   (c) highly desirable
   (d) impractical

8. Procedures used in a study should be described in detail so that:
   (a) validity of instrumentation is assured
   (b) a reader can determine the importance of the study
   (c) deficiencies in internal validity can be explained
   (d) replication is possible

9. The primary reason for considering threats to internal validity in a proposal is so that:
   (a) they can be defended against criticism
   (b) a small sample can be justified
   (c) steps can be taken to reduce them
   (d) weaknesses in instruments can be explained

10. The "data analysis" section of a proposal states:
   (a) how data collected will be analyzed
   (b) how the analyses were carried out
   (c) what the data demonstrate
   (d) what conclusions are justified by the data

11. Which of the following would <u>not</u> usually appear in a proposal budget?
   (a) Employee benefits
   (b) Travel
   (c) Personnel resumes
   (d) Indirect costs

12. Differences between a proposal and a report include all of the following <u>except</u>:
   (a) verb tense
   (b) results
   (c) conclusions
   (d) prior research

13. Contradictions are often found in proposals between:
   (a) sampling plan and instrumentation
   (b) sampling plan and control of extraneous variables
   (c) definitions and instrumentation
   (d) all of the above

14. The intent of the "review of related literature" in a proposal is to:
    (a) demonstrate the writer's ability to do a literature search
    (b) critically review all pertinent literature
    (c) show how the proposed study builds on previous knowledge
    (d) show where the proposed instrumentation came from

15. The purpose of operational definitions in a research proposal is to:
    (a) replace constitutive definitions
    (b) clarify constitutive definitions
    (c) clarify instrumentation
    (d) justify the importance of the planned-for study

16. The reader should be able to judge the external validity of a study when reading which of the following sections of a research report?
    (a) Statement of the problem
    (b) Review of the literature
    (c) Instrumentation
    (d) Sampling

17. When reading a research report, educators should:
    (a) accept the author's conclusions only if he or she is known to be an authority in the field
    (b) accept conclusions that agree with previous research
    (c) determine whether the conclusions are supported by the data of the study
    (d) accept the conclusions if they follow logically from the hypotheses of the study

18. When reading a research report in a highly regarded journal, educators should:
    (a) accept the author's conclusions without question if based on statistically significant results
    (b) accept those conclusions that agree with their own opinions
    (c) reject any conclusions that are based on inductive reasoning
    (d) evaluate the conclusions according to the correctness of the research methodology used in the study

19. When research results are the opposite of what was expected, the researcher should:
    (a) abandon the study
    (b) attempt to find what caused the study to go wrong
    (c) report the results the way they occurred
    (d) report that the instruments employed are inappropriate for measuring the variables involved

20. "Students who understand the reasoning underlying arithmetic processes will learn algebra more rapidly than will students who merely memorize the steps in the processes without understanding them." This statement will be tested with a logically sound research design and sampling plan. If the results are in agreement with the statement, it can be considered to be a(n):

(a) assumption on which hypotheses should be based
(b) proven generalization that can be added to existing theory
(c) single-variable hypothesis involving no cause-and-effect relationships
(d) tentatively confirmed hypothesis that should be subjected to further testing

---

CHAPTER TWENTY-ONE
DOING RESEARCH IN SCHOOLS

Chapter Objectives

Reading this chapter should enable students to:

•*describe* how the information they have acquired can be applied in their own circumstances.

•*describe* how each of the methods they have learned can be applied in schools and other settings.

•*evaluate* the relative appropriateness of different methodologies to particular research questions.

•*evaluate* the strengths and weaknesses of small-scale research.

Points to Stress

1. Research is not something to be done only by university professors and professionals who make their living as researchers.

2. There are all kinds of opportunities to investigate questions of interest and importance in schools and other settings.

3. All of the methodologies described in the text can be employed in school-based research.

4. Research on important questions can be conducted by practitioners in real-life situations.

5. Research in schools conducted by practitioners can lead to useful suggestions for practice.

Teaching Suggestions

1. Hold a class discussion with regard to question #2 under "For Review" on page 561 of the text.

2. Discuss each of the questions listed under "For Discussion" on page 561 of the text.

3. Encourage students to think back over the various ideas that were presented in the text. Which ones would they say are the most important for a person to master if he or she wishes to do quality research?

Answers to Discussion Questions

(Note to Instructor: Many of these "Questions for Discussion" are open-ended in nature and have no right answer. Students should be encouraged to offer as many alternative answers as they think plausible, and to explain the reasons for the answers they give.)

1. Which methodologies, other than the ones discussed, might be used in each of the hypothetical examples in this chapter? Answer: *Student ideas will vary here. Encourage them to speculate on how the examples presented might be conducted using a different methodology.*

2. What other methods might have been used in the DeMaria study? Answer: *Ms. DeMaria might have conducted a survey study, in which she might have*

administered a questionnaire to the teachers at the school to gain their impressions of the effects of the relaxation exercises on the students. She also might have interviewed both students and teachers about the effects of, and their reactions to, the relaxation exercises. Which, if any, would you recommend? Answer: Replies will vary here, but encourage students to explain their choice(s).

3. What do you think are the advantages of small-scale research? Answer: *More manageable, less cost, usually less time involved, quicker to implement and complete.* What are the disadvantages? Answer: *Limited in scope, difficult to generalize beyond the particular situation.*

TEST FOR CHAPTER TWENTY-ONE

There is no test for Chapter Twenty-One.

Part Six
How to Use the Problem Sheets

Located at the end of each chapter is a "research exercise" and an accompanying problem sheet for students to complete. Each of these exercises has been designed to help students learn the basic concepts and ideas presented in the corresponding chapters. These problem sheets may be used in two basic ways:

•*As a further vehicle for student learning.* When used in this way, students can be encouraged (although not required) to complete some or all of the problem sheets as a way of checking their understanding of important concepts and their ability to apply what they are learning to a specific, ongoing and meaningful task.

•*As a required assignment to obtain feedback from fellow students and the instructor.* When used in this way, many variations are possible in terms of: (a) the amount of time allocated to the problem sheets and the consequent quality of their final form; (b) the amount and nature of class time allocated to them; and (c) the amount and type of (student or instructor) feedback provided.

The authors of the text differ somewhat in their use of the problem sheets. Both of us use the problem sheets as required assignments to be completed during or shortly following class meetings on each chapter. Both of us use peer groups of 3-5 students to discuss and provide both feedback and assistance to other students. Class time is routinely allocated for group work on the material pertaining to each problem sheet. Students are instructed to allocate their time so as to hear from each group member and to be constructively critical. Class time is scheduled for some or all groups to report back to the total class on their progress and problems. Both of us circulate among the groups, responding to requests for assistance and participating in the group discussions.

Both of us also require students to turn in the problem sheets at one or two week intervals. We make a concerted effort to return them, with detailed comments, at the next class meeting. We have found that this periodic feedback is greatly appreciated by students, and contributes markedly to improved performance as the semester progresses.

We differ, however, in the relative weight we assign to the problem sheets, and the amount of class time that is given to working on them. One of us prefers to have a variety of activities scheduled during each class period and makes much use of visual aids (with the class as a whole), and uses handouts, case studies, and other kinds of materials for small group work. Peer group feedback, for this instructor, is only one of many class activities that takes place.

The other author devotes most of his class time to four main activities: (a) lecturing on topics of common difficulty for students; (b) answering questions of a general nature that students present; (c) responding to problems students are having with their problem sheets; and (d) peer feedback in small group. For this instructor, the problem sheets receive more emphasis in terms of class time and as the primary vehicle for learning and grading.

One of the authors uses each problem sheet pretty much as it is shown in the text, having found the allocated space to be, in general, sufficient for student responses. The other author requires more detail than can be encompassed in the space allocated, and hence uses a somewhat expanded format. Both of us require re-submission of problem sheets that are incomplete or misunderstood when first turned in. We present two examples of a student-completed set of problem sheets in Part Seven.

We have found students generally receptive to the peer group format. There are a few problems that, on occasion, we do encounter, however.

1. Some groups are not sufficiently critical, tending to provide a considerable amount of encouragement, but not much criticism. This can be remedied to a considerable extent by the instructor: (a) pointing out that *constructive* criticism early on saves much work later; and (b) reiterating that making mistakes and making them publicly with subsequent assistance is an excellent way to learn.

2. Sometimes a group is too negative. This, we think, is best handled by direct intervention on the part of the instructor and, if necessary, a restructuring of the group.

3. Occasionally, a group is too homogeneous--that is, all of the students in a group may find the content very difficult to understand. This becomes apparent both in the quality of the problem sheets submitted and through observation of the group during their discussions of the material. Such groups require additional help from the instructor. At the other extreme is the (usually rare) group comprised entirely of students who find the material easy to understand, and who are always finished early. Our approach to such a group is to encourage them to continue working until all members have the assignment completed and thoroughly understood, and then to permit them to leave for the remainder of the time allocated to group feedback.

It is desirable, of course, to structure the peer groups so that each has a range of skills and ability levels included, but we know of no way to ensure this other than by pretesting--which our students, at least, typically resent. Restructuring groups after aptitudes become known is difficult, because it interferes with the on-going involvement in the other members' topics that has already begun.

Part Seven
Examples of a Completed Set of Problem Sheets

What follows are two completed sets of problem sheets as developed by students in our research classes to fulfill the course requirements. The first set makes up a complete proposal for a correlational study, and illustrates the use of the problem sheets as they are presented in the text, without expansion. Each problem sheet is shown in its final form, following both in-class commentary and written comments by the instructor on earlier drafts submitted by the student and subsequently revised. These sheets are a straightforward proposal prepared by one of the more able students in the class. The original has been modified somewhat in order to provide a clearer illustration of the final product.

The second set pertains to an experimental study. Earlier drafts of some problem sheets are provided in order to illustrate instructor feedback and student use of such feedback to revise a first draft. These problem sheets were prepared by a student who initially had considerable difficulty, but eventually produced what we consider to be an acceptable proposal. The instructor's comments have been reproduced from notes to the student that were written on the student's original drafts in order to illustrate the instructor's thoughts at the time. Some modifications have been made to simplify the illustration.

Research Exercise One
What Kind of Research?

Think of a research idea or problem you would like to investigate. Using Problem Sheet #1, briefly describe the problem in a sentence or two. Then indicate the type of research methodology you would use to investigate this problem.

Problem Sheet #1
TYPE OF RESEARCH

I. A possible topic or problem I am thinking of researching is: *whether a woman's ideas about her body affect her self-esteem*

2. The type of research most appropriate to this topic or problem is: (*circle one*)

a. an experiment

b. a correlational study

c. a causal-comparative study

d. a survey utilizing a written questionnaire

e. a survey using interviews of several individuals

f. an ethnographic study

g. a case study

h. a content analysis

i. a historical study

Research Exercise Two
The Research Question

Using Problem Sheet #2, restate the problem question you listed in Research Exercise #1 in a sentence or two, and then formulate a research question which relates to this problem. Now list all of the key terms in the question that you think are not clear and which need to be defined. Define each of these terms both constitutively and operationally.

Problem Sheet #2
THE RESEARCH QUESTION

1. My research problem (restated) is: *the relationship between body-cathexis and self-esteem among college women*

2. My research question is: *What is the relationship between body-cathexis and self-esteem among college women?*

3. The following are the key terms in the problem or question which are not clear and which need to be defined:

a. *body-cathexis* d. ______
b. *self-esteem* e. ______
c. *college women* f. ______

4. Here are my constitutive definitions of these terms:

body-cathexis=*extent of satisfaction with various parts or processes of the body*

self-esteem=*the sum total of a person's feelings of personal worth and self-confidence*

college women=*female students enrolled at public or private universities or colleges*

5. Here are my operational definitions of these terms:

body-cathexis=score on the Body-Cathexis Scale developed by Secourd and Jourard--a 5 point *Likert scale rating on each of ten body characteristics*

self-esteem=*score on the Tennessee Self-Concept Scale--Counseling Form*

college women=*officially enrolled in at least one college course according to self-report and/or college records*

6. My justification for investigating this question/problem (why I would argue that it is an important question to investigate is as follows:

Social pressure to look good, specifically thinner, may cause women to have a lifetime of dissatisfaction with their bodies and with themselves in general. Many college women have unrealistic standards for an acceptable body. Self-esteem is seen by many authorities as

(Problem Sheet #2 continued)

essential for well-being and productive living. If it is shown that dissatisfaction with one's body is associated with low overall self-esteem, many recommendations might follow. For example, the fashion and clothing professions might examine the impact they have on women's lives. More specifically, a woman might begin to think that changing her ideas about her body rather than changing the appearance of her body could benefit her entire outlook on life.

Research Exercise Three
Ethics and Research

Using Problem Sheet #3, restate the research question you developed in Problem Sheet 2. Identify any possible ethical problems in carrying out such a study. How might such problems be remedied?

Problem Sheet #3
ETHICS AND RESEARCH

1. My research question is: *What is the relationship between body-cathexis and self-esteem among college women?*

2. The possibilities for harm to participants (if any) are: *none.*

I would handle these problems as follows: ______

3. The possibilities of problems of confidentiality (if any) are: *none*

4. The possibilities of problems of deception (if any) are: *none*

5. If you think your proposed study would fit the guidelines for exempt status, state why here.

Women participants will be asked only to fill out the two scales. Doing so will not put them at any risk. Confidentiality will be maintained. No deception is involved. It will be necessary to get permission to sample from registration lists at selected universities.

Research Exercise Four
The Research Hypothesis

Formulate a testable hypothesis related to the research question you developed in Research Exercise Three. Using Problem Sheet #4, state the hypothesis in a sentence or two, and indicate the more general research question which it reflects. Check to see if it suggests a relationship between at least two variables. If it does not, revise it so that it does. Now name these variables, and then indicate which is the independent variable and which is the dependent variable. Write a paragraph indicating why you think it is an important question to investigate, and identify any possible ethical problems posed by the research question. Lastly, list as many extraneous variables as you can think of that might affect the results of your study.

Problem Sheet #4
THE RESEARCH HYPOTHESIS

1. The hypothesis I wish to investigate is: *There is a positive relationship between body cathexis and self-esteem among college women.*

2. This hypothesis suggests a relationship between at least two variables.

They are: *body cathexis* and *self-esteem*

3. More specifically, the variables in my study are:

a. dependent: *self-esteem*

b. independent: *body cathexis*

4. Possible extraneous variables that might affect my results include: *age, health, actual body characteristics--e.g., height, weight, etc.*

Research Exercise Five
Review of the Literature

Using Problem Sheet #5, state again either your research problem or the hypothesis of your study. Then consult an appropriate general reference, and list at least three search terms that are relevant to your problem. Locate and read three primary sources (articles) which include studies related to your problem, taking notes as you read on note cards similar to the one shown in Figure 5.10. Attach each of your note cards (one per journal article) to Problem Sheet #5.

Problem Sheet #5
REVIEW OF THE LITERATURE

1. The question or hypothesis in my study is: *There is a positive relationship between body cathexis and self-esteem among college women.*

2. The general reference(s) I consulted was (were): *Education Index*

3. The search terms I used were:

a. *self-esteem, self-concept*

b. *body awareness; body cathexis*

4. The three journals I consulted were:

a. *Adolescence*

b. *Journal of Youth and Adolescence*

c. *Journal of Multicultural Counseling and Development*

5. The titles of the studies I read (note cards are attached) were:

a. *The relationship of self-esteem, maternal employment and work-family plans to sex role orientations of late adolescents*

b. *Recognition accuracy, stereotypic performance, aversion and subjective judgment of body appearance in adolescents and young adults*

c. *Self-esteem and selected clothing attributes of black adults: Implications for counseling*

Problem Sheet #5 (continued)

Example of Note Card for Problem Sheet #5

Keith, P.M. (1988). The relationship of self-esteem, maternal employment and work-family plans to sex role orientations of late adolescents. Adolescence, 92, pp. 959-966.

Problem: *See title*

Hypotheses: *Implied that orientation is related to other variables*

Procedures: *Sample was 206 males, 181 females in an introductory sociology class at a large midwestern university. A questionnaire was given that included: 36 item sex-role scale, a multi-item self-esteem scale; 10 items on male/female sharing of household tasks; and single items on whether women planned to work after marriage and after having children, and on occupations of parents.*

Findings: *Males showed more traditional sex-role orientation and higher self-esteem. Self-esteem slightly related to sex-role orientation for women (r=.27), but not for men.*

Conclusion: *Authors discuss importance of mother's working at length despite low correlations with other variables, all which were below .30.*

Research Exercise Six
Sampling Plan

Use Problem Sheet #6 to describe, as fully as you can, your sample--that is, the subjects whom you will have participate in your study. Describe the type of sample you plan to use and how you will obtain the sample. Indicate whether or not you expect your study to have population validity: if so, to what populations; if not, why it would not. Then indicate whether the study would have ecological validity: if so, to what settings; if not, why it would not.

Problem Sheet # 6
SAMPLING PLAN

l. My intended sample (subjects who would participate in my study) consists of (tell who and how many): *200 female college students*

2. Demographics (characteristics of the sample) are as follows:

a. age range: *18-45*

b. sex distribution: *all female*

c. ethnic breakdown: *representative of colleges in SF Bay Area--all major ethnic groups*

d. location (where are these subjects?): *S.F. Bay Area universities*

e. other (describe) characteristics not mentioned above that you deem important (use back if you need more space): ____

3. Type of sample: random _X_ stratified __ cluster _X_ convenience (accessible)____

other (describe): *cluster random selection of colleges; simple random selection of subjects*

4. I will obtain my sample by: *identifying all colleges in the 7 county S. F. Bay Area which have a residence (on-campus coursework) requirement (estimated at 30). I will randomly select 10 campuses. From student records, I will randomly select 30 women at each campus. This will give an initial sample of 300.*

5. External validity (I will generalize to the following population):

a. to what accessible population? *All women enrolled at the 10 campuses selected*

b. to what target population? *All women enrolled in college in S.F. Bay Area.*

c. if not generalizable, why not?____

6. Ecological validity (to what settings/conditions can you generalize?):

a. generalizable to what setting(s)? *Two and four year residential colleges.*

b. generalizable to what conditions? *No special limitations on conditions*

c. if not generalizable, why not?____

____

Research Exercise Seven
Instrumentation

> Decide on the kind of instrument you will use to measure the dependent variable(s) in your study. Using Problem Sheet #7, name all of the instruments you plan to use in your study. If you plan to use one or more already existing instruments, describe each. If you will need to develop an instrument, give two examples of the kind of questions you would ask (or tasks you would have students perform) as a part of each instrument. Indicate how you would describe and organize the data on each of the variables yielding numerical data.

Problem Sheet #7
INSTRUMENTATION

1. The instrument I plan to use to measure my dependent variable is the: *Tennessee Self Concept Scale--Counseling Form*

2. Other instruments I plan to use would be: *the Body-Cathexis Scale (Secourd and Jourard)*

3. If I need to develop an instrument, here are two examples of the kind of questions I would ask (or tasks I would have students perform) as part of my instrument:

a. *instrument to be developed to obtain evidence of validity of the Body-Cathexis Scale.*

b. *a series of projective cartoon similar to the one shown below:*

I can't wait to get my swim suit

These are the existing instruments I plan to use: *See 1, 2 above*

4. I would describe each variable yielding numerical data as follows:

	variable #1		variable #2	other
	Self-esteem		*Body Cathexis*	
quantitative? or categorical?	*quantitative*		*quantitative*	
nominal? or ordinal? or interval? or ratio?	*ordinal/interval*		*ordinal/interval*	

(Problem Sheet #7 continued)

5. For each variable yielding numerical data, I will treat it as follows:

raw score	___√________	___√________	____________
age/grade equivalents	____________	____________	____________
percentile	____________	____________	____________
standard score	____________	____________	____________

Research Exercise Eight
Instrument Validity and Reliability

Use Problem Sheet #8 to describe how you plan to check on the validity and reliability of scores obtained with your instruments. If you plan to use an existing instrument, summarize what you have been able to learn about the validity and reliability of results obtained with it. If you plan to develop an instrument, explain how you will attempt to ensure validity and reliability. In either case, explain how you will empirically check validity and reliability.

Problem Sheet #8
INSTRUMENT VALIDITY AND RELIABILITY

1. I plan to use the following existing instruments:

Tennessee Self-Concept Scale

Body-Cathexis Scale (Secourd & Jourard)

In summary, I have learned the following about the validity and reliability of scores obtained with these instruments: *the Tennessee S-C Scale is reviewed favorably in MMY. It appears to yield scores for typical populations (such as mine) that are adequately reliable. Evidence of validity for all such self-report scales is questionable. Less is known about the Body Cathexis Scale.*

2. I plan to develop the following instruments:

a. *Series of projective cartoons (to get evidence on validity of Body Cathexis Scale)*

b. *Essay to get evidence on validity of Self-Concept Scale*

I will try to ensure reliability and validity of results obtained with these instruments by:

(1) using the Counseling Form of the Tenn. S-C Scale which is less time consuming. I will delete items that relate specifically to one's body since this would overlap my second variable (body cathexis).

(2) modifying the Body-Cathexis Scale to shorten it, clarify choice alternatives and also clarify the instructions. I realize that shortening these scales may reduce reliability, but I think they will still contain a sufficient number of items. Shortening seems desirable in order to foster cooperation of subjects and therefore improve validity. I recognize that these changes make previous data on reliability and validity highly questionable.

(Problem Sheet #8 continued)

3. For each instrument I plan to use:

a. This is how I will collect evidence to check internal consistency: *For the Tennessee Self-Concept Scale, I will obtain a split half (odd-even) reliability coefficient. For the Body-Cathexis Scale, I will also obtain a reliability coefficient (odd-even).*

b. This is how I will collect evidence to check reliability over time (stability): *For the Tenn. Self-Concept Scale,. I will administer the scale twice, with a one month time interval inbetween, to a convenience sample (one or two English classes at each college). This second sample is less satisfactory but necessary since re-administration to my primary sample is not feasible as they will be contacted individually. For the Body-Cathexis Scale, I will administer the scale twice, with a one month time interval inbetween, to the same convenience sample just described. Both scales (self-esteem and body cathexis) will be combined into one scale for purposes of administration and then scored separately.*

c. This is how I will collect evidence to check validity: *At the first administration of the TSC, students will be asked to write a brief essay describing themselves. These will be scored for self-esteem and compared with their scores on the TSC. For the Body-Cathexis Scale, a projective cartoon test portraying situations involving body satisfaction (developed by the researcher) will be given. Scores on this test will be compared with Body-Cathexis scores. I may have to use different classes for each scale in getting evidence of validity.*

Research Exercise Nine
Descriptive Statistics

> Using Problem Sheet #9, state again the question or hypothesis of your study, and list your variables. Then indicate how you would summarize the results for each variable. Lastly, indicate how you would describe the relationship between variables one and two.

Problem Sheet #9
DESCRIPTIVE STATISTICS

1. The question or hypothesis of my study is: *There is a positive relationship between body cathexis and self-esteem among college women.*

2. My variables are: (1) *body cathexis*
(2) *self-esteem* (others)________________

3. I consider variable #1 to be: quantitative ✓ or categorical ____

4. I consider variable #2 to be: quantitative ✓ or categorical ____

5. I would summarize the results for each variable as follows:

	Variable #1 *body cathexis*	Variable #2 *self-esteem*	Other ________
frequency polygon	✓	✓	
mean	✓	✓	
median	✓	✓	
range			
standard deviation			
frequency table			
bar graph			
pie chart			

6. I will describe the relationship between variables 1 and 2 by a (indicate by a check mark):

comparison of frequency polygons	______
comparison of averages	______
crossbreak tables(s)	______
correlation coefficient	✓
scatterplot	✓

Research Exercise Ten
Inferential Statistics

> Using Problem Sheet #10, once again state the question or hypothesis of your study. Summarize the descriptive statistics you would use to describe the relationship you are hypothesizing. Tell whether you would or would not do a significance test and/or calculate a confidence interval, and if not, why. Lastly, describe the type of sample used in your study, and explain any limitations that are placed on your using inferential statistics due to the nature of the sample.

Problem Sheet #10
INFERENTIAL STATISTICS

1. The question or hypothesis of my study is: *There is a positive relationship between body cathexis and self-esteem among college women.*

2. The descriptive statistic(s) I would use to describe the relationship I am hypothesizing would be: *Scatterplot, Pearson correlation coefficient*

3. The appropriate inference technique for study would be: *t test for r*

4. I would use a parametric √ or a nonparametric ___ technique because: *the assumption of an interval scale seems reasonable.*

5. I would √ or would not ___ do a significance test because: *I want to know the probability that the population r is zero (.00).*

6. I would √ or would not ___ calculate a confidence interval because: *I want to know the values of r that are probable in the population.*

7. The type of sample used in my study is: *two-stage random*

8. The type of sample used in my study places the following limitation(s) on my use of inferential statistics: *The sample is random, but small at cluster stage (10 colleges out of an estimated 30). Thus the resultant probability based on my total n of 200 is somewhat misleading and should be qualified.*

Research Exercise Eleven
Statistics in Perspective

Using Problem Sheet #11, once again state the question or hypothesis of your study. Summarize the descriptive and inferential statistics you would use to describe the relationship you are hypothesizing, and then tell how you evaluate the magnitude of any relationship you might find.

Problem Sheet #11
STATISTICS IN PERSPECTIVE

1. The question or hypothesis of my study is: *There is a positive relationship between body cathexis and self-esteem among college women.*

2. My expected relationship(s) would be described using the following descriptive statistics: *Scatterplot, Pearson correlation coefficient*

3. The inferential statistics I would use are: *t test for r*

4. I would evaluate the magnitude of the relationship(s) I find by: *examining the scatterplot and subsequently obtaining either the Pearson r or Eta, or both. If either is .40 or higher, I will consider my hypothesis supported.*

5. Indicate any changes in your use of descriptive or inferential statistics as described in Problem Sheets 8 and 9: *I would determine from the scatterplot whether Eta should be calculated.*

Research Exercise Twelve
Internal Validity

State the question or hypothesis of your study at the top of Problem Sheet #12. Then, in the spaces indicated, place an X after each of the threats to internal validity that apply to your study, explain why they are threats, and describe how you intend to control for those most likely to occur (i.e., prevent their having an effect on the outcome of your study).

Problem Sheet #12
INTERNAL VALIDITY

1. My question or hypothesis is: *There is a positive relationship between body cathexis and self-esteem among college women.*

2. I have placed an **X** in the blank in front of each threat listed below that applies to my study. I explain why I think each one is a problem and then explain how I would attempt to control for the threat.

Threats: X Subject Characteristics X Mortality ___ Location
X Instrumentation ___ Testing ___ History ___ Maturation
___ Subject Attitude ___ Regression ___ Implementation X Other (Specify)

Threat 1: *Subject characteristics* Why? *Age, health, actual body characteristics may explain any relationship I find.*

I will control by: *obtaining this information for each subject and controlling statistically*

Threat 2: *Loss of Subjects* Why? *Some subjects will probably not return scales, and they are probably those who would score lower on both scales.*

I will control by: *encouraging all subjects to respond. Loss of subjects would probably lower my correlation.*

Threat 3: *Instrumentation* Why? *Respondents may "psych out" my hypothesis and alter responses accordingly.*

I will control by: *mixing items from the two scales together for administration but scoring them separately. The item format is the same for both scales.*

Threat 4: *Other* Why? *The time of the year data is collected might affect responses since women may be affected by heavily advertised swim suits, etc.*

I will control by: *avoiding data collection during spring or early summer months.*

I will control by: *not collecting data during spring or early summer*

Research Exercise Fourteen
Correlational Research

NOTE: You should complete Problem Sheet #14 only if you are planning a correlational study. If your intended study involves a different methodology, you will find a similar problem sheet at the end of the chapter that deals with that methodology. You might wish to consider, however, whether your research question could be investigated by means of a correlational study.

> Using Problem Sheet #14, once again state the question or hypothesis of your study. Then describe, briefly but thoroughly, the procedures of your study, including analysis of results -- that is, what you intend to do, when, where, and how. Lastly, indicate any unresolved problems you see at this point in your planning.

Problem Sheet #14
CORRELATIONAL RESEARCH

1. The question or hypothesis of my study is: *There is a positive relationship between body cathexis and self-esteem among college women.*

2. A brief summary of what I intend to do, when, where, and how is as follows:
Once subjects have been selected, each will be contacted by phone (numbers available from the Registrar) and cooperation solicited. Confidentiality will be assured. I will then mail the form containing both the Self-Esteem and Body-Cathexis Scales, along with a demographics questionnaire asking about subjects' age, health status, height, weight and other descriptive characteristics. I will establish a number code so that I can re-contact those subjects who do not respond within two weeks.

I will request permission to administer the combined scales along with the validity instruments to one or two English classes on each campus.

3. The major problems I foresee at this point include the following: *I may have difficulty getting access to registration lists in which case I may have to try to persuade someone in the registrar's office to select names for me. I may end up being able to get my sample from only one campus. I may have difficulty getting classes for checking validity. I may have more lost data than I anticipate.*

SET # 2

PROBLEM SHEETS FOR AN EXPERIMENTAL STUDY

Research Exercise One
What Kind of Research?

Think of a research idea or problem you would like to investigate. Using Problem Sheet #1, briefly describe the problem in a sentence or two. Then indicate the type of research methodology you would use to investigate this problem.

Problem Sheet #1
TYPE OF RESEARCH
(First draft)

1. A possible topic or problem I am thinking of researching is: *How awareness of the values of other cultures results in the development of self-concept and how this awareness can be developed by the multicultural curriculum in second grade.*

(**Instructor's comments:** *Needs to be clarified. Do you have a specific curriculum in mind? Do you intend to study its effects? If so, do you intend to study both "awareness" and "self-concept"? I suggest you focus on one or the other. This is a different study from one which relates awareness* to *self-concept*).

2. The type of research most appropriate to this topic or problem is: (*Circle one*)

   a. An experiment
   b. A correlational study
   c. A causal-comparative study
   d. A survey utilizing a written questionnaire
   e. A survey using interviews of several individuals
   f. An ethnographic study
   g. A case study
   h. A content analysis
   i. A historical study

(**Instructor's comments:** *Maybe—if you plan to compare students receiving the curriculum with those who do not* and *if you can locate examples of each.)*

3. What questions, if any, might a critical researcher raise with regard to your study? *None*

(**Instructor's comments:** *Multicultural curricula are controversial. Your values and intent should be made clear—perhaps in Problem Sheet 3 under "justification."*)

Research Exercise One
What Kind of Research?

> Think of a research idea or problem you would like to investigate. Using Problem Sheet #1, briefly describe the problem in a sentence or two. Then indicate the type of research methodology you would use to investigate this problem.

Problem Sheet #1
TYPE OF RESEARCH
(Second draft)

1. A possible topic or problem I am thinking of researching is: *The effects of curricula on awareness of the values of other cultures and on self-concept*

2. The type of research most appropriate to this topic or problem is: (*Circle one*)

   a. An experiment [boxed]
   b. A correlational study
   c. A causal-comparative study
   d. A survey utilizing a written questionnaire
   e. A survey using interviews of several individuals
   f. An ethnographic study
   g. A case study
   h. A content analysis
   i. A historical study

3. What questions, if any might a critical researcher raise with regard to your study? *Some critical researchers might disagree with the values and intentions implied in my study. I would argue that such studies would promote fairer treatment of all segments of society. I will explain further in Problem Sheet 3.*

Research Exercise Two
The Research Question

Using Problem Sheet #2, restate the problem question you listed in Research Exercise #1 in a sentence or two, and then formulate a research question which relates to this problem. Now list all of the key terms in the question that you think are not clear and which need to be defined. Define each of these terms both constitutively and operationally.

Problem Sheet #2
THE RESEARCH QUESTION
(First draft)

1. My research problem (restated) is: *The effects of curricula on awareness of the values of other cultures.*

2. My research question is: *Whether the curriculum I am developing (for my thesis) will increase awareness of the values of other cultures and improve self-concept.*

(**Instructor's comments:** *I still think you should choose awareness* or *self-concept in order to simplify your task for this course. Do you intend to include a control group?*)

3. The following are the key terms in the problem or question which are not clear and which need to be defined:

a. *Awareness* *c.* ______

b. *Self-concept* *d.* ______

(**Instructor's comments:** *You must define the term "awareness of values of other cultures." Also you must define "the curriculum."*)

4. Here are my constitutive definitions of these terms:

a. ***Awareness:*** *Vigilance in observing or alertness in drawing inferences from what one experiences will help children become more aware of different cultures. Synonyms: cognizant, conscious, aware.*

(**Instructor's comments:** *The first part is not a definition and it is circular. You must explain what you mean by "awareness of the values of other cultures."*)

b. ***Self-concept:*** *the mental image one has of oneself.*

(**Instructor's comments:** *Much too ambiguous. Try to be more specific.*)

Problem Sheet #2 continued

5. Here are my operational definitions of these terms:

   a. ***Awareness:*** *(1) Administer a verbal questionnaire and examine children's responses as a group; (2) observe the children's behavior and their involvement during the activities.*

(**Instructor's comments:** *Describes what you will do, but needs more detail. What verbal or other behaviors will you be looking at? If you plan to develop an instrument, refer to it here.*)

   b. ***Self-concept:*** *I have not found an instrument yet.*

6. My justification for investigating this question/problem (why I would argue that it is an important question to investigate) is as follows:

   One of the characteristics of California's present educational environment is the increasing number of students from various ethnic backgrounds. Also, the number of interracial marriages has increased rapidly in the last decade. In order to help today's children to succeed in obtaining social harmony and happiness in their future lives, they need to know, understand, and respect each other's values.

(**Instructor's comments:** *You must show why they need these things—you can't assume it is self-evident.*)

Research Exercise Two
The Research Question

Using Problem Sheet #2, restate the problem question you listed in Research Exercise #1 in a sentence or two, and then formulate a research question which relates to this problem. Now list all of the key terms in the question that you think are not clear and which need to be defined. Define each of these terms both constitutively and operationally.

Problem Sheet #2
THE RESEARCH QUESTION
(Second draft)

1. My research problem (restated) is: *The effects of curricula on awareness of the values of other cultures.*

2. My research question is: *Whether students exposed to a multicultural curriculum will increase their respect for other cultures.*

3. The following are the key terms in the problem or question which are not clear and which need to be defined:

   a. *Multicultural curriculum* ______ *c.* ______

   b. *Respect for other cultures* ______ *d.* ______

4. Here are my constitutive definitions of these terms:

   a. ***Multicultural curriculum:*** *a variety of lessons about the many cultural values unique to each ethnic group. Units are designed for second grade and include information and activities on the Native American, African, Mexican, Chinese, Jewish, and Japanese cultures.*

   b. ***Respect for other cultures:*** *the degree of understanding and acceptance for cultures different from one's own.*

   (**Instructor's comments:** *The terms "understanding" and "acceptance" are pretty ambiguous.*)

5. Here are my operational definitions of these terms:

   a. ***Multicultural curriculum:*** *The teacher will be observed using the materials and activities provided by the researcher.*

   b. ***Respect for other cultures:*** *The score on a rating scale developed by the researcher (This is illustrated subsequently in Problem Sheet 6)*

Problem Sheet #2 continued

6. My justification for investigating this question/problem (why I would argue that it is an important question to investigate) is as follows:

This research deals with one of today's most controversial issues, the multiracial mixture of classes in schools. This nation was established by people from many different cultures. California has always been one of the states where immigrants could find a new life. Today, immigrants are coming in large numbers from Mexico, Asia, and many other parts of the world. Newly arriving children must often suppress their own cultural values in order to be accepted; this must have a negative effect on their sense of self-respect. Further, children of the dominant culture need to develop respect for the values of people from different backgrounds. Respect is the core of positive human relationships and fosters harmonious bonds between individuals. This curriculum is intended to provide respect for self and others from all other cultures represented in our classrooms.

Research Exercise Three
Ethics and Research

Using Problem Sheet #3, restate the research question you developed in Problem Sheet 2. Identify any possible ethical problems in carrying out such a study. How might such problems be remedied?

Problem Sheet #3
ETHICS AND RESEARCH
(First draft)

1. My research question is: *Whether students exposed to a multicultural curriculum will increase their respect for other cultures.*

2. The possibilities for harm to participants (if any) are as follows: *None.*

(**Instructor's comment:** *What about denying a potentially valuable experience to the group which does not get the curriculum?*)

I would handle these problems as follows: —

3. The possibilities of problems of confidentiality (if any) are as follows: *Students might not want their scores made public.*

I would handle these problems as follows: *All information will be kept confidential.*

4. The possibilities of problems of deception (if any) are as follows: *None; no one will be deceived.*

I would handle these problems as follows: —

5. If you think your proposed study would fit the guidelines for exempt status, state why here. *Because neither the curriculum nor the assessment of "respect" depart from customary school practice.*

(**Instructor's comment:** *I agree, but some administrators and parents might not. You might be required to get consent from parents.*)

Research Exercise Three
Ethics and Research

Using Problem Sheet #3, restate the research question you developed in Problem Sheet 2. Identify any possible ethical problems in carrying out such a study. How might such problems be remedied?

Problem Sheet #3
ETHICS AND RESEARCH
(Second draft)

1. My research question is: *Whether students exposed to a multicultural curriculum will increase their respect for other cultures.*

2. The possibilities for harm to participants (if any) are as follows: *Only that the comparison group does not get the benefit of the new curriculum.*

   I would handle these problems as follows: *I would arrange to have the comparison group receive the curriculum after my study is completed.*

3. The possibilities of problems of confidentiality (if any) are as follows: *Students might not want their scores made public.*

   I would handle these problems as follows: *All information will be kept confidential.*

4. The possibilities of problems of deception (if any) are as follows: *None; no one will be deceived.*

   I would handle these problems as follows: —

5. If you think your proposed study would fit the guidelines for exempt status, state why here. *Because neither the curriculum nor the assessment of "respect" depart from customary school practice. If necessary, I would get informed consent from parents.*

Research Exercise Four
The Research Hypothesis

Formulate a testable hypothesis related to the research question you developed in Research Exercise Three. Using Problem Sheet #4, state the hypothesis in a sentence or two, and indicate the more general research question which it reflects. Check to see if it suggests a relationship between at least two variables. If it does not, revise it so that it does. Now name these variables, and then indicate which is the independent variable and which is the dependent variable. Write a paragraph indicating why you think it is an important question to investigate, and identify any possible ethical problems posed by the research question. Lastly, list as many extraneous variables as you can think of that might affect the results of your study.

Problem Sheet #4
THE RESEARCH HYPOTHESIS

1. The hypothesis I wish to investigate is: *Second-grade students who are exposed to a multicultural curriculum will demonstrate greater respect for different cultures than students not exposed to this curriculum.*

2. This hypothesis suggests a relationship between at least two variables. They are: *multicultural curriculum versus no multicultural curriculum; amount of respect for different cultures.*

3. More specifically, the variables in my study are:

   a. ***Dependent:*** *respect for different cultures.*

   b. ***Independent:*** *multicultural curriculum versus no multicultural curriculum.*

4. Possible extraneous variables that might affect my results include: *the ethnic mix of the comparison classrooms; teaching style and cultural knowledge.*

(**Instructor's comments:** *You also need to be concerned about the prior level of "respect" in your comparison classes.*)

Research Exercise Five
Review of the Literature

Using Problem Sheet #5, state again either your research problem or the hypothesis of your study. Then consult an appropriate general reference, and list at least three search terms that are relevant to your problem. Locate and read three primary sources (articles) which include studies related to your problem, taking notes as you read on note cards similar to the one shown in Figure 5.10. Attach each of your note cards (one per journal article) to Problem Sheet #5.

Problem Sheet #5
REVIEW OF THE LITERATURE

1. The hypothesis I wish to investigate is: *Second-grade students who are exposed to a multicultural curriculum will demonstrate greater respect for different cultures than students not exposed to this curriculum.*

2. The general reference(s) I consulted was (were): *Education Index.*

3. The search terms I used were:
   a. *Multicultural curriculum*
   b. *Cross-cultural respect*
   c. *Self-esteem (before deleting from my hypothesis)*

4. The three journals I consulted were:
   a. *The Social Studies*
   b. *Day Care Early Education*
   c. *Harvard Educational Review*

5. The titles of the studies I read (note cards are attached) were:
   a. *Strategies for implementing a pluralistic curriculum in the social studies*
   b. *Multicultural education: A pathway to global harmony*
   c. *An analysis of multicultural education in the United States.*

Problem Sheet #5 (continued)

Example of Note Card for Problem Sheet 5

Steeter, C. E., and Grant, C. A. (1987). An analysis of multicultural education in the United States. *Harvard Educational Review, 57*,421–444.

Problem: To review books and articles published in the United States regarding multicultural education in grades K–12.

Hypotheses or objectives: To see if trends were evident.

Procedures: Content analysis.

Findings: Multicultural education has many meanings, the common thread is benefit to people of color. Connections between goals and recommended practices are generally vague or weak. Weak connections to theory. The multicultural method is the most successful at relating goals to theory and practice. The focus is predominantly on the classroom teacher—other power groups are ignored. Most teaching guides are for elementary grades and most are for single lessons. Little research on practice or outcomes.

Conclusion: The field is in need of funding and a journal.

(**Instructor's comments:** *You need more detail on the content analysis. Also, the reference to the multicultural method is unclear—the most successful of what?*)

Revision of Note Card for Problem Sheet 5

Steeter, C. E., and Grant, C. A. (1987). An analysis of multicultural education in the United States. *Harvard Educational Review, 57*,421–444.

Problem: To review books and articles published in the United States regarding multicultural education in grades K–12.

Hypotheses or objectives: To see if trends were evident.

Procedures: Content analysis: 89 articles and 38 books were reviewed. Five different methods were identified: "Teaching the culturally different," "Human relations," "Single-group studies," "Multicultural education," and "Education that is multicultural and social reconstructionist." The authors used 14 categories of analysis including "goals," "scope," "theory," and "implementation" in order to compare the five methods and arrive at overall generalizations.

Findings: Multicultural education has many meanings, the common thread is benefit to people of color. Connections between goals and recommended practices are generally vague or weak. Weak connections to theory. The multicultural method is the most successful at relating goals theory and practice. The focus is predominantly on the classroom teacher—other power groups are ignored. Most teaching guides are for elementary grades and most are for single lessons. Little research on practice or outcomes.

Conclusion: The field is in need of funding and a journal.

Research Exercise Six
Sampling Plan

> Use Problem Sheet #6 to describe, as fully as you can, your sample--that is, the subjects whom you will have participate in your study. Describe the type of sample you plan to use and how you will obtain the sample. Indicate whether or not you expect your study to have population validity: if so, to what populations; if not, why it would not. Then indicate whether the study would have ecological validity: if so, to what settings; if not, why it would not.

Problem Sheet # 6
SAMPLING PLAN
(First draft)

1. My intended sample (subjects who would participate in my study) consists of (tell *who* and *how many*): *Ten second-grade classes in five schools; each school will have one curriculum and one no-curriculum class.*

(**Instructor's comments:** *Better to have a larger sample of schools, if feasible.*)

2. Demographics (characteristics of the sample) are as follows:
   a. Age range: *Second-graders*
   b. Sex distribution: *Male and female*
   c. Ethnic breakdown: *Various—representative of San Francisco schools.*
   d. Location (where are these subjects?): *San Francisco public schools.*
   e. Other (describe) characteristics not mentioned above that you deem important (use back if you need more space): ______

3. Type of sample: random __X__ stratified ____ cluster __X__ convenience(accessible) ____
   other (describe): ______

4. I will obtain my sample by: *Identifying all primary schools in San Francisco Bay Area and randomly selecting 10. I will write a letter to the principal of each school explaining my study. I expect at least five acceptances. I will then use both second grades in each school, one to receive the curriculum and the other to be in the control group.*

(**Instructor's comments:** *Better to try to get all to cooperate. Why so? What about schools that might have fewer than (or more than) two second-grade classes? How many schools do you estimate in the population?*)

Problem Sheet #6 (continued)

5. External validity (I will generalize to the following population):

a. To what accessible population? *All second-graders in San Francisco public schools because my sample is picked randomly. Most of the schools have similar characteristics, use the same basic curriculum and textbooks.*

(**Instructor's comments:** *Your randomness applies only to picking five schools. Remember that randomness is not effective with small numbers. Also, you cannot assume that all schools are similar in ways affecting your study just because they are similar in* some *ways.*)

b. To what target population? *All second-graders in multiethnic urban schools in United States*

(**Instructor's comments:** *Multiethnic urban schools can differ considerably—you are using only one geographic area.*)

c. If not generalizable, why not? ________

6. Ecological validity (to what settings/conditions can you generalize?):

a. Generalizable to what setting(s)? *All elementary schools in San Francisco*

b. Generalizable to what conditions? *No special limitations on conditions*

c. If not generalizable, why not? ________

Research Exercise Six
Sampling Plan

Use Problem Sheet #6 to describe, as fully as you can, your sample--that is, the subjects whom you will have participate in your study. Describe the type of sample you plan to use and how you will obtain the sample. Indicate whether or not you expect your study to have population validity: if so, to what populations; if not, why it would not. Then indicate whether the study would have ecological validity: if so, to what settings; if not, why it would not.

Problem Sheet # 6
SAMPLING PLAN
(Second draft)

1. My intended sample (subjects who would participate in my study) consists of (tell *who* and *how many*): *Ten second-grade classes receiving the multicultural curriculum and 10 that do not. Approximately 600 students in each method group.*

2. Demographics (characteristics of the sample) are as follows:

   a. Age range: *Second-graders*

   b. Sex distribution: *Male and female*

   c. Ethnic breakdown: *Various—representative of San Francisco schools*

   d. Location (where are these subjects?): *San Francisco public schools*

   e. Other (describe) characteristics not mentioned above that you deem important (use back if you need more space): _____

3. Type of sample: random *X* stratified _____ cluster *X* convenience(accessible) _____

   other (describe): *Cluster random sample of 10 schools. One second grade in each school will be in each method group.*

4. I will obtain my sample by: *Identifying all primary schools in San Francisco (estimated at 60). Select those having two or more second-grade classes. Randomly select 10 schools from these. If a school has more than two second-grade classes, randomly pick two.*

5. External validity (I will generalize to the following population):

   a. To what accessible population? *All second-graders in San Francisco public schools*

(Problem Sheet #6 continued)

(**Instructor's comments:** *Improved by increase to 10 schools, but recognize that a random sample of 10 out of 60 may not be representative.*)

b. To what target population? *Second-grade classrooms having a similar ethnic mix and in urban schools.*

(**Instructor's comments:** *Still highly questionable—how does one determine "similarity"?—but improved.*)

c. If not generalizable, why not? ______

6. Ecological validity (to what settings/conditions can you generalize?):

   a. Generalizable to what setting(s)? *Elementary schools in San Francisco*

   b. Generalizable to what conditions? *No special limitations on conditions*

   c. If not generalizable, why not? ______

Research Exercise Seven
Instrumentation

Decide on the kind of instrument you will use to measure the dependent variable(s) in your study. Using Problem Sheet #7, name all of the instruments you plan to use in your study. If you plan to use one or more already existing instruments, describe each. If you will need to develop an instrument, give two examples of the kind of questions you would ask (or tasks you would have students perform) as a part of each instrument. Indicate how you would describe and organize the data on each of the variables yielding numerical data.

Problem Sheet #7
INSTRUMENTATION
(First draft)

1. The instrument I plan to use to measure my dependent variable is: *the Respect for Cultures Scale, which I would develop*

2. Other instruments I plan to use would be: *None.*

(**Instructor's comments:** *What about checking for validity?*)

3. If I need to develop an instrument, here are two examples of the kind of questions I would ask (or tasks I would have students perform) as part of my instrument:

Example of items for Native American culture. Each item is rated from 1 to 5 as follows:

1 = Should not be allowed	*Scoring would be as follows:*
2 = Should be discouraged	*1 and 5 = 0 points*
3 = Should be permitted	*2 and 4 = 1 point*
4 = Should be encouraged	*3 = 2 points*
5 = Should be required	

a. Making musical instruments from natural materials such as stick rattles, cocoon rattles, and bird-bone whistles

b. Dancing with feather masks and painted bodies for both happy and sad occasions.

c. Living close to nature, by the ocean or in the woods.

Note: I will develop 10 items for each of the six cultures. They will be based on cultural practices included in the curriculum.

(**Instructor's comments:** *Promising idea. Make clear the rationale for scoring, i.e., acceptance rather than requirement or prohibition. Will second-graders understand the items—are they read to them? Will they understand the response choices? Also, what will you do to review and improve these items?*)

(Problem Sheet #7 continued)

4. These are the existing instruments I plan to use: None.

5. I would describe each variable yielding numerical data as follows:

	Variable 1	Variable 2	Other variable(s)
	Respect		
Quantitative or categorical	Quantitative		
Nominal or ordinal or interval or ratio	interval		

6. For each variable yielding numerical data, I will treat it as follows:

Raw score	✓		
Age/grade equivalents			
Percentile			
Standard score			

Research Exercise Seven
Instrumentation

Decide on the kind of instrument you will use to measure the dependent variable(s) in your study. Using Problem Sheet #7, name all of the instruments you plan to use in your study. If you plan to use one or more already existing instruments, describe each. If you will need to develop an instrument, give two examples of the kind of questions you would ask (or tasks you would have students perform) as a part of each instrument. Indicate how you would describe and organize the data on each of the variables yielding numerical data.

Problem Sheet #7
INSTRUMENTATION
(Second draft)

1. The instrument I plan to use to measure my dependent variable is: *The Respect for Cultures Scale.*

2. Other instruments I plan to use would be: *An observation checklist filled out by the teacher, as a means of checking for validity.*

3. If I need to develop an instrument, here are two examples of the kind of questions I would ask (or tasks I would have students perform) as part of my instrument:

Example of items for Native American culture. Each item is rated from 1 to 5 as follows:

1 = Should not be allowed	*Scoring would be as follows:*
2 = Should be discouraged	*1 and 5 = 0 points*
3 = Should be permitted	*2 and 4 = 1 point*
4 = Should be encouraged	*3 = 2 points*
5 = Should be required	

a. Making musical instruments from natural materials such as stick rattles, cocoon rattles, and bird-bone whistles

b. Dancing with feather masks and painted bodies for both happy and sad occasions.

c. Living close to nature, by the ocean or in the woods.

Note: I will develop 10 items for each of the six cultures. They will be based on cultural practices included in the curriculum.

The rationale for scoring is that tendencies to either prohibit or require the particular behaviors described indicate lack of respect, whereas a willingness to allow the behavior shows respect. Each of the items will be read aloud to the

(Problem Sheet #7 continued)

class. At the start of testing, the response choices will be gone over with several examples to make sure students understand the task before them.

I will develop 10 items for each of the six cultures. They will be based on the cultural practices included in the curriculum. These items will be reviewed by knowledgeable professors and fellow teachers for appropriateness of content and format.

(**Instructor's comments:** *This test may prove difficult for second-graders. You would want to do a fair amount of tryout before using it in your study.*)

4. These are the existing instruments I plan to use: *None.*

5. I would describe each variable yielding numerical data as follows:

	Variable 1 *Respect*	Variable 2	Other
Quantitative or categorical	*Quantitative*		
Nominal or ordinal or interval or ratio	*interval*		

6. For each variable yielding numerical data, I will treat it as follows:

Raw score	✓		
Age/grade equivalents			
Percentile			
Standard score			

Research Exercise Eight
Validity and Reliability

Use Problem Sheet #8 to describe how you plan to check on the validity and reliability of scores obtained with your instruments. If you plan to use an existing instrument, summarize what you have been able to learn about the validity and reliability of results obtained with it. If you plan to develop an instrument, explain how you will attempt to ensure validity and reliability. In either case, explain how you will empirically check validity and reliability.

Problem Sheet #8
VALIDITY AND RELIABILITY
(First draft)

1. I plan to use the following existing instruments: *Not applicable, as I am developing my instrument.*

   In summary, I have learned the following about the validity and reliability of scores obtained with these instruments:

   N/A

2. I plan to develop the following instruments:

   A series of 60 rating scale items to measure "respect for cultures"; a set of behavior rating items to be used by teachers to check validity of the Respect scale

   I will try to ensure reliability and validity of results obtained with these instruments by: *having both instruments reviewed by my colleagues. I will try out both instruments before using them in my study.*

3. For each instrument I plan to use:

   a. This is how I will collect evidence to check internal consistency: *For the Respect scale, I will obtain a split-half reliability coefficient by dividing the text into odd and even halves and giving the 30-item tests on two different days.*

   (**Instructor's comments:** *This will check reliability over content* and *time? Why so?*)

   b. This is how I will collect evidence to check reliability over time (stability): *I will compare pretests to posttests given one semester later.*

   (**Instructor's comments:** *For both curriculum and noncurriculum groups? Is using the former a good idea?*)

(Problem Sheet #8 continued)

c. This is how I will collect evidence to check validity:

I will compare posttest scores on my scale to teacher ratings of each student based on observation during the teaching of each of the units.

Examples of rating scale items are:	*low*				*high*
(1) Degree of involvement in the activity	*1*	*2*	*3*	*4*	*5*
(2) Degree of interest in the folk stories	*1*	*2*	*3*	*4*	*5*
(3) Degree of completeness of work	*1*	*2*	*3*	*4*	*5*
(5) Degree of popularity of culture center	*1*	*2*	*3*	*4*	*5*

(**Instructor's comments:** *These items do* not *have content validity as indicators of "respect." A child could have high interest but low respect. Also, it is not a good idea to assess respect* during *the units since your primary instrument is given before and after the curriculum units.*)

Research Exercise Eight
Validity and Reliability

Use Problem Sheet #8 to describe how you plan to check on the validity and reliability of scores obtained with your instruments. If you plan to use an existing instrument, summarize what you have been able to learn about the validity and reliability of results obtained with it. If you plan to develop an instrument, explain how you will attempt to ensure validity and reliability. In either case, explain how you will empirically check validity and reliability.

Problem Sheet #8
VALIDITY AND RELIABILITY
(Second Draft)

1. I plan to use the following existing instruments: *Not applicable, as I am developing my instrument.*

   In summary, I have learned the following about the validity and reliability of scores obtained with these instruments:
   N/A

2. I plan to develop the following instruments:
   A series of 60 rating scale items to measure "respect for cultures"; a set of behavior rating items to be used by teachers to check validity of the Respect scale

   I will try to ensure reliability and validity of results obtained with these instruments by: *having both instruments reviewed by my colleagues. I will try out both instruments before using them in my study.*

3. For each instrument I plan to use:

   a. This is how I will collect evidence to check internal consistency: *For the Respect scale, I will obtain a split-half reliability coefficient by scoring pretests separately on odd and even items.*

   b. This is how I will collect evidence to check reliability over time (stability): *I will compare pretest scores to scores on the posttest given one semester later for the control group. I want to know how stable scores are in the absence of a specific intervention.*

   c. This is how I will collect evidence to check validity: *I will compare posttest scores on my scale to teacher observations of each student during the 3 weeks before the end of the semester. The teachers will be asked to assign points to each student each time they observe them reacting to expressions of a culture different from their own. Points will be assigned as follows:*

(Problem Sheet #8 continued)

+1 point—any indication of acceptance or support for the behavior

−1 point—any indication of rejection or teasing resulting from the behavior

Examples of cultural expression:

Child brings ethnic foods for snack or lunch.

Child talks about family customs during sharing time.

Child uses new form of "goodbye" or "good morning" in another language.

Child brings examples of cultural art from home.

(**Instructor's comments:** *Promising idea. It may be difficult to get teachers to do this, however. Also, some children may "stand out" more than others. This should be pretested. You could change the format to the more customary rating scale based on teacher recall of each child's behavior.*)

Research Exercise Nine
Descriptive Statistics

Using Problem Sheet #9, state again the question or hypothesis of your study, and list your variables. Then indicate how you would summarize the results for each variable. Lastly, indicate how you would describe the relationship between variables one and two.

Problem Sheet #9
DESCRIPTIVE STATISTICS

1. The hypothesis of my study is: *Second-grade students who are exposed to a multicultural curriculum will demonstrate greater respect for different cultures than students not exposed to this curriculum.*

2. My variables are: (1) *Respect for different cultures;* (2) *multicultural versus usual curriculum.*

3. I consider variable 1 to be: quantitative ✓ or categorical _____

4. I consider variable 2 to be: quantitative _____ or categorical ✓

5. I would summarize the results for each variable as follows:

	Variable 1 *"respect"*	Variable 2	Other
Freq. polygon	✓		
Mean	✓		
Median	✓		
Range			
Standard deviation	✓		
Frequency table			
Bar graph			
Pie chart			

6. I will describe the relationship between variables 1 and 2 by a (use a check mark):

Comparison of frequency polygons	✓
Comparison of averages	✓
Crossbreak tables(s)	
Correlation coefficient	
Scatterplot	

Research Exercise Ten
Inferential Statistics

Using Problem Sheet #10, once again state the question or hypothesis of your study. Summarize the descriptive statistics you would use to describe the relationship you are hypothesizing. Tell whether you would or would not do a significance test and/or calculate a confidence interval, and if not, why. Lastly, describe the type of sample used in your study, and explain any limitations that are placed on your using inferential statistics due to the nature of the sample.

Problem Sheet #10
INFERENTIAL STATISTICS

1. The hypothesis of my study is: *Second-grade students who are exposed to a multicultural curriculum will demonstrate greater respect for different cultures than students not exposed to this curriculum.*

2. The descriptive statistic(s) I would use to describe the relationship I am hypothesizing would be: *a comparison of polygons and averages.*

3. The appropriate inference technique for study would be: *a t test for means.*

4. I would use a parametric ✓ or a nonparametric ____ technique because: *I think my Respect scale is interval and I want to use all the information available.*

5. I would ✓ or would not ____ do a significance test because: *I want to know if the difference in means would happen more than 5 in 100 samples if there is no difference in the population.*

6. I would ✓ or would not ____ calculate a confidence interval because: *I want to know the difference in means that is likely in the population.*

7. The type of sample used in my study is: *cluster random.*

8. The type of sample used in my study places the following limitation(s) on my use of inferential statistics: *None, because the sample is random in terms of clusters (schools), and 10 out of the estimated 60 is sizable. My total sample in each group should be around 300.*

(**Instructor's comments:** Unless *you are refused access to some schools, in which case your sample is no longer random. Also, remember that 10 out of 60 is not a large sample of schools.*)

Research Exercise Eleven
Statistics in Perspective

Using Problem Sheet #11, once again state the question or hypothesis of your study. Summarize the descriptive and inferential statistics you would use to describe the relationship you are hypothesizing, and then tell how you evaluate the magnitude of any relationship you might find.

Problem Sheet #11
STATISTICS IN PERSPECTIVE

1. The hypothesis of my study is: *Second-grade students who are exposed to a multicultural curriculum will demonstrate greater respect for different cultures than students not exposed to this curriculum.*

2. My expected relationship(s) would be described using the following descriptive statistics: *A comparison of polygons and means.*

3. The inferential statistics I would use are: *A t test for means.*

4. I would evaluate the magnitude of the relationship(s) I find by: *Comparing means using an effect size (delta).*

5. Indicate any changes in your use of descriptive or inferential statistics as described in Problem Sheets 8 and 9: *Addition of effect size.*

(**Instructor's comments:** *In addition you could analyze your data more thoroughly by:*
(1) obtaining medians in addition to means.
(2) using a nonparametric inference test.
(3) comparing your two classes within *each school.*
(4) comparing your two methods groups using the mean (or median) score for each class *as the unit of analysis* (n = *10 in each group).*
(5) analyzing data separately for "dominant culture" students and for "minority culture" students. Your justification for doing this study suggests this, in fact.)

Research Exercise Twelve
Internal Validity

State the question or hypothesis of your study at the top of Problem Sheet #12. Then, in the spaces indicated, place an X after each of the threats to internal validity that apply to your study, explain why they are threats, and describe how you intend to control for those most likely to occur (i.e., prevent their having an effect on the outcome of your study).

Problem Sheet #12
INTERNAL VALIDITY
(First Draft)

1. The hypothesis of my study is: *Second-grade students who are exposed to a multicultural curriculum will demonstrate greater respect for different cultures than students not exposed to this curriculum.*

2. I have placed an **X** in the blank in front of each threat listed below that applies to my study. I explain why I think each one is a problem and then explain how I would attempt to control for the threat.

Threats: *X* Subject Characteristics ___ Mortality *X* Location *X* Instrumentation ___ Testing *X* History ___ Maturation *X* Subject Attitude ___ Regression ___ Implementation ___ Other (Specify) ___

Threat 1: *Subject characteristics* Why? *Diversity of ethnic composition in classrooms and teacher style, and knowledge may influence "respect."*

How control? *I cannot control ethnic mix because I want random samples. Teacher style and knowledge should not be controlled because they should share what they know with their students.*

(**Instructor's comments:** *There are ways of equating your groups on ethnic mix that you should consider. How are you deciding which class in each school gets which method? Teacher style and knowledge* should *be the same overall for your two methods groups. If not, you cannot be confident that any differences in "respect" are due to your curriculum!)*

Threat 2: *Location* Why? *The existence of more resources, such as more parent involvement in school activities, could affect respect. Support by the principal can influence the effectiveness of the curriculum.*

How control? *I will send a letter to the principals requesting their cooperation and selecting the sample that might control this problem.*

Problem Sheet #12 continued

(**Instructor's comments:** *Changes such as parent support that occur* because *of your curriculum are part of its intended effect, not an alternative explanation of results. Is it likely that the two classes in each school would differ in resources? If principals are not supportive, your hypothesis is* less *likely to be supported since your curriculum may not get a fair trial. Again, how you decide which class in each school gets which methods makes a difference.*)

Threat 3: *History* Why? *A parent's special help in demonstrating cultural activities might favor my hypothesis since the students would get more exposure to different cultures.*

How control? *Parent participation is valuable and should not be controlled.*

(**Instructor's comments:** *Since such parent participation is* not *a component of your curriculum, it should be controlled. If not, differences in "respect" may be due to this influence rather than your curriculum,* unless *they result* from *your curriculum. In the absence of your curriculum, why would you expect more parent involvement in one method group than in the other?*)

Threat 4: *Subject attitude* Why? *The special attention received by students might account for their gain in "respect."*

How control? *Trying not to have the units appear "special," but rather a normal part of the ongoing curriculum.*

Threat 5: *Instrumentation* Why? *Not used to taking such an instrument.*

How control? *To prevent distortion, I will administer the respect scale to all classes. I should have good rapport with students since I will visit each class often, both during and after each unit.*

(**Instructor's comments:** *But you have a personal interest in the outcome that could affect the way you administer the scales. Also, you will* not *be known to the control classes.*)

Research Exercise Twelve
Internal Validity

State the question or hypothesis of your study at the top of Problem Sheet #12. Then, in the spaces indicated, place an X after each of the threats to internal validity that apply to your study, explain why they are threats, and describe how you intend to control for those most likely to occur (i.e., prevent their having an effect on the outcome of your study).

Problem Sheet #12
INTERNAL VALIDITY
(Second Draft)

1. The hypothesis of my study is: *Second-grade students who are exposed to a multicultural curriculum will demonstrate greater respect for different cultures than students not exposed to this curriculum.*

2. I have placed an **X** in the blank in front of each threat listed below that applies to my study. I explain why I think each one is a problem and then explain how I would attempt to control for the threat.

Threats: _X_ Subject characteristics ___ Mortality _X_ Location _X_ Instrumentation ___ Testing _X_ History ___ Maturation _X_ Subject Attitude ___ Regression ___ Implementation ___ Other (Specify) ___

Threat 1: *Subject characteristics* Why? *Diversity of ethnic composition in classrooms and teacher style and knowledge may influence "respect."*

How control? *Random assignment of one of the two classes at each school to each curriculum group. With a total of 10 classes in each curriculum group, the method groups should be equated overall. In addition, I will compare the classes at each school on the "Respect" pretest. If there are differences, I will match the groups statistically.*

(**Instructor's comments:** *Differences in teacher background and teaching style should also be equated by the random assignment of classes.*)

Threat 2: *Location* Why? *The existence of more resources such as more parent involvement in school activities could affect respect. Support by the principal can influence the effectiveness of the curriculum.*

How control? *The random assignment of classes within each school. Also I would not expect the classes in the same school to be different in resources affecting "respect" unless it is a desired side effect of my curriculum.*

Problem Sheet #12 continued

Threat 3: *History* Why? *A parent's special help in demonstrating cultural activities might favor my hypothesis since the students would get more exposure to different cultures.*

How control? *The random assignment of classes within each school. I would not expect the classes to be different anyway.*

Threat 4: *Subject attitude* Why? *The special attention received by students might account for their gain in "respect."*

How control? *Trying not to have the units appear "special," but rather a normal part of the ongoing curriculum.*

Threat 5: *Instrumentation* Why? *Not used to taking such an instrument.*

How control? *I will have an outside examiner who knows nothing about my hypothesis administer the pre- and posttests to all classes and go over the end-of-semester observation method with each teacher. I will make sure that both classes at each school are tested the same day, one after the other and in the morning.*

Research Exercise Thirteen
Experimental Research

NOTE: You should complete Problem Sheet #13 only if you are planning an experimental study. If your intended study involves a different methodology, you will find a similar problem sheet at the end of the chapter that deals with that methodology. You might wish to consider, however, whether your research question could be investigated by means of an experiment.

> Using Problem Sheet #13, once again state the question or hypothesis of your study. Then describe, briefly but thoroughly, the procedures of your study, including analysis of results--that is, what you intend to do, when, where, and how. Lastly, indicate any unresolved problems you see at this point in your planning.

Problem Sheet #13
EXPERIMENTAL RESEARCH
(First Draft)

1. The hypothesis of my study is: *Second-grade students who are exposed to a multicultural curriculum will demonstrate greater respect for different cultures than students not exposed to this curriculum.*

2. A brief summary of *what* I intend to do, *when*, *where*, and *how* is as follows: *I will develop the multicultural curriculum by gathering information about the six cultural groups and develop a unit on each group focusing on values that are important to the culture. Activities and materials will center on art, music, literature, food, clothing, customs, rituals, holidays, and other important events.*

   I will meet with the 10 "curriculum" teachers to go over the units and help them plan to teach the units. Each unit should take about 2 weeks, though a longer time would be better.

   My examiner will administer the pretest to all 20 classes during the third week of the fall semester. Posttesting will be done the second week before the semester ends. Four weeks before the semester ends, my examiner will meet with each of the 20 teachers to go over the observation method.

(**Instructor's comments:** *What will you do to make sure your "curriculum" teachers actually implement your curriculum as you intend?*)

Problem Sheet #13 continued

3. The experimental design I intend to use is: *a variation of the matching-only pretest-posttest design. I will match my groups statistically rather than mechanically. I am also randomly assigning my previously existing classes in each school to the method groups, which means I can claim my students are randomly assigned.*

(**Instructor's comments:** *You need to change your wording. You can't claim that your students are randomly assigned—although your design does provide a sizable amount of randomness which* helps *equate your groups overall. This is much less true if you compare classes* within *each school!*)

4. The major problems I foresee at this point include the following: *I don't think I will have trouble getting support from the school district since they are interested in such materials being developed. With their support, I don't see problems getting the cooperation of principals and teachers, although I will be sure to contact them all personally, I don't see the need to obtain consent because my units will consist of typical class activities which some teachers do anyway. I don't see any problems with confidentiality and I am not using any deception.*

(**Instructor's comments:** *What if your control group teachers start using your curriculum? I think you may have problems with your instruments—see comments on Problem Sheets 7 and 8.*)

Research Exercise Thirteen
Experimental Research

NOTE: You should complete Problem Sheet #13 only if you are planning an experimental study. If your intended study involves a different methodology, you will find a similar problem sheet at the end of the chapter that deals with that methodology. You might wish to consider, however, whether your research question could be investigated by means of an experiment.

> Using Problem Sheet #13, once again state the question or hypothesis of your study. Then describe, briefly but thoroughly, the procedures of your study, including analysis of results--that is, what you intend to do, when, where, and how. Lastly, indicate any unresolved problems you see at this point in your planning.

Problem Sheet #13
EXPERIMENTAL RESEARCH
(Second Draft)

1. The hypothesis of my study is: *Second-grade students who are exposed to a multicultural curriculum will demonstrate greater respect for different cultures than students not exposed to this curriculum.*

2. A brief summary of *what* I intend to do, *when*, *where*, and *how* is as follows: *I will develop the multicultural curriculum by gathering information about the six cultural groups and develop a unit on each group focusing on values that are important to the culture. Activities and materials will center on art, music, literature, food, clothing, customs, rituals, holidays, and other important events.*

   I will meet with the 10 "curriculum" teachers to go over the units and help them plan to teach the units. Each unit should take about 2 weeks though a longer time would be better.

   My examiner will administer the pretest to all 20 classes during the third week of the fall semester. Posttesting will be done the second week before the semester ends. Four weeks before the semester ends, my examiner will meet with each of the 20 teachers to go over the observation method. I will maintain contact with the experimental teachers by visiting them once every 2 weeks to help them and to make sure my curriculum is used.

3. The experimental design I intend to use is: *a variation of the matching-only pretest-posttest design. I will match my groups statistically on the pretest. I am also randomly assigning my two previously existing classes in each school to the method groups (multicultural curriculum versus control). This helps equate my groups, especially when I combine all 10 classes using each method.*

Problem Sheet #13 continued

4. The major problems I foresee at this point include the following: *I don't think I will have trouble getting support from the school district since they are interested in such materials being developed. With their support, I don't see problems getting the cooperation of principals and teachers although I will be sure to contact them all personally. I don't see the need to obtain consent because my units will consist of typical class activities which some teachers do anyway. I don't see any problems with confidentiality and I am not using any deception. I will explain to the control teachers that they should not use my curriculum during fall semester. They will be encouraged to use it during spring semester and I will offer to help them.*

   I recognize that my instruments may not work as I intend, but I have no choice since I cannot locate any appropriate existing instruments.

Part Eight
Transparency Masters

CUT ALONG THIS LINE

Research Exercise One: What Kind of Research?

Think of a research idea or problem you would like to investigate. Using Problem Sheet 1, briefly describe the problem in a sentence or two. Then indicate the type of research methodology you would use to investigate this problem.

PROBLEM SHEET 1
Type of Research

1. A possible topic or problem I am thinking of researching is: ______________________________

____

____

____

2. The type of research that seems most appropriate to this topic or problem is: (*circle one*)

   a. An experiment.

   b. A correlational study.

   c. A causal-comparative study.

   d. A survey using a written questionnaire.

   e. A survey using interviews of several individuals.

   f. An ethnographic study.

   g. A case study.

   h. A content analysis.

   i. A historical study.

Figure 1.2

The Research Process

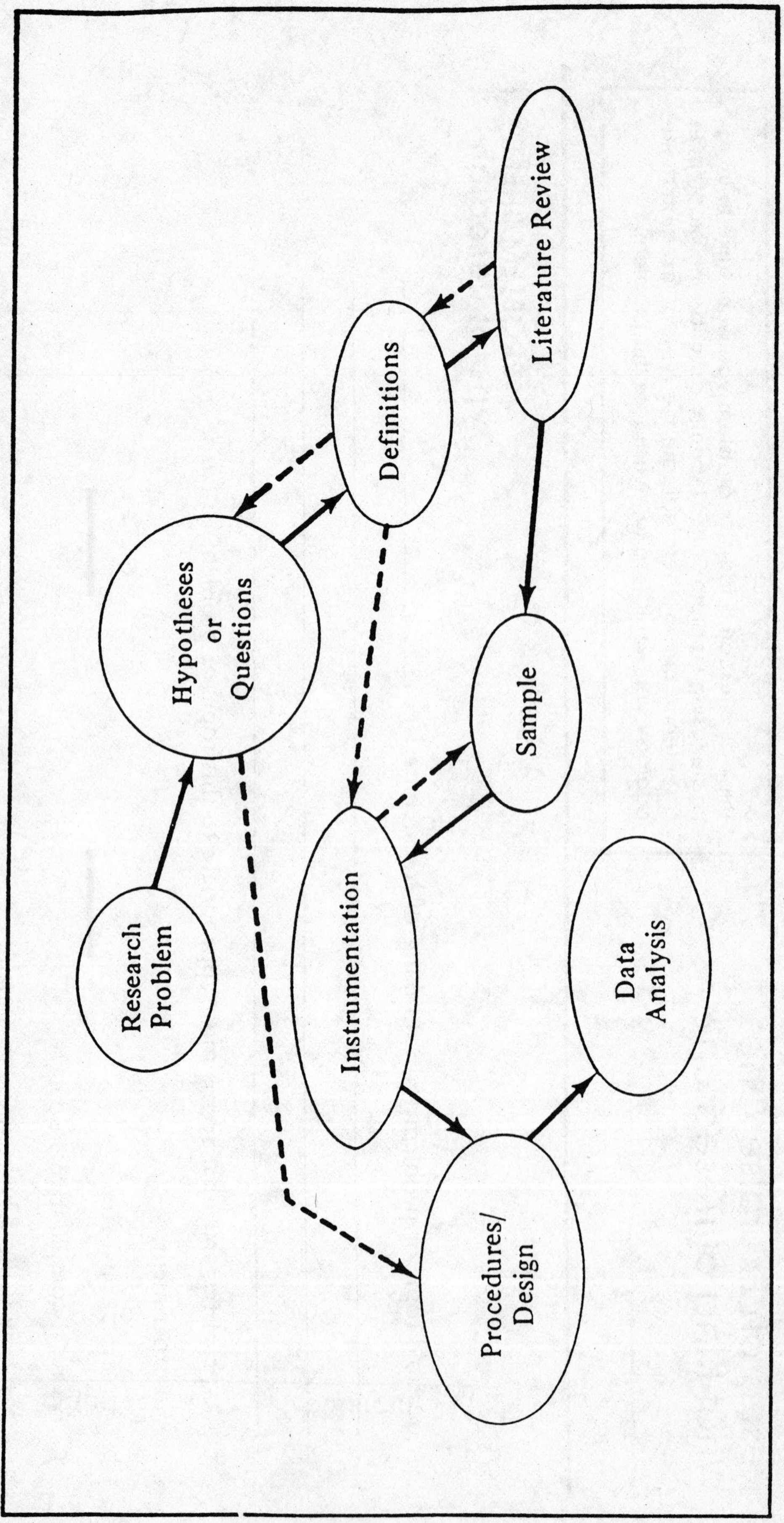

Research Problem

Hypotheses or Questions

Definitions

Literature Review

Sample

Instrumentation

Procedures/ Design

Data Analysis

Figure 2.1

CUT ALONG THIS LINE

Illustration of Relationship between Voter Gender and Party Affiliation[2]

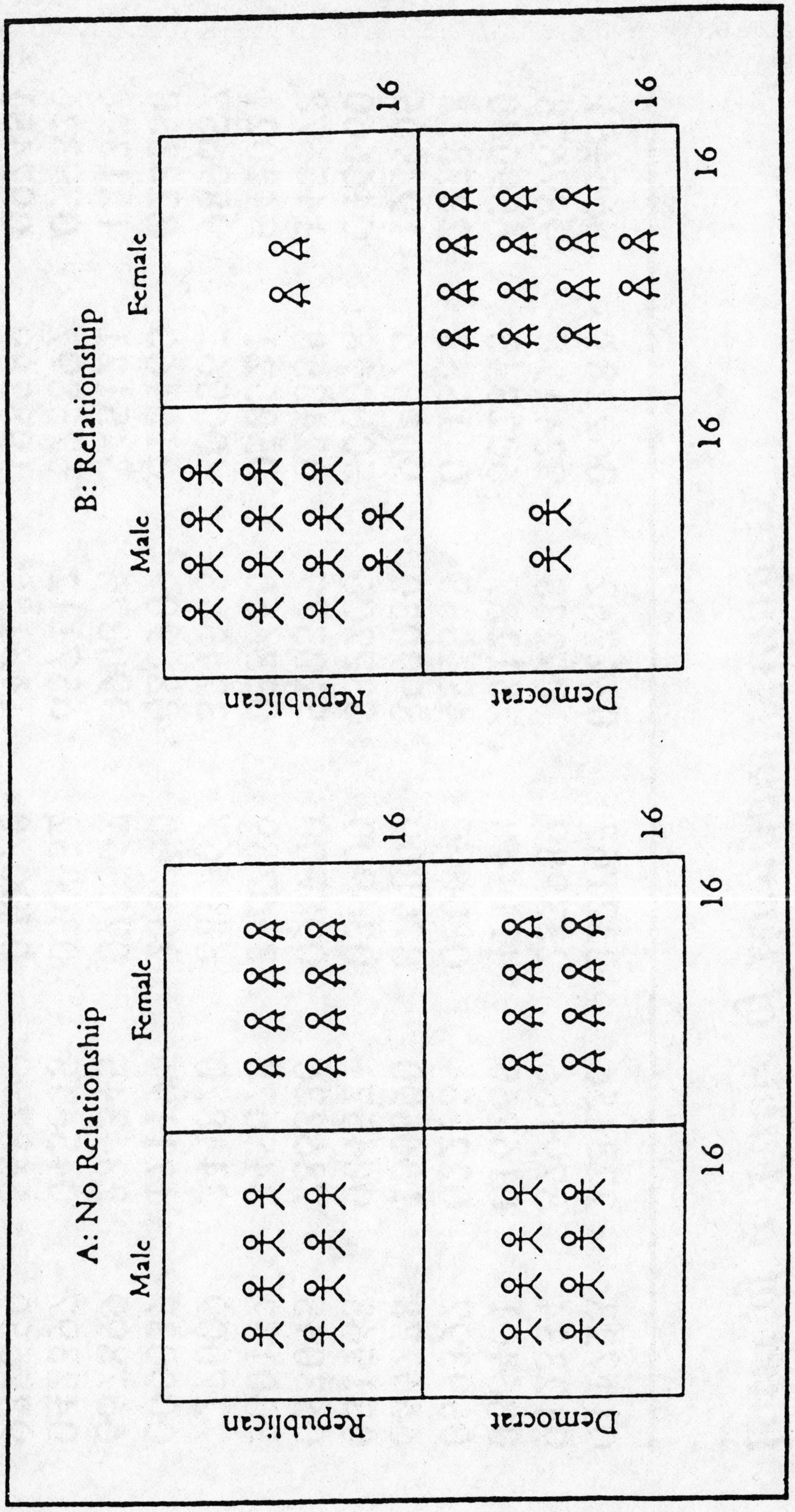

A: No Relationship

	Male	Female	
Republican	8	8	16
Democrat	8	8	16
	16	16	

B: Relationship

	Male	Female	
Republican	14	2	16
Democrat	2	14	16
	16	16	

Table 6.1

Part of a Table of Random Numbers

011723	223456	222167	032762	062281	565451
912334	379156	233989	109238	934128	987678
086401	016265	411148	251287	602345	659080
059397	022334	080675	454555	011563	237873
666278	106590	879809	899030	909876	198905
051965	004571	036900	037700	500098	046660
063045	786326	098000	510379	024358	145678
560132	345678	356789	033460	050521	342021
727009	344870	889567	324588	400567	989657
000037	121191	258700	088909	015460	223350
667899	234345	076567	090076	345121	121348
042397	045645	030032	657112	675897	079326
987650	568799	070070	143188	198789	097451
091126	021557	102322	209312	909036	342045

Table 6.2
A Hypothetical Population of 99 Students

Student Number	Sex	School	IQ	Student Number	Sex	School	IQ
01	F	Adams	134	51	M	Beals	110
02	F	Adams	133	52	M	Beals	110
03	F	Adams	130	53	M	Beals	109
04	F	Adams	127	54	M	Beals	108
05	F	Adams	123	55	M	Beals	107
06	M	Adams	123	56	M	Beals	106
07	M	Adams	121	57	M	Beals	101
08	M	Adams	120	58	M	Beals	101
09	F	Adams	119	59	M	Beals	98
10	M	Adams	118	60	M	Beals	97
11	F	Adams	117	61	F	Beals	91
12	F	Adams	117	62	F	Beals	86
13	M	Adams	115	63	F	Beals	83
14	M	Adams	111	64	F	Cortez	137
15	M	Adams	109	65	M	Cortez	136
16	M	Adams	108	66	F	Cortez	133
17	M	Adams	108	67	F	Cortez	130
18	F	Adams	106	68	F	Cortez	128
19	F	Adams	105	69	F	Cortez	125
20	F	Adams	104	70	F	Cortez	125
21	F	Adams	103	71	M	Cortez	122
22	F	Adams	101	72	F	Cortez	121
23	F	Adams	101	73	M	Cortez	118
24	M	Adams	101	74	F	Cortez	118
25	M	Adams	100	75	M	Cortez	113
26	M	Adams	98	76	F	Cortez	113
27	M	Adams	97	77	M	Cortez	111
28	M	Adams	97	78	F	Cortez	111
29	M	Adams	96	79	F	Cortez	107
30	F	Adams	95	80	F	Cortez	106
31	F	Adams	89	81	F	Cortez	106
32	F	Adams	88	82	F	Cortez	105
33	F	Adams	85	83	F	Cortez	104
34	F	Beals	133	84	F	Cortez	103
35	F	Beals	129	85	F	Cortez	102
36	F	Beals	129	86	M	Cortez	102
37	F	Beals	128	87	M	Cortez	100
38	F	Beals	127	88	M	Cortez	100
39	F	Beals	127	89	M	Cortez	99
40	F	Beals	126	90	M	Cortez	99
41	M	Beals	125	91	M	Cortez	99
42	M	Beals	124	92	F	Cortez	98
43	M	Beals	117	93	M	Cortez	97
44	M	Beals	116	94	F	Cortez	96
45	M	Beals	115	95	F	Cortez	95
46	M	Beals	114	96	F	Cortez	93
47	M	Beals	114	97	F	Cortez	85
48	M	Beals	113	98	M	Cortez	83
49	M	Beals	111	99	M	Cortez	83
50	M	Beals	111				

Figure 6.2

Random Sampling Methods

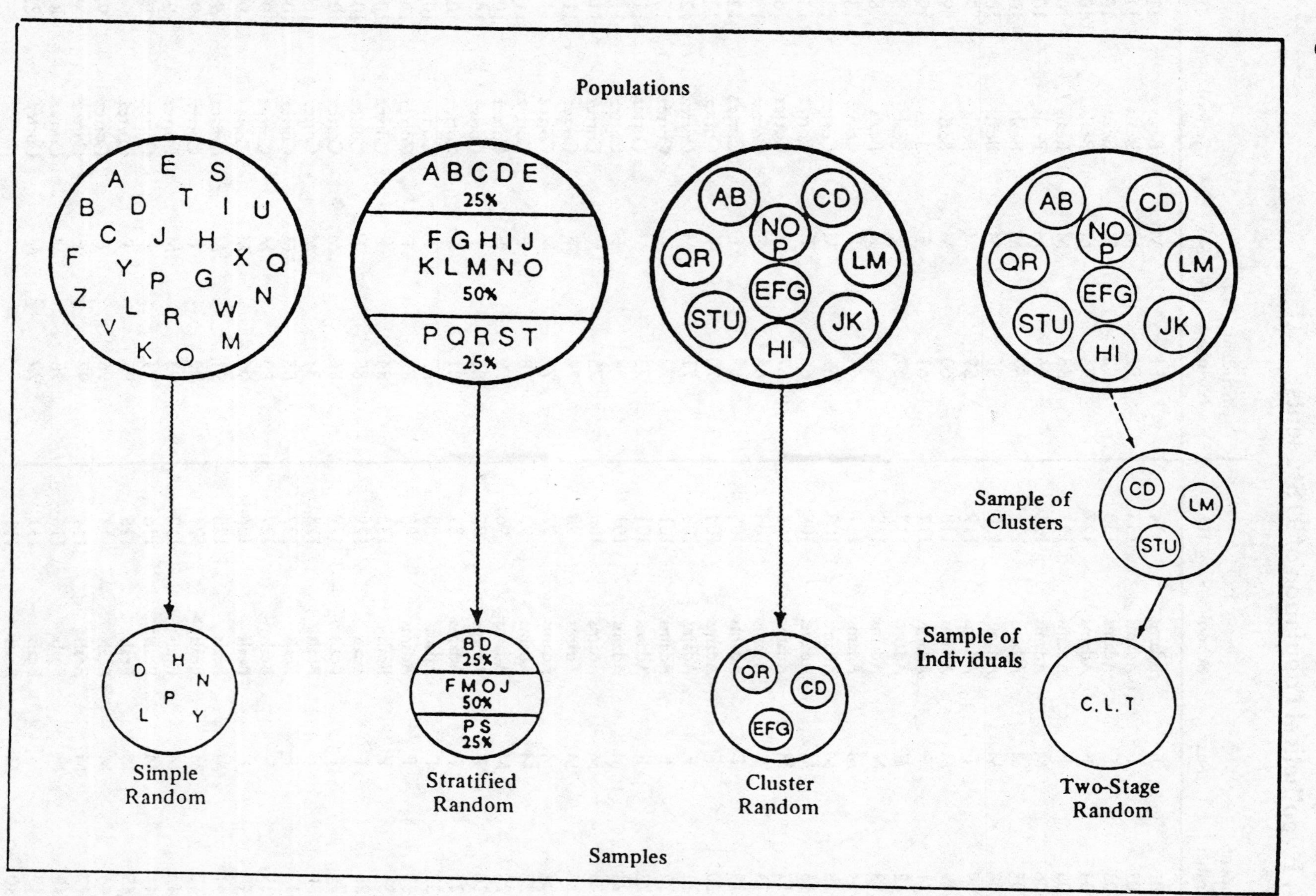

Figure 6.3

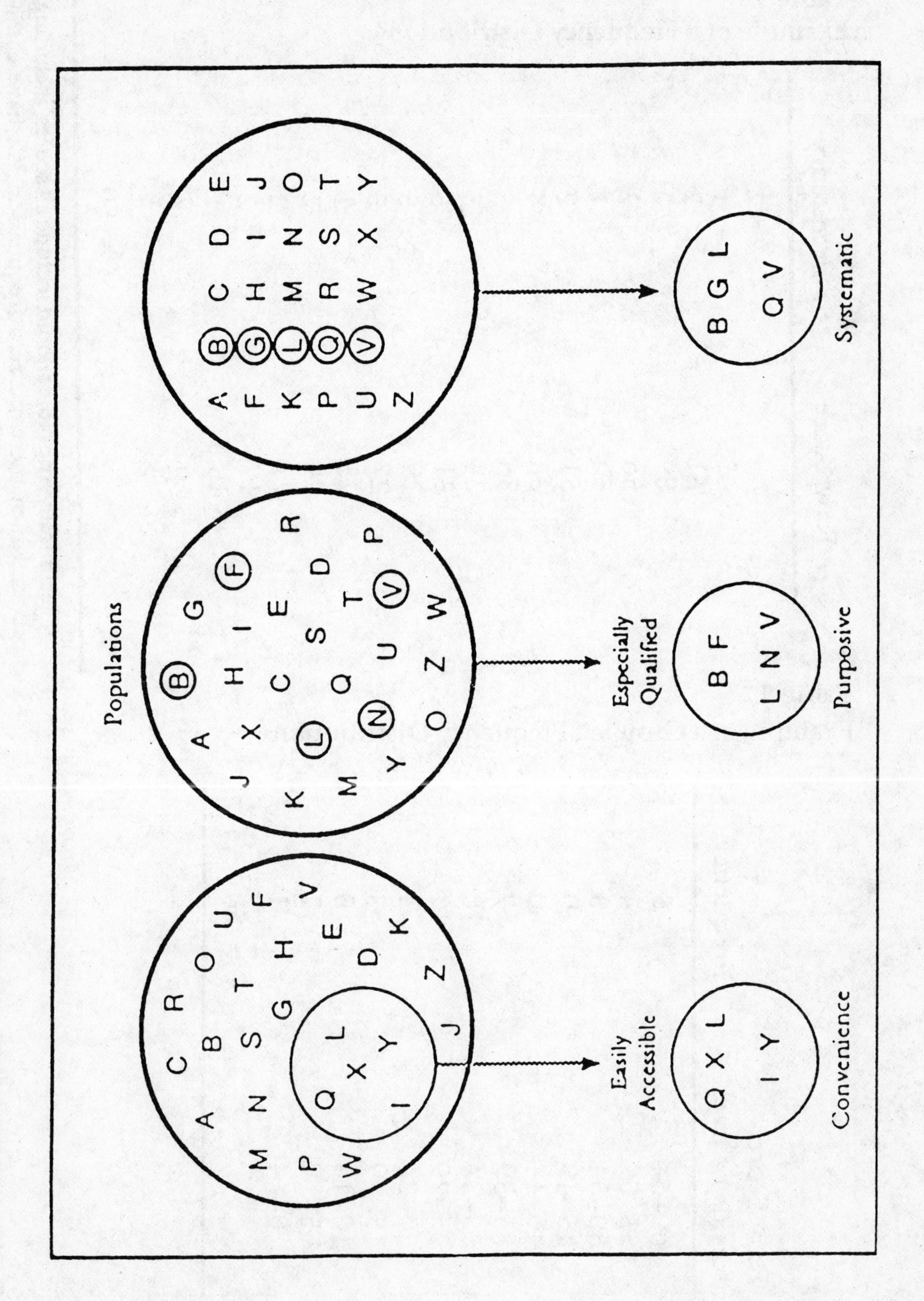
Nonrandom Sampling Methods
Populations
Easily Accessible
Q X L
I Y
Convenience
Especially Qualified
B F
L N V
Purposive
B G L
Q V
Systematic

Table 9.1
Example of a Frequency Distribution[a]

Raw Score	Frequency
64	2
63	1
61	2
59	2
56	2
52	1
51	2
38	4
36	3
34	5
31	5
29	5
27	1
25	2
24	2
21	2
17	1
15	2
6	1
3	
	n = 50

[a] Technically, the table should include all scores, including those for which there are zero frequencies. We have eliminated those to simplify the presentation.

Table 9.2
Example of a Grouped Frequency Distribution

Raw Scores (Intervals of five)	Frequency
60–64	5
55–59	4
50–54	3
45–49	0
40–44	0
35–39	7
30–34	10
25–29	11
20–24	4
15–19	3
10–14	0
5– 9	2
0– 4	1
	n = 50

Figure 9.8

The Normal Curve

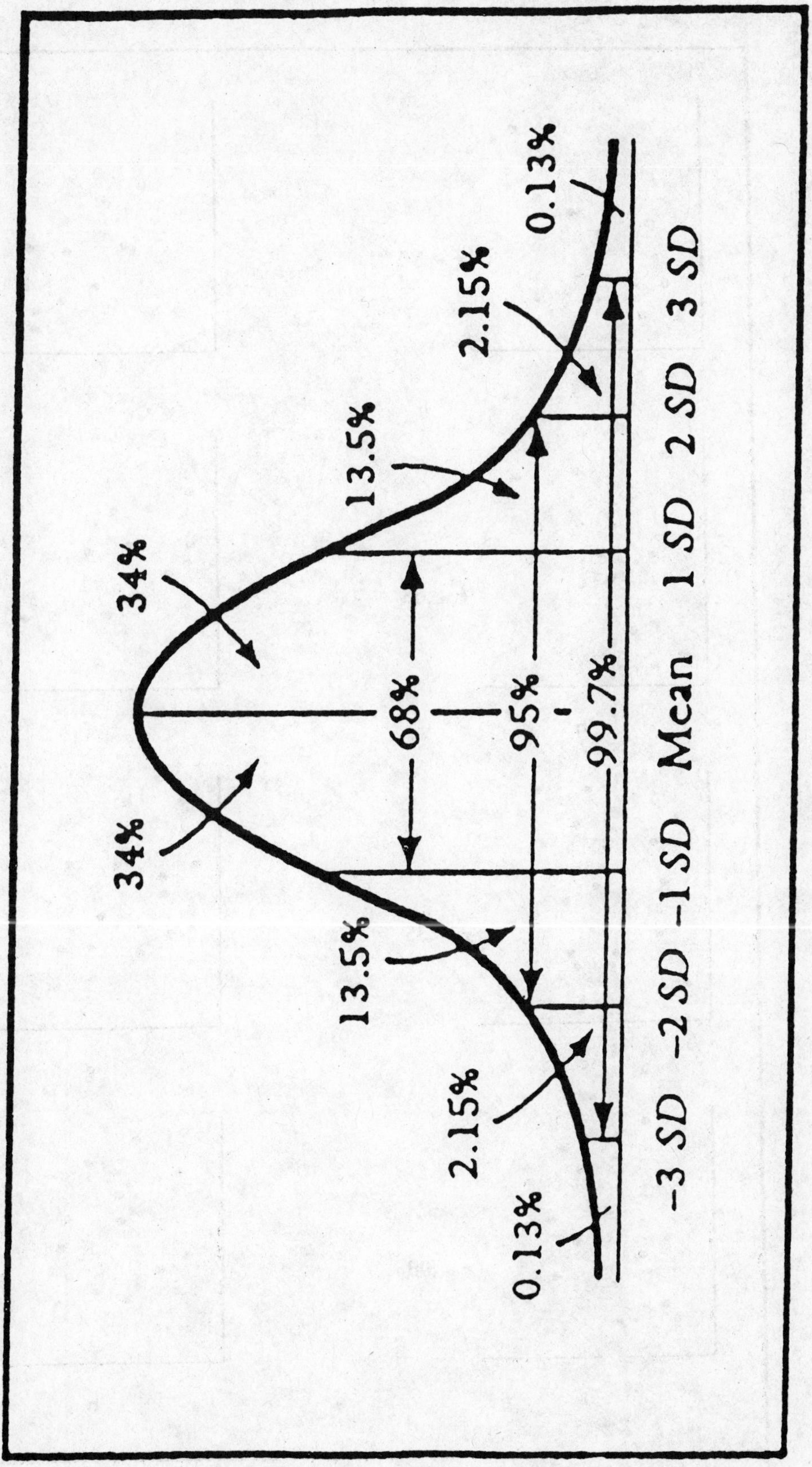

0.13%
2.15%
13.5%
34%
34%
13.5%
2.15%
0.13%
68%
95%
99.7%
−3 SD −2 SD −1 SD Mean 1 SD 2 SD 3 SD

Figure 9.16
Examples of Scatterplots

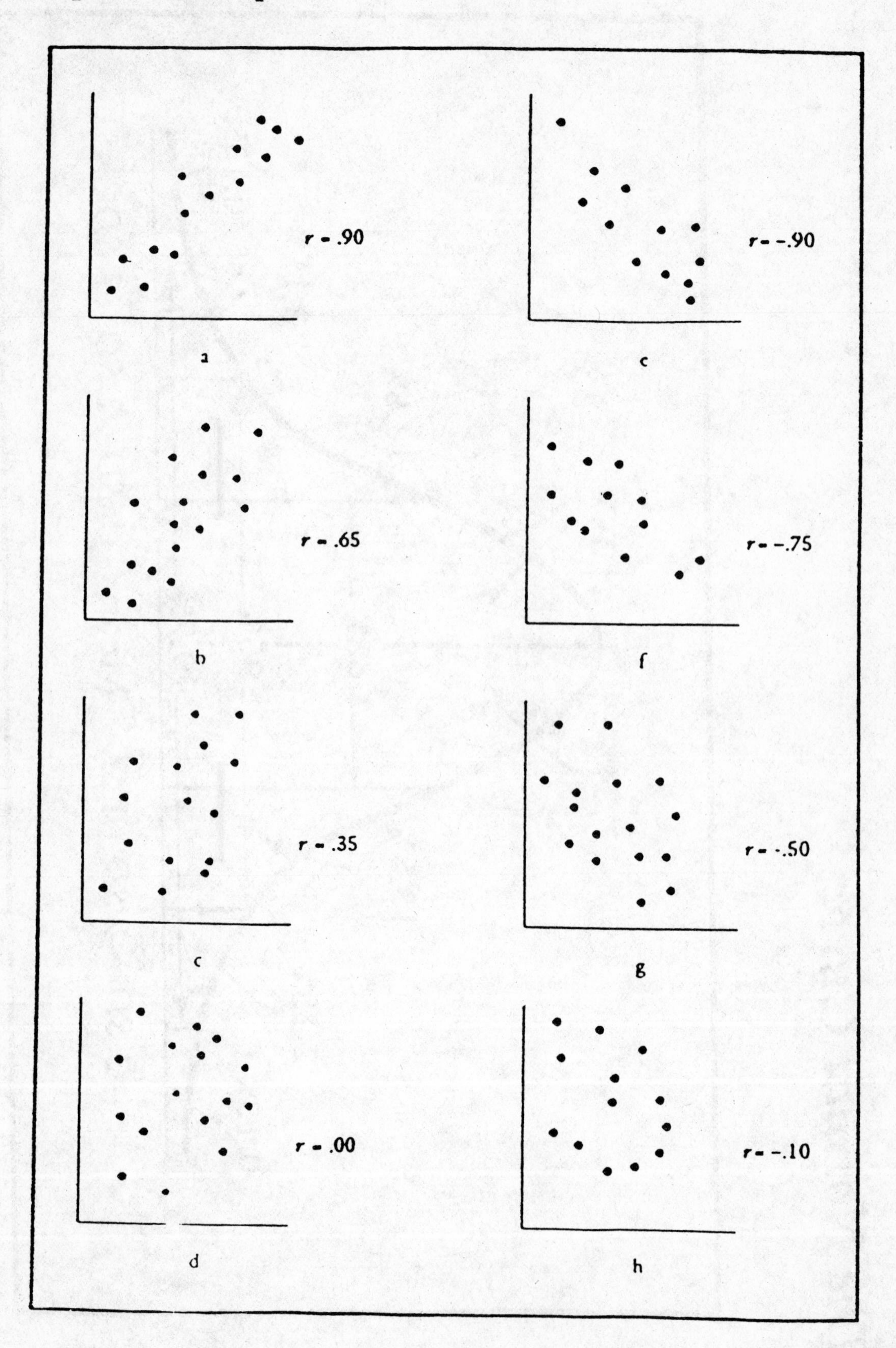

Figure 9.17

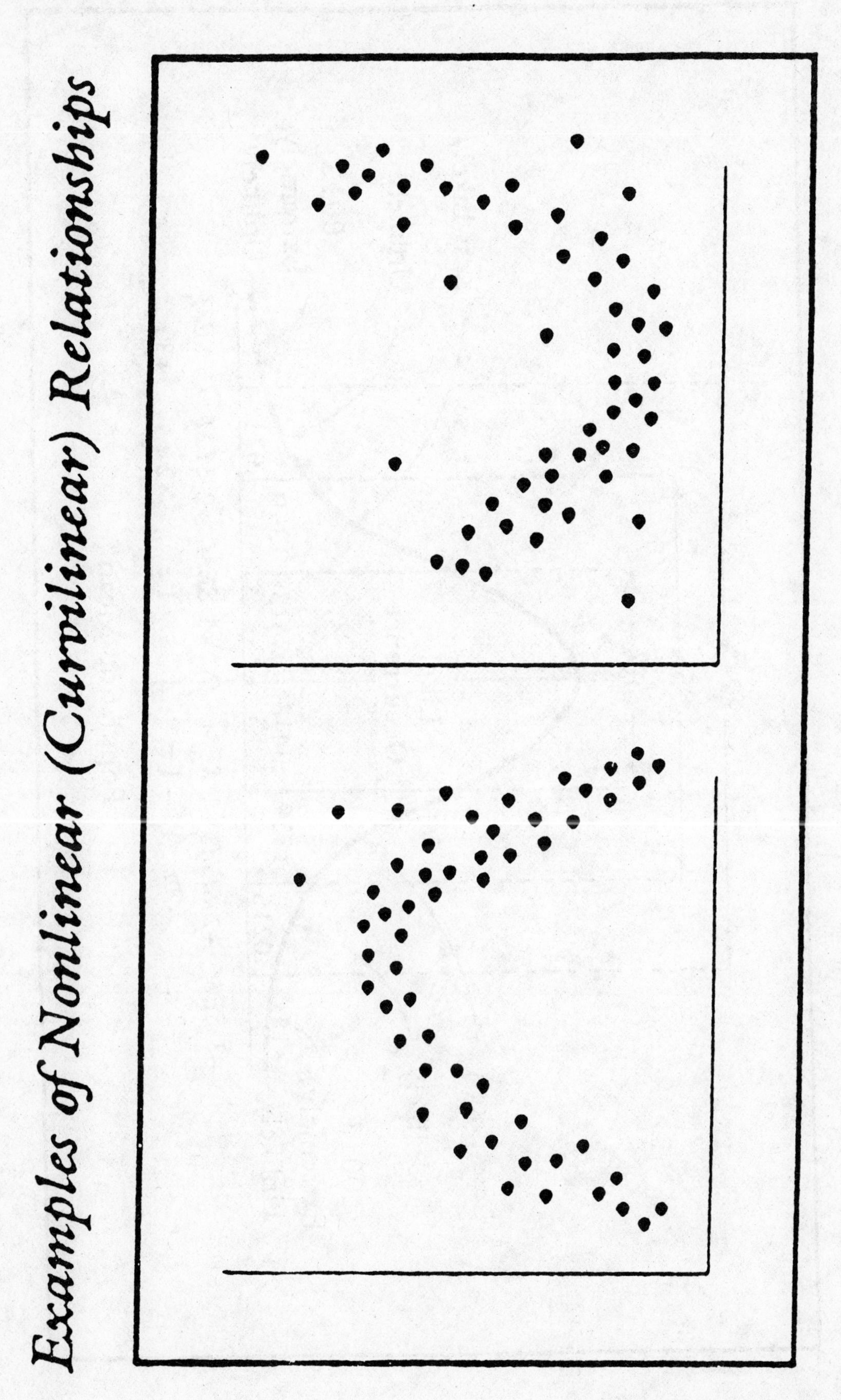

Figure 9.3

Distribution of Sample Means[1]

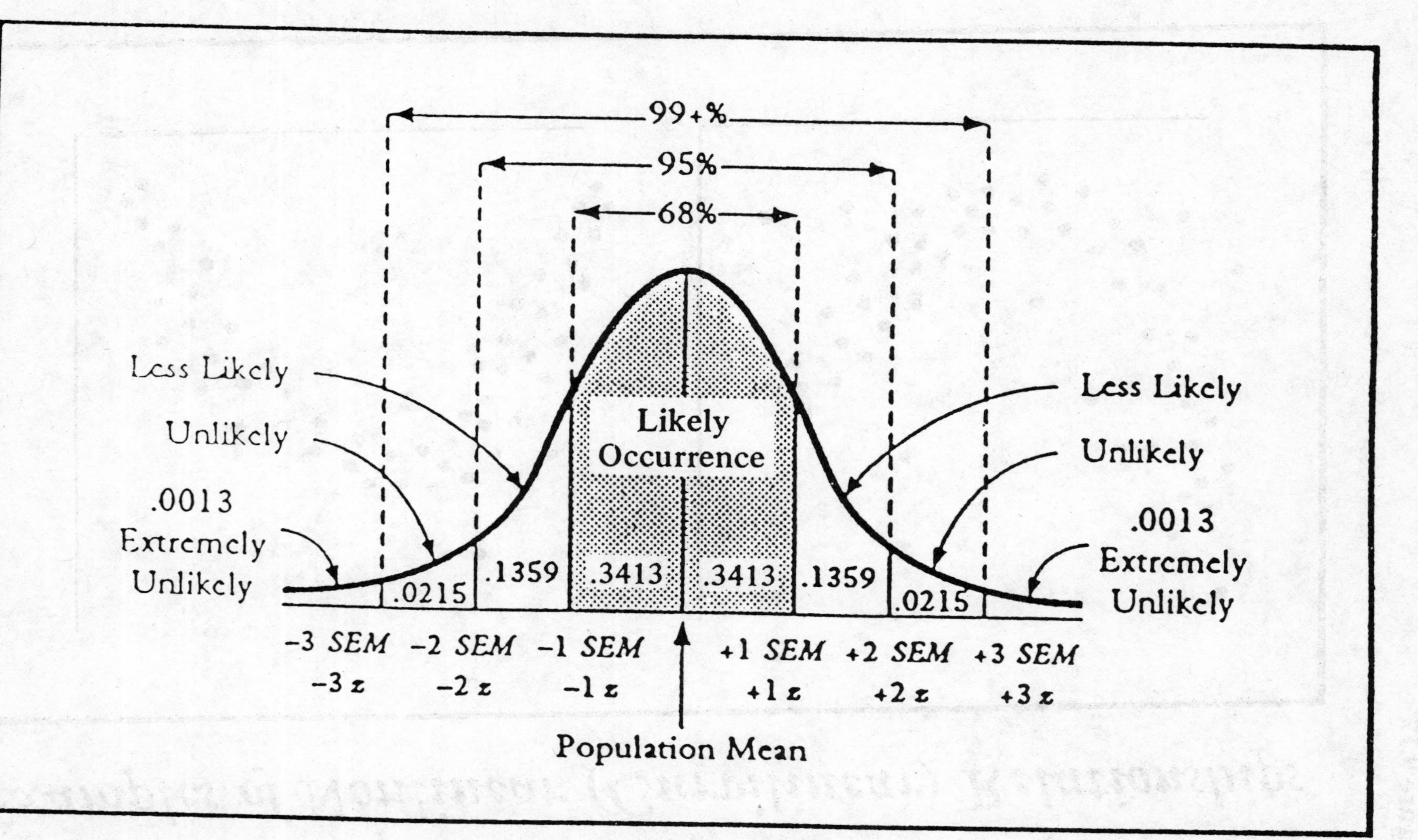

[1] Notice that these values are approximate.

Figure 10.4

The 95 Percent Confidence Interval

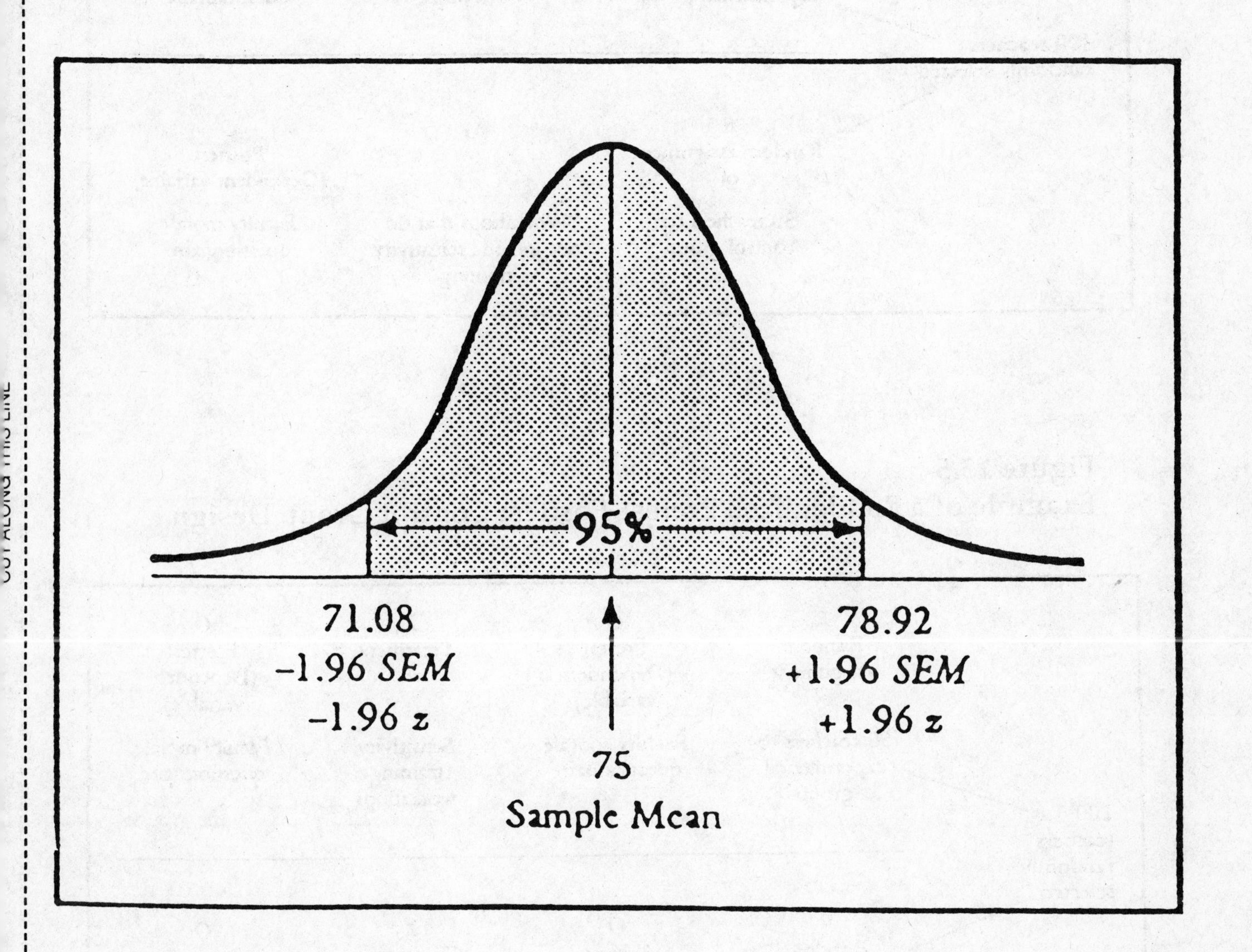

Figure 13.4
Example of a Randomized Posttest-Only Control Group Design

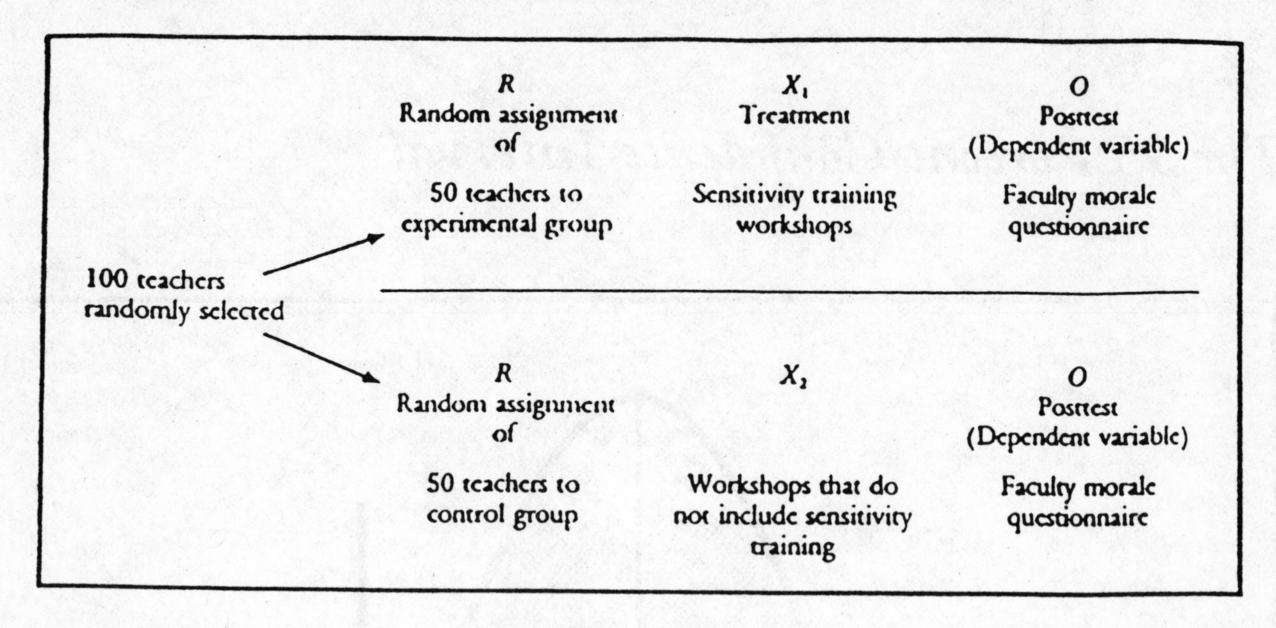

Figure 13.5
Example of a Randomized Pretest-Posttest Control Group Design

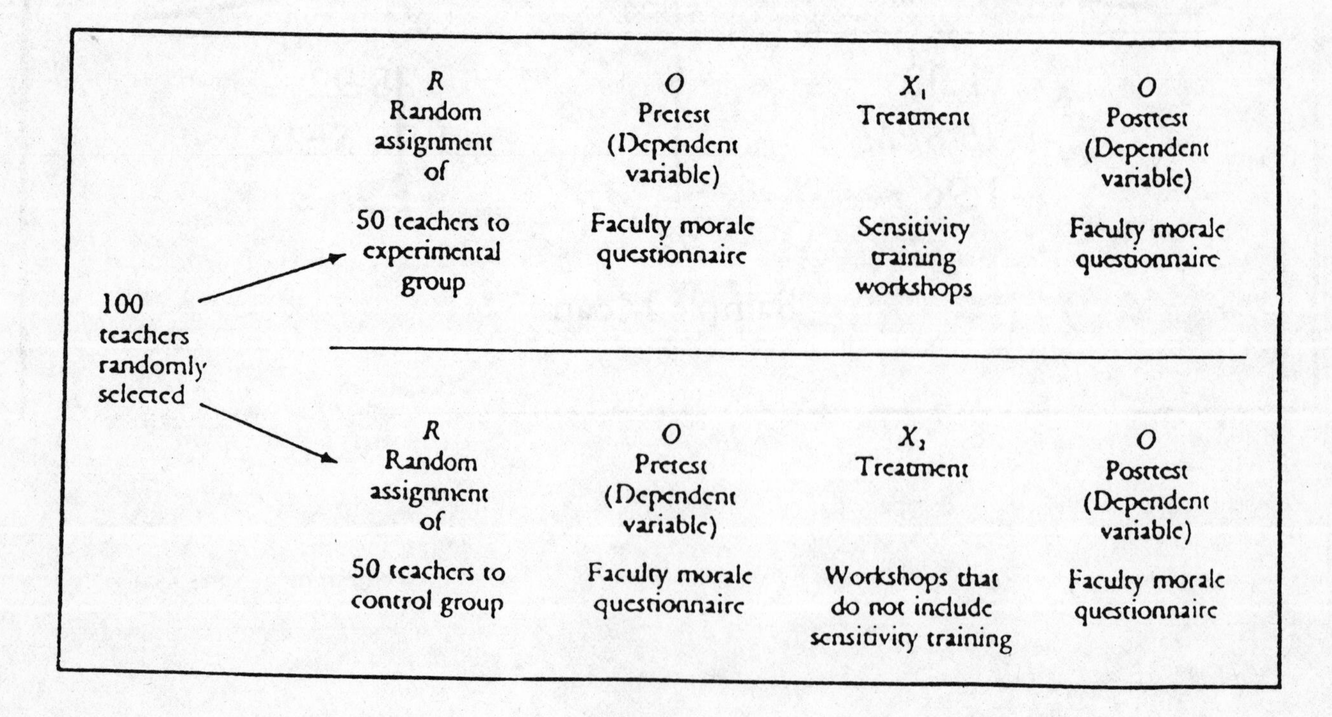

Figure 13.6
Example of a Randomized Solomon Four-Group Design

	R	*O*	X_1 / X_2	*O*
100 teachers randomly selected, then divided into four groups				
	R Random assignment of	*O* Pretest (Dependent variable)	X_1 Treatment	*O* Posttest (Dependent variable)
→	25 teachers to experimental group (Group I)	Faculty morale questionnaire	Sensitivity training workshops	Faculty morale questionnaire
	R Random assignment of	*O* Pretest (Dependent variable)	X_2 Treatment	*O* Posttest (Dependent variable)
→	25 teachers to control group (Group II)	Faculty morale questionnaire	Workshops that do not include sensitivity training	Faculty morale questionnaire
	R Random assignment of		X_1 Treatment	*O* Posttest (Dependent variable)
→	25 teachers to experimental group (Group III)		Sensitivity training workshops	Faculty morale questionnaire
	R Random assignment of		X_2 Treatment	*O* Posttest (Dependent variable)
→	25 teachers to control group (Group IV)		Workshops that do not include sensitivity training	Faculty morale questionnaire

Figure 13.7

Example of a Randomized Posttest-Only Control Group Design, Using Matched Subjects

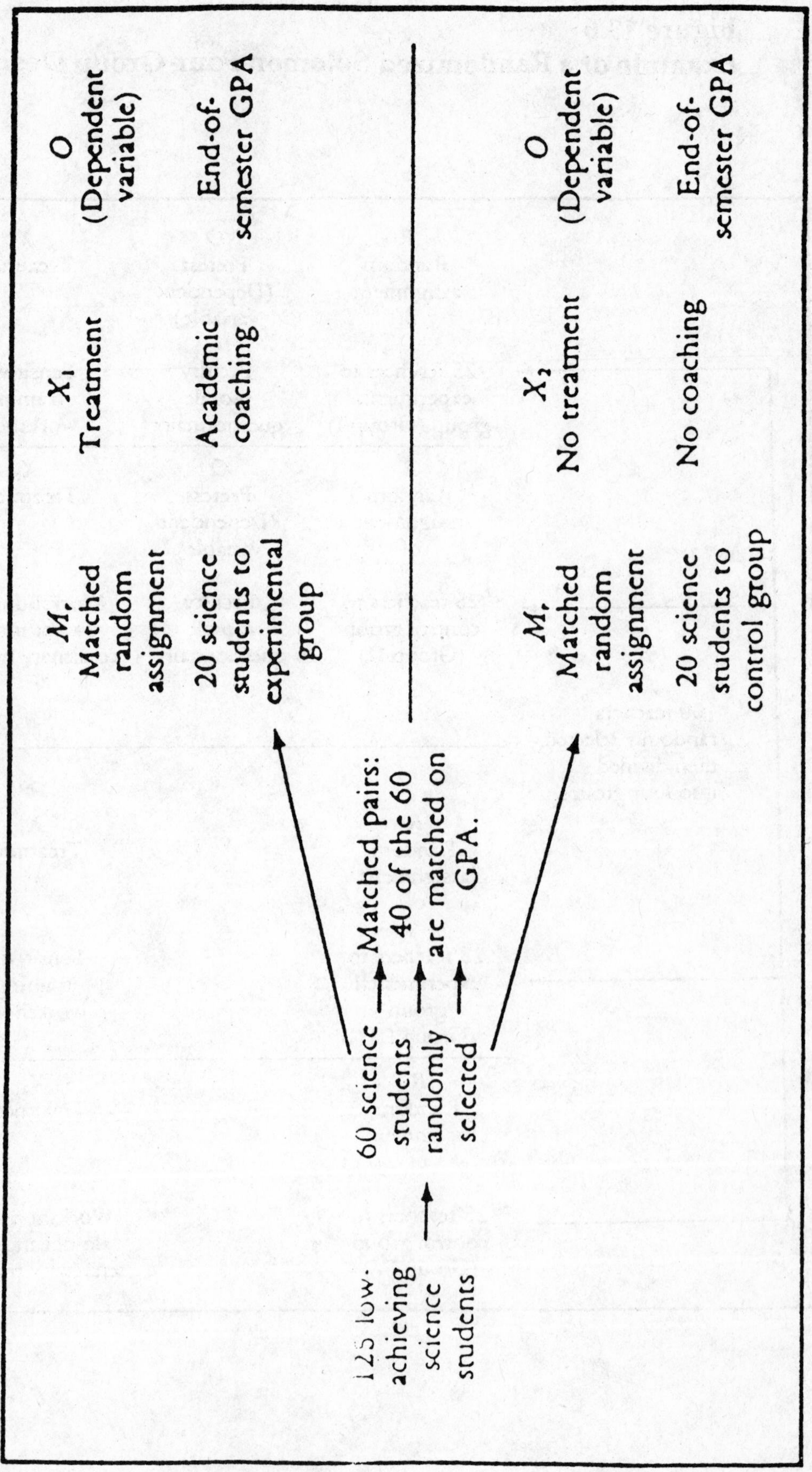

125 low-achieving science students → 60 science students randomly selected → Matched pairs: 40 of the 60 are matched on GPA.

M_r Matched random assignment	X_1 Treatment	O (Dependent variable)
20 science students to experimental group	Academic coaching	End-of-semester GPA

M_r Matched random assignment	X_2 No treatment	O (Dependent variable)
20 science students to control group	No coaching	End-of-semester GPA

Figure 13.11
Illustration of Interaction and No Interaction in a 2x2 Factorial Design

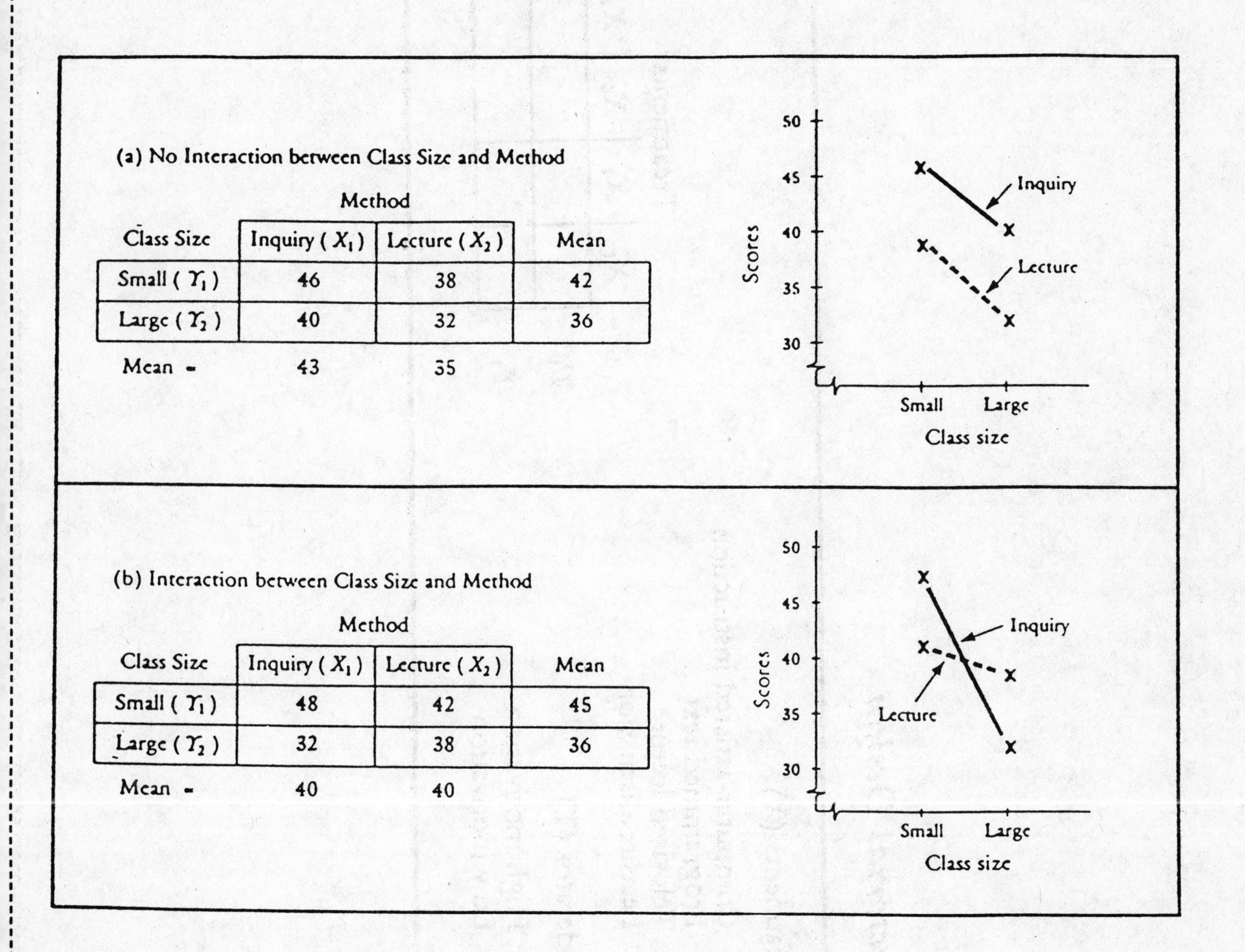

(a) No Interaction between Class Size and Method

Class Size	Method: Inquiry (X_1)	Lecture (X_2)	Mean
Small (Y_1)	46	38	42
Large (Y_2)	40	32	36
Mean =	43	35	

(b) Interaction between Class Size and Method

Class Size	Method: Inquiry (X_1)	Lecture (X_2)	Mean
Small (Y_1)	48	42	45
Large (Y_2)	32	38	36
Mean =	40	40	

Figure 13.12

Example of a 4 by 2 Factorial Design

R	X_1	Y_1	O
R	X_2	Y_1	O
R	X_3	Y_1	O
R	X_4	Y_1	O
- - -	- - -	- - -	- - -
R	X_1	Y_2	O
R	X_2	Y_2	O
R	X_3	Y_2	O
R	X_4	Y_2	O

Treatments (X)

X_1 Computer-assisted instruction
X_2 Programmed text
X_3 Televised lecture
X_4 Lecture-discussion

Moderator (Y)

Y_1 High motivation
Y_2 Low motivation

	Treatments			
	X_1	X_2	X_3	X_4
Y_1				
Y_2				

Single-Subject Designs

(a) A-B Design—One Baseline Period with One Treatment Period

O O O O	*X O X O X O X O*
baseline period A	treatment period B

(b) A-B-A Design—Two Baseline Periods with One Treatment Period

O O O O	*X O X O X O X O*	*O O O O*
baseline period A	treatment period B	baseline period A

(c) A-B-A-B Design—Two Baseline Periods with Two Treatment Periods

O O O O	*X O X O X O X O*	*O O O O*	*X O X O X O X O*
baseline period A	treatment period B	baseline period A	treatment period B

CUT ALONG THIS LINE

A Multiple-Baseline Design

Behavior one	O O O O X O X O X O X O X O X O X O X O X O
Behavior two	O O O O O O O X O X O X O X O X O X O X O
Behavior three	O O O O O O O O O O X O X O X O X O X O

Figure 13.16
Illustration of Multiple Baseline Designs

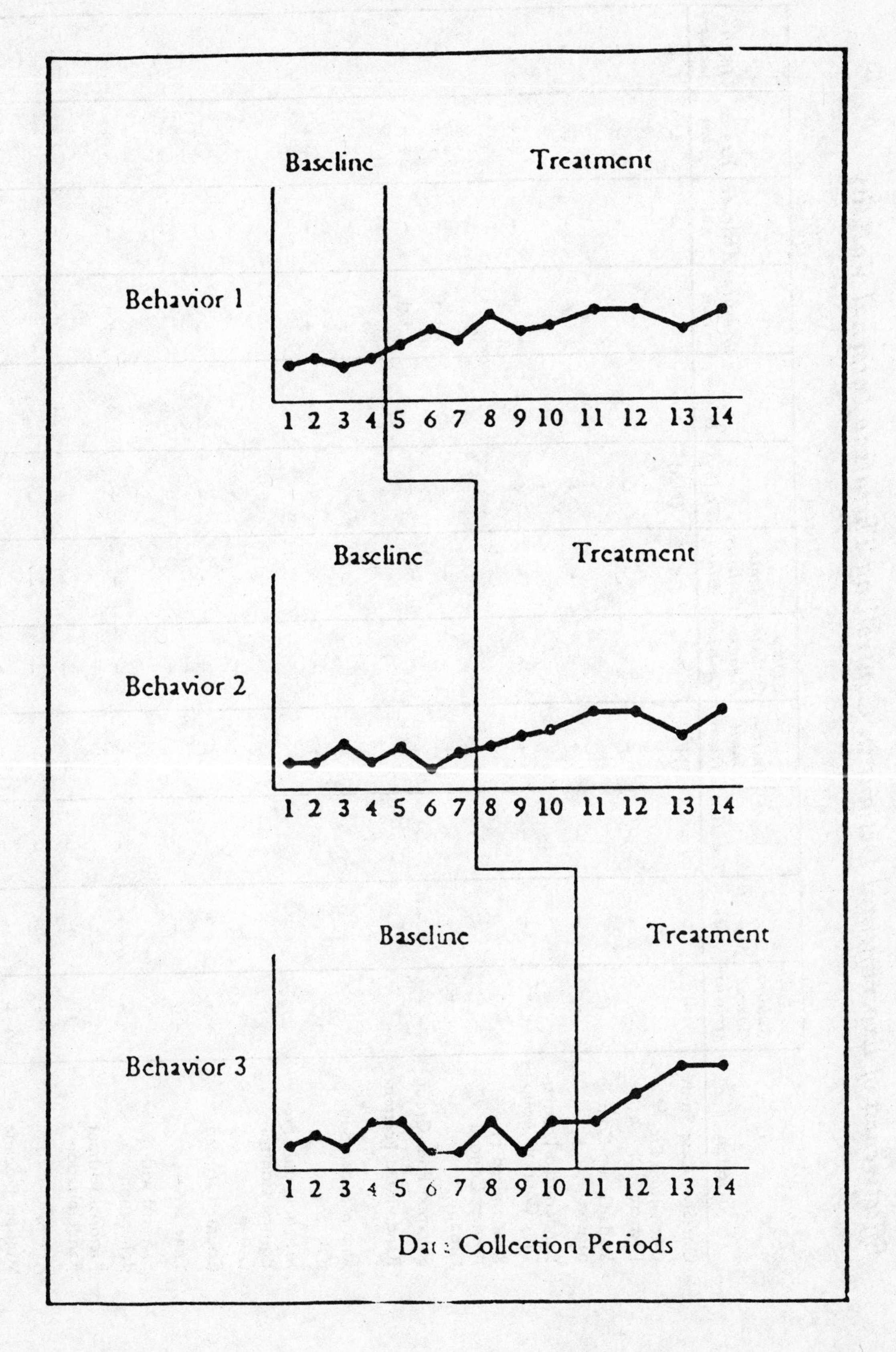

Table 13.1

Effectiveness of Experimental Designs in Controlling Threats to Internal Validity

Design	Threat: Subject Characteristics	Mortality	Location	Instrument Decay	Data Collector Characteristics	Data Collector Bias	Testing	History	Maturation	Attitudinal	Regression	Implementer
One-Shot Case Study	−	−	−	(N/A)	−	−	(NA)	−	−	−	−	−
One Group Pre-Posttest	−	+	−	−	−	−	−	−	−	−	−	−
Static-Group Comparison	−	−	−	+	−	−	+	+	+	−	−	−
Randomized Posttest-Only Control Group	++	+	−	+	−	−	+	+	++	−	++	−
Randomized Pre-Posttest Control Group	++	+	−	+	−	−	−	+	++	−	++	−
Solomon Four-Group	++	++	−	+	−	−	+	+	++	−	++	−
Randomized Posttest-Only Control Group with Matched Subjects	++	+	−	+	−	−	+	+	++	−	++	−
Matching only Pre-Posttest Control Group	+	+	−	+	−	−	+	+	+	−	+	−
Counterbalanced	++	++	−	+	−	−	−	++	++	−	++	−
Time-Series	++	−	−	−	−	−	−	+	+	−	++	−
Factorial with Randomization	++	++	−	++	−	−	+	+	++	−	++	−
Factorial without Randomization	?	?	−	++	−	−	+	+	+	−	?	−
A-B-A-B	++	++	−	−	−	−	−	++	+	−	+	−
Multiple Baseline	++	++	−	−	−	−	−	++	+	−	+	−

Key: (++) = strong control, threat unlikely to occur; (+) = some control, threat may possibly occur; (−) = weak control, threat likely to occur; (?) = can't determine; (NA) = threat does not apply.

Figure 14.1

Scatterplot Illustrating a Correlation of +1.00

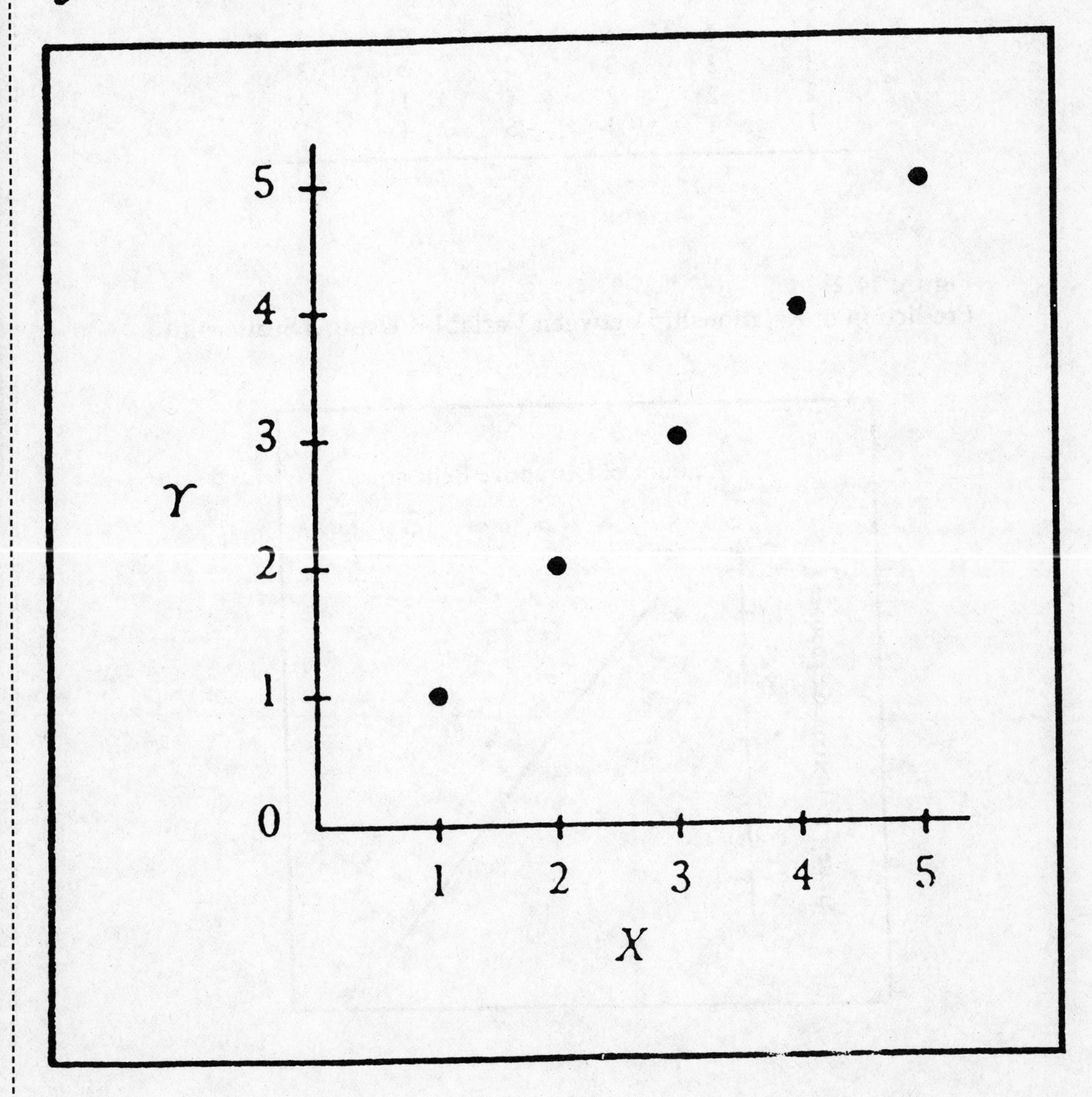

Table 14.1
Three Sets of Data Showing Different Directions and Degrees of Correction

(A) $r = +1.00$		(B) $r = -1.00$		(C) $r = 0$	
X	*Y*	*X*	*Y*	*X*	*Y*
5	5	5	1	2	1
4	4	4	2	5	2
3	3	3	3	3	3
2	2	2	4	1	4
1	1	1	5	4	5

Figure 14.2
Prediction of Relationship between Variables Using a Scatterplot

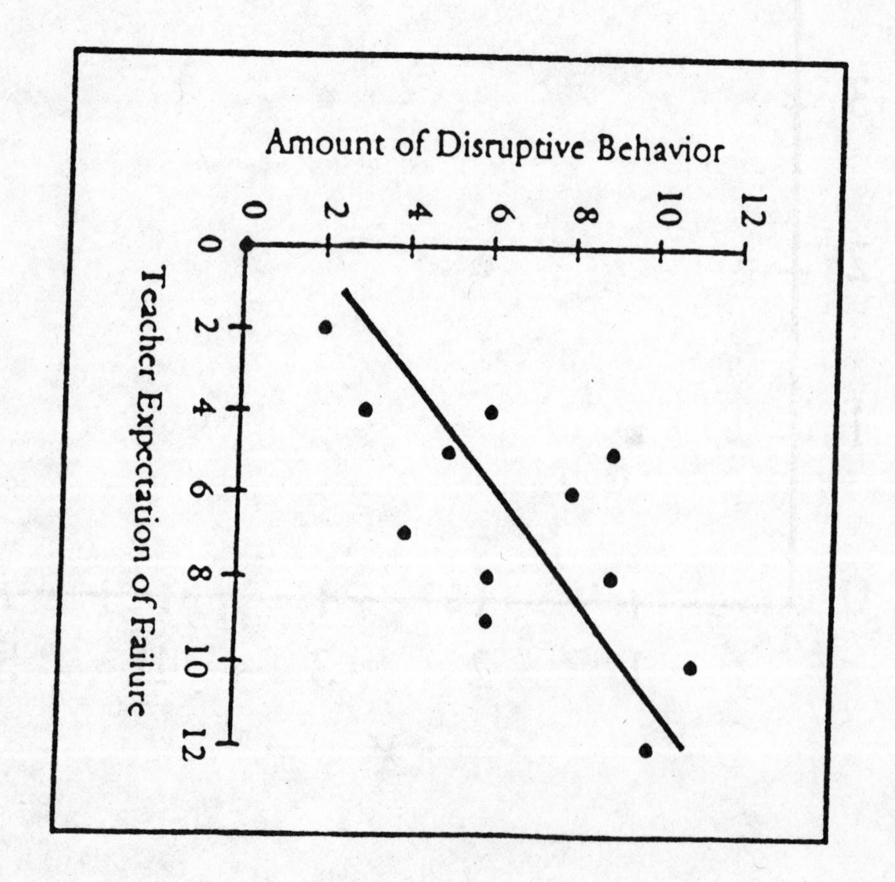

Figure 14.6

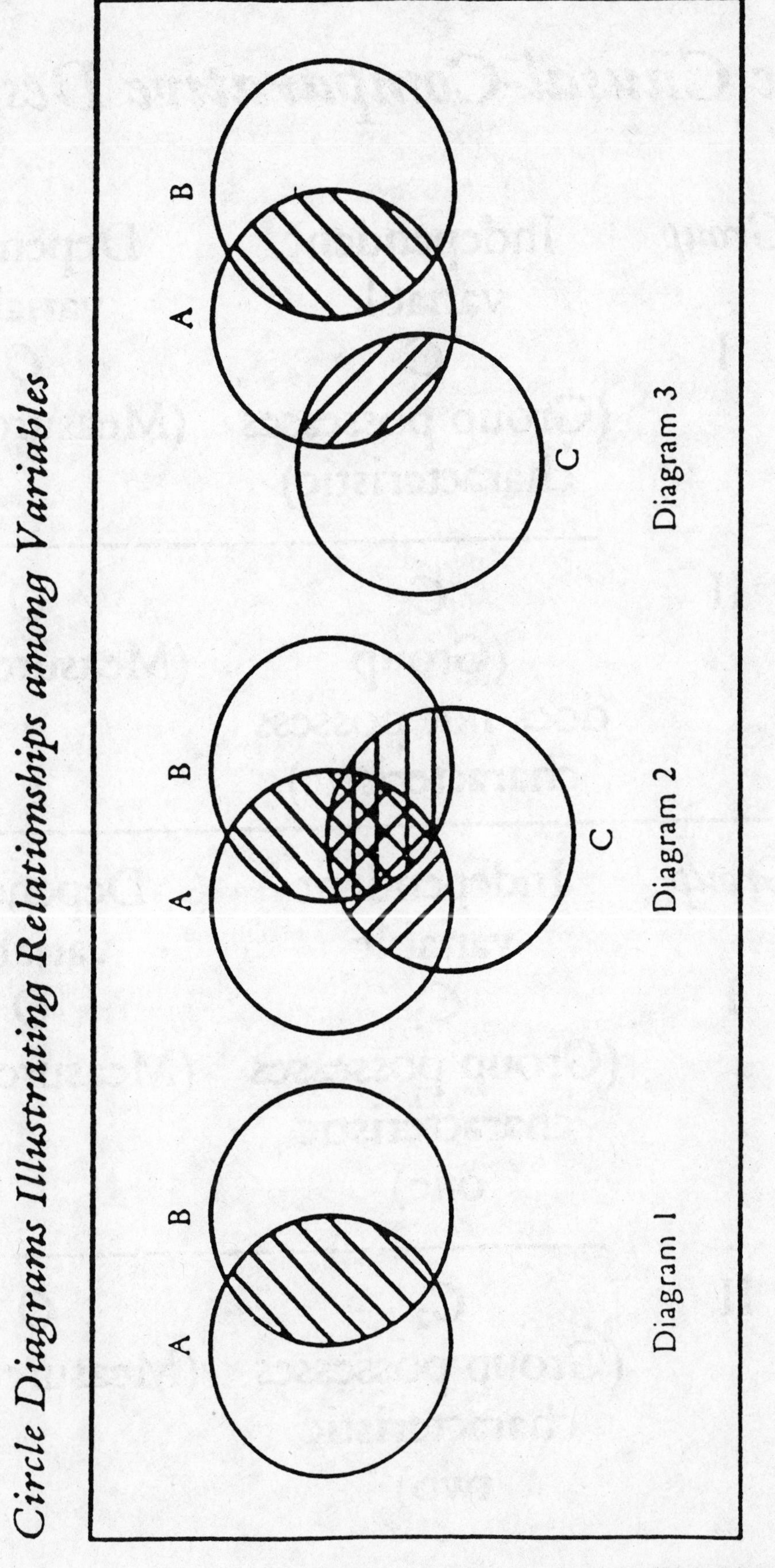
Circle Diagrams Illustrating Relationships among Variables
A
B
Diagram 1
A
B
C
Diagram 2
A
B
C
Diagram 3

Illustration of Causal-Comparative Designs

Basic Causal-Comparative Designs

(a)

Group	Independent variable	Dependent variable
I	C (Group possesses characteristic)	O (Measurement)
II	C (Group does not possess characteristic)	O (Measurement)

(b)

Group	Independent variable	Dependent variable
I	C_1 (Group possesses characteristic one)	O (Measurement)
II	C_2 (Group possesses characteristic two)	O (Measurement)

Figure 15.1

Example of the Basic Causal-Comparative Designs

(a)	*Group*	Independent variable	Dependent variable
	I	C Dropouts	O Level of self-esteem
	II	$(-C)$ Nondropouts	O Level of self-esteem

(b)	*Group*	Independent variable	Dependent variable
	I	C_1 Counselors	O Amount of job satisfaction
	II	C_2 Teachers	O Amount of job satisfaction

CUT ALONG THIS LINE

Figure 16.1

Example of Several Contingency Questions in an Interview Schedule

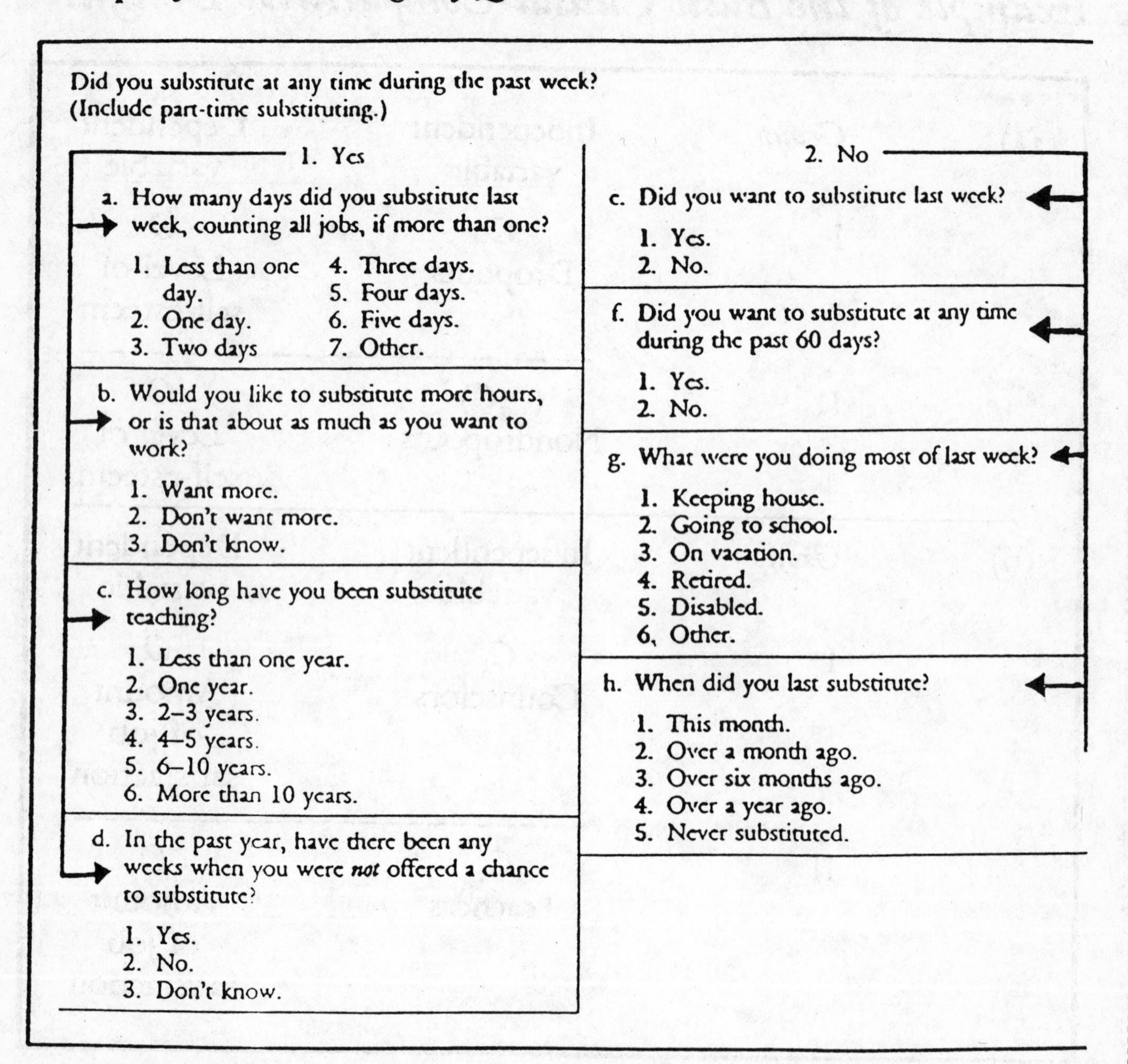

Did you substitute at any time during the past week?
(Include part-time substituting.)

1. Yes

a. How many days did you substitute last week, counting all jobs, if more than one?

1. Less than one day.
2. One day.
3. Two days
4. Three days.
5. Four days.
6. Five days.
7. Other.

b. Would you like to substitute more hours, or is that about as much as you want to work?

1. Want more.
2. Don't want more.
3. Don't know.

c. How long have you been substitute teaching?

1. Less than one year.
2. One year.
3. 2–3 years.
4. 4–5 years.
5. 6–10 years.
6. More than 10 years.

d. In the past year, have there been any weeks when you were *not* offered a chance to substitute?

1. Yes.
2. No.
3. Don't know.

2. No

e. Did you want to substitute last week?

1. Yes.
2. No.

f. Did you want to substitute at any time during the past 60 days?

1. Yes.
2. No.

g. What were you doing most of last week?

1. Keeping house.
2. Going to school.
3. On vacation.
4. Retired.
5. Disabled.
6. Other.

h. When did you last substitute?

1. This month.
2. Over a month ago.
3. Over six months ago.
4. Over a year ago.
5. Never substituted.

Adapted from Earl S. Babbie. (1973). *Survey research methods*. Belmont, CA: Wadsworth. p. 149.

CUT ALONG THIS LINE

Table 16.1

Advantages and Disadvantages of Survey Data Collection Methods

	Direct Administration	Telephone	Mail	Interview
Comparative cost	lowest	about the same		high
Facilities needed?	yes	no	no	yes
Require training of questioner?	yes	yes	no	yes
Data collection time	shortest	short	longer	longest
Response rate	very high	good	poorest	very high
Group administration possible?	yes	no	no	yes
Allow for random sampling?	possibly	yes	yes	yes
Require literate sample?	yes	no	yes	no
Permit follow-up questions?	no	yes	no	yes
Encourage response to sensitive topics?	somewhat	somewhat	best	weak
Standardization of responses	easy	somewhat	easy	hardest

Figure 18.1

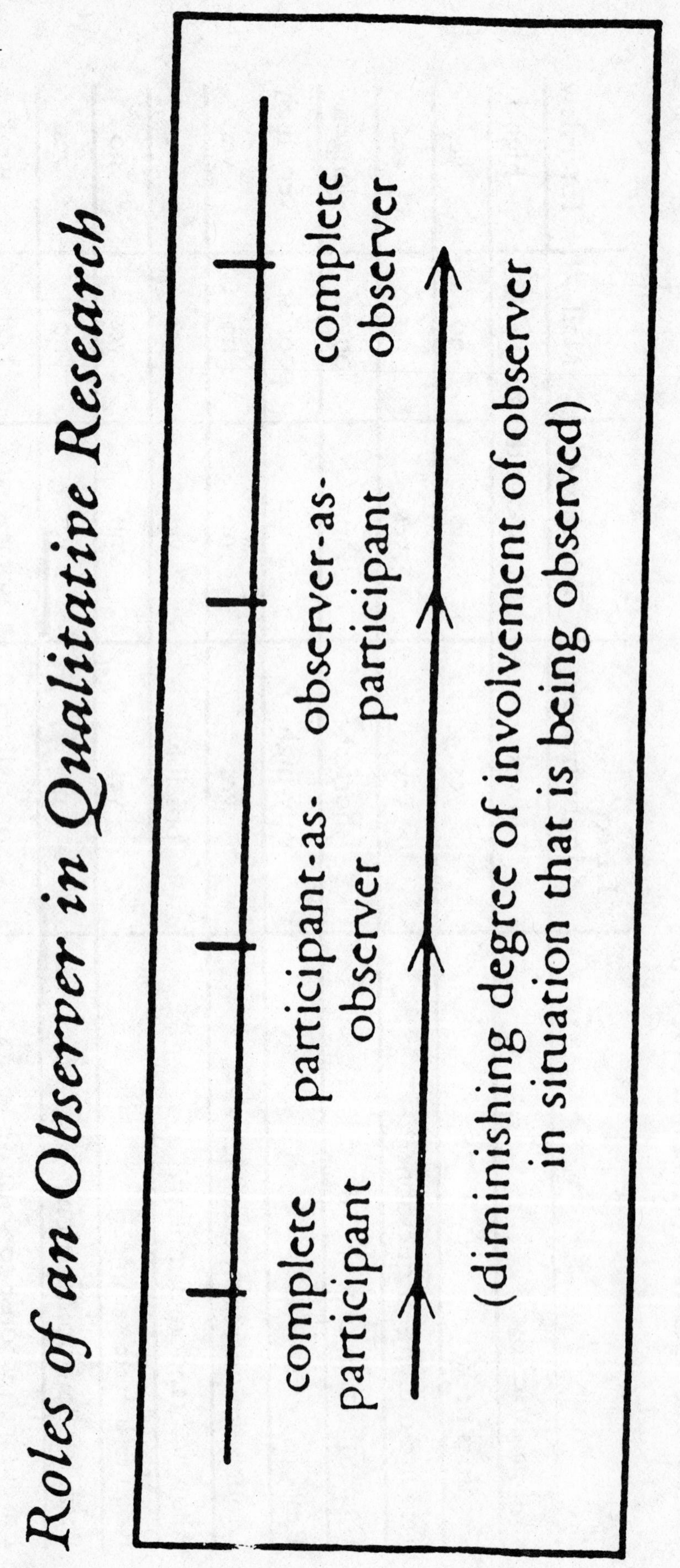

CUT ALONG THIS LINE

Part Nine
Answer Key:
Chapter Test Questions

Chapter One

1.	b	11.	d	21.	a
2.	d	12.	b	22.	c
3.	c	13.	a	23.	b
4	a	14.	b	24.	c
5.	c	15.	d	25.	a
6.	c	16.	b		
7.	c	17.	c		
8.	b	18.	a		
9.	d	19.	d		
10.	a	20.	a		

Chapter Two

1.	b	11.	d
2.	d	12.	c
3.	c	13.	c
4	a	14.	b
5.	c	15.	b
6.	a	16.	a
7.	d		
8.	c		
9.	a		
10.	a		

Chapter Three

1. d
2. c
3. b
4. d
5. c
6. d
7. d
8. a
9. c
10. b

Chapter Four

1.	d	11.	b	21.	d
2.	b	12.	d	22.	c
3.	c	13.	d	23.	b
4	a	14.	a		
5.	c	15.	c		
6.	a	16.	b		
7.	d	17.	a		
8.	b	18.	b		
9.	c	19.	d		
10.	a	20.	c		

Chapter Five

1.	a	11.	b
2.	c	12.	c
3.	b	13.	a
4	d	14.	d
5.	a	15.	c
6.	c	16.	c
7.	a	17.	b
8.	a	18.	c
9.	b	19.	d
10.	b	20.	b

Chapter Six

1.	a	11.	c	21.	c
2.	d	12.	d	22.	a
3.	d	13.	c	23.	a
4	d	14.	a	24.	d
5.	c	15.	d	25.	d
6.	c	16.	a	26.	b
7.	c	17.	b		
8.	b	18.	a		
9.	c	19.	d		
10.	a	20.	a		

Chapter Seven

1.	c	11.	a	21.	b
2.	c	12.	c	22.	a
3.	c	13.	c	23.	c
4	c	14.	a	24.	c
5.	a	15.	b	25.	d
6.	c	16.	d		
7.	b	17.	c		
8.	b	18.	a		
9.	d	19.	c		
10.	c	20.	b		

Chapter Eight

1.	a	11.	a
2.	c	12.	b
3.	c	13.	c
4	c	14.	b
5.	b	15.	b
6.	a	16.	a
7.	d	17.	c
8.	b	18.	b
9.	b	19.	b
10.	d	20.	d

Chapter Nine

1.	a	11.	d	21.	d
2.	d	12.	b	22.	b
3.	c	13.	b	23.	d
4	c	14.	a	24.	a
5.	b	15.	d	25.	b
6.	a	16.	d	26.	c
7.	b	17.	b	27.	d
8.	a	18.	c		
9.	d	19.	a		
10.	c	20.	a		

Chapter Ten

1.	c	11.	b	21.	d
2.	a	12.	a	22.	c
3.	d	13.	b	23.	a
4	c	14.	c	24.	c
5.	a	15.	a	25.	b
6.	b	16.	b		
7.	c	17.	d		
8.	a	18.	d		
9.	d	19.	b		
10.	a	20.	b		

Chapter Eleven

1.	b	11.	c
2.	a	12.	d
3.	c	13.	b
4	c	14.	d
5.	b	15.	d
6.	b	16.	a
7.	d	17.	b
8.	b	18.	c
9.	b	19.	b
10.	a	20.	a

Chapter Twelve

1.	c	11.	d	21.	a
2.	d	12.	c	22.	b
3.	b	13.	d	23.	c
4	c	14.	b	24.	a
5.	a	15.	d	25.	c
6.	d	16.	b		
7.	c	17.	c		
8.	b	18.	d		
9.	b	19.	a		
10.	c	20.	b		

Chapter Thirteen

1.	b	11.	b	21.	b
2.	b	12.	c	22.	a
3.	a	13.	b	23.	a
4	b	14.	d	24.	d
5.	c	15.	d	25.	c
6.	b	16.	c	26.	d
7.	c	17.	b	27.	c
8.	d	18.	d	28.	c
9.	a	19.	a		
10.	c	20.	c		

Chapter Fourteen

1.	d	11.	a
2.	c	12.	c
3.	a	13.	d
4	a	14.	c
5.	c	15.	c
6.	a	16.	d
7.	d	17.	c
8.	a	18.	a
9.	c	19.	d
10.	c	20.	c

Chapter Fifteen

1.	b	11.	a
2.	a	12.	c
3.	a	13.	d
4	c	14.	b
5.	d	15.	b
6.	c	16.	b
7.	a	17.	d
8.	b	18.	d
9.	c	19.	c
10.	a	20.	b

Chapter Sixteen

1.	c	11.	b
2.	c	12.	d
3.	a	13.	b
4	d	14.	b
5.	d	15.	c
6.	a	16.	b
7.	b	17.	c
8.	d	18.	c
9.	a	19.	a
10.	a	20.	d

Chapter Seventeen

1.	d	11.	b
2.	c	12.	b
3.	b	13.	c
4	a	14.	d
5.	b	15.	a
6.	d	16.	a
7.	c	17.	d
8.	d	18.	d
9.	c	19.	a
10.	b	20.	c

Chapter Eighteen

1.	d	11.	c	21.	b
2.	d	12.	c	22.	a
3.	b	13.	b	23.	d
4	b	14.	a	24.	c
5.	a	15.	d		
6.	c	16.	c		
7.	d	17.	c		
8.	a	18.	d		
9.	d	19.	a		
10.	b	20.	b		

Chapter Nineteen

1.	a	11.	b
2.	a	12.	c
3.	a	13.	b
4	c	14.	a
5.	d	15.	c
6.	a	16.	d
7.	c	17.	b
8.	b	18.	b
9.	d	19.	c
10.	b	20.	a

Chapter Twenty

1.	d	11.	c
2.	b	12.	d
3.	b	13.	d
4	a	14.	c
5.	d	15.	b
6.	b	16.	d
7.	c	17.	c
8.	d	18.	d
9.	c	19.	c
10.	a	20.	d

Chapter Twenty-One

There is no test for Chapter Twenty-One

Part Ten
Two Additional Studies
(with our analysis of each)

<u>Study #1</u>: ***Effects of choice making on the serious problem behaviors of students with severe handicaps*** **(a single-subject study).**

<u>Study #2</u>: ***Pupil occupancy time in classroom settings across cultures*** **(an observational study).**

APPENDIX F

Analysis of a Single-Subject Study

From: Journal of Applied Behavior Analysis, 23(4):515–524, 1990.

Effects of Choice Making on the Serious Problem Behaviors of Students with Severe Handicaps

Kathleen Dyer
The May Institute

Glen Dunlap
Florida Mental Health Institute
University of South Florida

Vincent Winterling
University of Kentucky

Abstract

This study assessed the impact of choice making on the serious problem behaviors of 3 students with severe autism and/or mental retardation. In the context of within-subject reversal designs, the results showed consistently reduced levels of problem behaviors (e.g., aggression) when the students were given opportunities

This investigation was supported by Cooperative Agreement G0087CO234 from the National Institute on Disability and Rehabilitation Research. However, the opinions expressed herein do not necessarily reflect the opinions or policies of the supporting agency, and no official endorsement should be inferred.

The authors are grateful to Jeff Amero and Michele Taylor for serving as teachers, and to Cynthia Dollman, Mark Ellison, Beth Brookfield, Jennifer Karr, Jenny Turner, Paul Reedy, Kit Hoffman, Jeffrey K. Withstandly, and Lynn Foster Johnson for assistance in data collection and manuscript and figure preparation. Appreciation is extended to Steven C. Luce and Edward K. Morris for their helpful comments.

Correspondence and requests for reprints should be sent to Kathleen Dyer, The May Institute, Box 703, 100 Sea View Street, Chatham, Massachusetts 02633, or to Glen Dunlap, Department of Child & Family Studies, Florida Mental Health Institute, University of South Florida, Tampa, Florida 33612-3899.

to make choices among instructional tasks and reinforcers. Additional data showed no systematic differences in the rate of correct responding between the two conditions. The results are discussed in relation to the continuing search for effective, nonintrusive solutions to the occurrence of serious problem behavior.

Descriptors: *severely handicapped, choice behavior, problem behavior, autistic children*

The importance of these behaviors with this population could be emphasized.

A growing emphasis of research and practice has been on the development of effective, nonintrusive techniques for managing the serious problem behaviors of persons with developmental disabilities (Horner et al., in press). Numerous authors have argued in favor of restricting the use of invasive procedures and promoting the development of positive, educative approaches to behavior managment (e.g., Evans and Meyer, 1985; Lovaas and Favell, 1987). It has been recognized by many that continued progress in this area will rely on applied research designed to delineate and document interventions that are both effective and respectful of a person's dignity (Bannerman, Sheldon, Sherman, and Harchick, 1990; Dunlap, 1985; Horner et al., in press).

One rapidly expanding research emphasis has been on the effects of learners' preferences and choicemaking opportunities (Guess, Benson, and Siegel-Causey, 1985; Houghton, Bronicki and Guess, 1987; Kishi, Teeluck-singh, Zollers, Park-Lee, and Meyer, 1988; Parsons and Reid, 1990; Shevin and Klein, 1984). The success of procedures using choice and preference for individuals with severe handicaps has been documented in studies showing reductions in social avoidance behavior (Koegel, Dyer, & Bell, 1987), increases in spontaneous communication (Dyer, 1987; Peck, 1985), and improvements in task performance (Mithaug & Mar, 1980; Parsons, Reid, Reynolds, and Bumgarner, 1990). There has also been some suggestion that choice making may result in reductions in serious problem behaviors. For example, Dyer (1987) showed that when children with autism were given choices of preferred rewards, decreases were shown in stereotyped self-stimulatory behaviors that had been reduced previously only with contingent restraint. This study also indicated that there were improvements in other problem behaviors, but these indications came from global ratings of on-task behavior rather than from direct observations of specific responses. Therefore, the purpose of the present experiment was to expand the literature on choice making by focusing explicitly on the serious problem behaviors (including aggression and self-injury) of school-age students with severe handicaps. In this case, a choice-making package was implemented in which students were permitted to make selections of rewards as well as the tasks and materials with which they would be engaged.

Clear focus.

METHOD

Definitions would help here.

Subjects

Three children (Lori, Mary, and George) participated in this experiment. All of the children exhibited high levels of serious disruptive behavior such as aggression, self-injury, and tantrums. The behaviors resulted in placement in a residential treatment center for Lori and Mary. George had also been institutionalized because of his problem behaviors, but at the time of this study he was living at home and receiving assessment and training services from a university-based program. Lori was 5 years old, and Mary and George were 11. Lori was diagnosed as having a developmental delay with autistic features, Mary as having pervasive developmental delay with autistic features, and George as having severe mental retardation. On the Vineland Social Maturity Scale, Lori and Mary were estimated to have social age scores of 1.8 years and 1.0 years, respectively. George received an adaptive behavior composite of 1.5 years on the Vineland Adaptive Behavior Scales. Lori was nonverbal and used gestures and a small number of signs to communicate. Mary had a vocabulary of approximately 10 words that served requesting functions. George was primarily echolalic, but he occasionally used phrases of two to four words to express needs and desires.

No mention is made of the intended population.

Good descriptions.

Before the experimental sessions were conducted, each child received pretraining on how to express choices. Lori and Mary were taught to point to a preferred object when presented with two objects and the statement, "Show me which one you want." For George, the pretraining involved teaching him to discriminate such questions as "What do you want to work on?" and to limit his selections to the materials that were available and designated as options. Prior to the experiment, the children were also exposed to sessions in which definitions of the dependent variables wre developed and the teachers were trained to use the procedures.

Not clear.

Setting

All sessions were conducted with one-to-one teacher-student ratios in rooms located on the campuses of the residential center or the university. The rooms contained at least one table, several chairs, instructional tasks, and videotape equipment. Sessions ranged in length from 10 to 20 min, with no more than four sessions per day and 5 days between sessions.

Selection of Tasks and Reinforcers

During all sessions in each experimental condition, three to four educational tasks were used for each student. The students had demonstrated the ability to perform each of the tasks during previous educational activities. The tasks involved prevocational and preacademic skills and were selected because they could be handled easily in table work sessions and because they were judged by the students' teachers to be of approximately equivalent preference.

Also used in each session were three to five preferred stimuli that were reported by the children's teachers to be functional reinforcers in other contexts. These preferred stimuli were used as reinforcers for correct performance on instructional tasks. The schedules of reinforcement, determined by the teachers, were variable-ratio schedules (e.g., VR3, VR 5) that were maintained throughout all phases of the experiment. Table 1 lists the tasks and reinforcers available for each child.

Reinforcement is provided as an intermittent pattern.

Dependent Variables

The primary dependent variable in this experiment was the percentage of intervals that included instances of serious problem behavior. Problem behaviors were defined individually for each child and included aggression (biting, hitting, kicking, pinching, and scatching) and object misuse (throwing, tearing, banging, and destroying objects) for all 3 children, tantrums (screaming, whining, and crying) and bolting (moving more than 2 ft from the table) for Lori and George, and self-injury (slapping the face or body, punching self, head banging, elbow and wrist banging, and forcefully pressing objects to the face) for Lori. For a self-hit or self-slap to be scored, it had to be forceful and be initiated from a distance of more than 6 in. Measures of problem behavior were obtained with a 30-s continuous-interval system of data recording.

Ambiguous.

To obtain measures of task performance, correct responses were counted

TABLE 1

Tasks and Reinforcers for Each Student in Each of the Experimental Conditions

Student	Tasks	Reinforcers
Lori	Nine-piece puzzle	Soda
	Inserting sticks into a slot	Crackers
	Shape box	M&M candies
Mary	Seven-piece puzzle	Teddy bear
	Inserting pennies into a bank	Cookie
	Inserting buttons into a slot	Juice
George	Large form puzzle	Crackers
	Stacking disks onto a spindle	Soda
	Sorting spoons by color	Juice
	Labeling picutre cards[a]	Candy
		Potato sticks

[a] Used only in the final choice condition.

and then translated into measures of rate for each task. To be scored as a correct response, performance on the educational materials had to conform to the task definitions. Responses that were prompted with physical assistance were not counted as correct. Response definitions for each child's tasks are as follows:

A second dependent variable.

Lori. A correct response on the puzzle was scored when Lori placed one puzzle piece into its accompanying space on the template. The stick task involved inserting sticks into a small hole on top of a can. A correct response for this task was scored when one stick was put completely into the slot. A correct response on the shape box was scored when Lori placed a block into its accompanying hole in a container.

Mary. A correct response on the puzzle was scored when Mary placed one puzzle piece into its accompanying space on the template. The button task involved inserting buttons into a small hole on top of a can, with a correct response being scored when one button was put completely through the slot. A correct response on the penny task was scored when Mary put a penny into a slot in a bank.

George. A correct response on the puzzle task was scored when a puzzle piece was inserted into its appropriate place. A correct response on the stacking spindles was counted when a donut-shaped disk was placed successfully on a spindle. Plastic spoons were sorted by color and a correct response was recorded when a spoon was placed in its appropriate receptable. Responses to the picture cards were scored as correct when George accurately labeled a picture upon request.

Reliability of Dependent Variables

Reliability measures were obtained for each of the dependent variables during the experiment or from videotape obtained throughout each experimental condition. Interobserver agreement on the occurrence of problem behaviors was assessed for 21% of the experimental sessions, and reliability of the task performance data was assessed for 61% of the sessions. An agreement in the recording of problem behavior was counted when two independent observers scored a 30-s interval in an identical manner.

Interobserver agreement for problem behavior was calculated by dividing the number of agreements by the sum of agreements plus disagreements and multiplying the obtained quotient by 100. Percentage agreement for problem behavior was 92% (range, 75% to 100%); occurrence reliability was 92% (range, 75% to 100%); nonoccurrence reliability was 91% (range, 75% to 100%). Reliability for rate of correct responding was calculated by dividing the smallest frequency count (obtained by one observer) by the largest frequency count (obtained by the other observer) and multiplying the quotient by 100. Percentage agreement for rate of correct responding was 96% (range, 80% to 100%).

Observer agreement only.

Design and Experimental Conditions

Modified AB-A-B design.

To demonstrate replicability of treatment effects, reversal designs (Barlow and Hersen, 1984) were used, with the order of conditions alternated across children. For each child, two conditions were presented, a choice condition and a no-choice condition. In the choice condition, the child was provided with opportunities to choose from the available selection of tasks and reinforcers. George indicated his selections verbally, and Mary and Lori indicated their selections by pointing. If a task was completed during a session, the child was asked to choose new materials. The children were also permitted to continue work on the same materials if they chose. Also, if the child voluntarily requested a change in materials, such a change was permitted. Reinforcers were also selected, but the opportunity to select a reinforcer was provided in accordance with the prevailing reinforcement schedule.

Defines choice vs. no-choice.

In the no-choice condition, the same tasks and reinforcers were provided, but always according to an independent schedule and always at the teacher's initiation. To keep the teaching sessions as natural as possible, the specific scheduling of tasks in some of the no-choice conditions was left to the discretion of the teacher. In other no-choice conditions, teachers were given explicit instructions to maintain an equal balance of tasks within the sessions. Any expression of choice that occurred during this condition was followed by a brief explanation that the schedule must be followed (e.g., "We need to do this other work now.")

Why?

In all experimental conditions, problem behaviors were addressed according to guidelines set forth in each child's regular program. In general, problem behaviors were ignored whenever possible and aggressive responses were blocked in a protective manner. For all 3 children, physical prompts were used occasionally to continue instruction. For example, if the child engaged in excessive motor activity that prevented attending to task-related instructions, he or she was prompted with verbal and occasional physical guidance to sit quietly. In accordance with her ongoing habilitation plan, some of Mary's problem behaviors were managed with additional contingencies. Specifically, Mary's aggression was followed by a brief regime of contingent exercise, and her instances of object misuse were followed by 5 s of corrective positive practice. All procedures were used in the same manner across all conditions in the experiment.

Teachers and Observers

All teachers had extensive experience in the use of behavioral techniques with severely handicapped children, including a minimum of 1 year supervised practicum in clinic settings. The observers had extensive backgrounds in the recording of operationally defined behavior of children with disabilities. Before any experimental data were recorded, each observer was trained to record each of the dependent variables until interobserver agreement reached at least 80% for three consecutive practice sessions. To control for the potential effects of experimenter bias, the teachers were naive with respect to the experimental hypothesis for 59% of the experimental sessions.

What about observers?

Why not 100%?

RESULTS

The data points in Figure 1 show the percentage of intervals with problem behavior during each session for each experimental condition in the reversal analyses. Each child exhibited lower levels of problem behavior during the choice condition. When choices were first presented to Mary, her problem behavior decreased to a low of 5% during the last session in the condition. A reversal to the no-choice condition resulted in an immediate increase in problem behavior, with an average of 78% across the condition. During the subsequent choice condition, Mary's problem behavior decreased to a low of 0%. The remaining two graphs reveal essentially the same effects for the other 2 children. That is, the choice condition always produced lower levels of problem behavior than did the no-choice condition.

For George and Mary, a subset of their problem behavior (i.e., aggression) was considered to be a most urgent and severe problem (Lori did not display aggression during the experiment). To assess the potential effects of choice on George and Mary's aggressive behaviors, the videotapes were reviewed, and the data on aggressive behavior were separated from the pool of problem behaviors for these 2 children. The shaded portions of Figure 1 show the results of this analysis. Both Mary and George showed higher levels of aggression in the no-choice condition than in the choice condition. Mary's aggressive behavior decreased to 0 during the last two sessions of both choice conditions, and George's did not display any aggressive behavior during any of the sessions in the choice condition.

Data for rate of correct unprompted responding across all experimental conditions are shown in Table 2. These data show no consistent differences in rate of responding across the conditions.

Very low rate of correct response.

Data were also collected on the relative proportions of tasks and reinforcers that were presented by the teachers in the no-choice condition and those that were presented (i.e., selected by the children) in the choice condition. These data are shown in Table 3. All of the children selected all of the tasks in the choice condition that were presented in the no-choice condition. Although there was some evidence of preference (e.g., Mary appeared to favor the pennies and buttons over the puzzle), in general there were few consistent differences across tasks and conditions.

The data for reinforcer presentation and selection are also presented in Table 3. All of the children selected all of the reinforcers in the choice

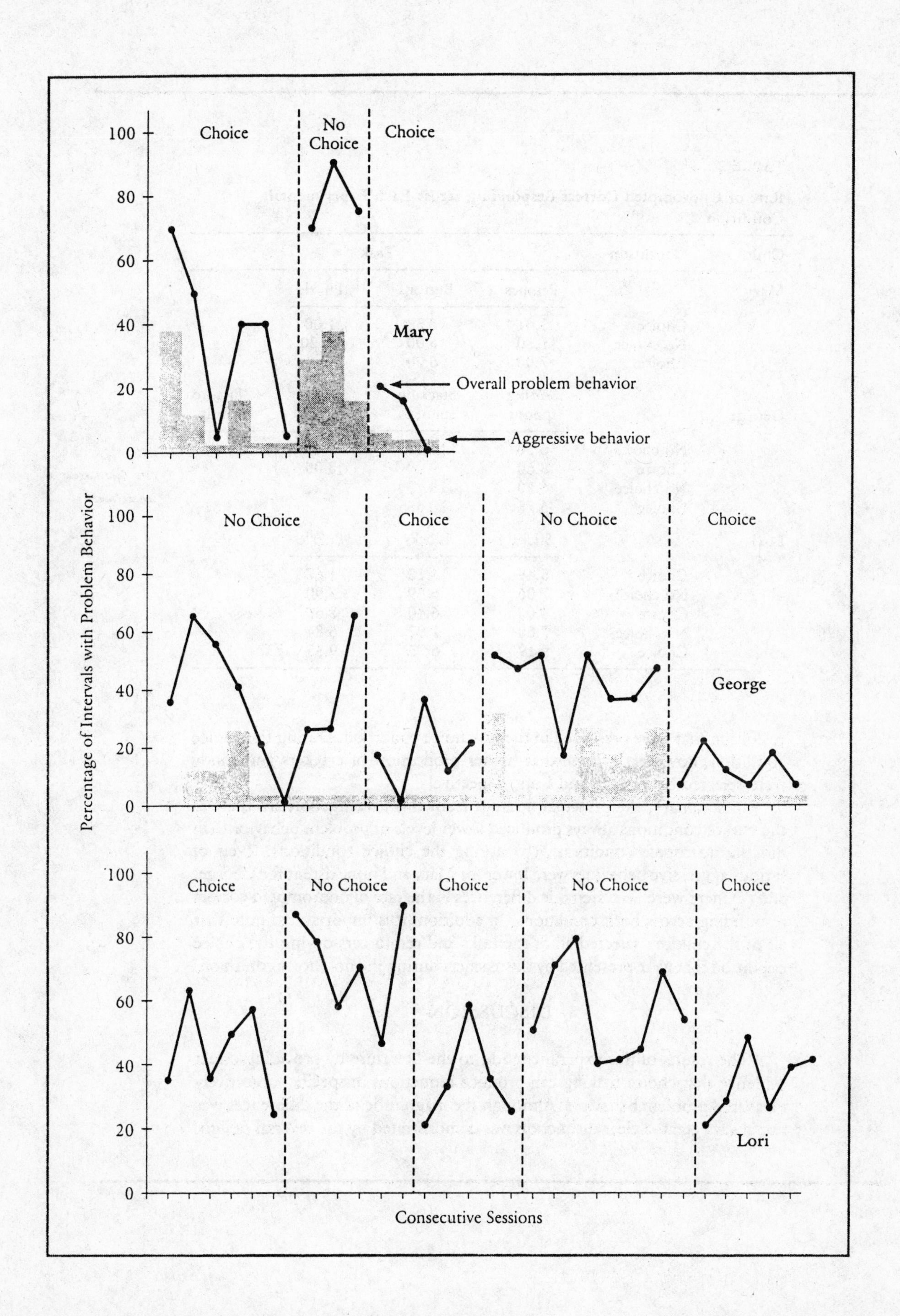
Percentage of Intervals with Problem Behavior
Choice
No Choice
Choice
Mary
Overall problem behavior
Aggressive behavior
No Choice
Choice
No Choice
Choice
George
Choice
No Choice
Choice
No Choice
Choice
Lori
Consecutive Sessions
0
20
40
60
80
100

TABLE 2

Rate of Unprompted Correct Responding across Each Experimental Condition

Child	Condition	Task			
Mary		Pennies	Buttons	Puzzle	
	Choice	3.61	7.58	1.00	
	No choice	5.30	6.00	0.20	
	Choice	7.00	6.00		
George		Sorting spoons	Stacking spindles	Rubber puzzles	Picture cards
	No choice	6.36	10.49	7.89	
	Choice	8.60	9.00	8.00	
	No choice	6.70	10.47		
	Choice	6.75	10.65		3.81
Lori		Sticks	Blocks	Puzzle	
	Choice	5.49	4.13	1.67	
	No choice	7.06	6.89	7.90	
	Choice	8.07	6.40	8.60	
	No choice	7.00	7.02	6.84	
	Choice	9.19	6.75	9.55	

Are these means of percentages?

condition that were presented in the no-choice condition. During the choice condition, however, a somewhat higher proportion of crackers and candy were selected by George and Lori, respectively.

In summary, the principal findings from this investigation are that (a) the choice conditions always produced lower levels of problem behavior than did the no-choice conditions, (b) during the choice conditions, levels of serious aggressive behaviors were lower for Mary and nonexistent for George, and (*c*) there were no systematic differences in the rate of unprompted correct responding across both conditions. In addition, it is important to note that all of the children selected all of the tasks and reinforcers during the choice condition that were presented by the teachers during the no-choice condition.

DISCUSSION

The results of this experiment add to the literature by providing direct evidence that choice making can produce reductions in specific, objectively measured problem behaviors. Although the magnitude of the differences was not always great, a clear distinction was demonstrated by the reversal design.

TABLE 3

Relative Proportion of Therapist Presentation and Child Selection of Tasks and Reinforcers

Child	Condition	Tasks				Reinforcers				
Mary		Pennies	Buttons	Puzzle		Cookie	Juice	Stuffed animals		
	Choice	.29	.59	.12		.50	.20	.30		
	No choice	.25	.25	.50		.67	.33			
	Choice	.40	.40	.20		.42	.13	.45		
George		Sorting spoons	Stacking spindles	Rubber puzzles	Picture cards	Crackers	Candy	Soda	Juice	Potato sticks
	No choice	.41	.45	.14		.26	.35	.0	.39	.0
	Choice	.60	.27	.13		.83	.0	.07	.10	.0
	No choice	.50	.46	.04		.36	.29	.0	.35	.0
	Choice	.17	.33		.50	.60	.05	.11	.03	.21
Lori		Sticks	Blocks	Puzzles		Candy	Crackers	Soda		
	Choice	.41	.24	.35		.65	.16	.19		
	No choice	.38	.27	.35		.33	.33	.34		
	Choice	.32	.27	.41		.78	.12	.10		
	No choice	.31	.34	.35		.35	.28	.37		
	Choice	.36	.21	.43		.69	.21	.10		

Additionally, whereas other studies used preference assessments that were conducted before each session (Dyer, 1987; Koegel at al., 1987), this study showed that simply providing choices of preferred reinforcers and maintenance tasks during the session reduced problem behavior. Thus, it may not be necessary to conduct daily preference assessments to achieve positive results. Indeed, such assessments can be time consuming and, thus, impractical for many practitioners in applied settings. The present procedure of making choices available on a continuing basis was demonstrated to be effective and may be more efficient than previously reported strategies.

It is important to note that although the provision of choice-making opportunities systematically influenced problem behavior, there were no effects on the rate of responding on the instructional tasks. Similar results were found by Cox (1988), who suggested that systematic differences in performance across choice and no-choice conditions might not occur in tasks that have been previously acquired by the study participants. Thus, it is important to evaluate the effects of this procedure on new skills.

Because the independent variable in this study was a package that permitted choices of both reinforcers and tasks, the effects of each element on problem behavior cannot be separated. However, the data on the children's selection of tasks and reinforcers offer some suggestions. Specifically, because Mary selected the puzzle at a relatively low rate during the choice condition, it is possible that this task was less preferred and that the problem behavior served an escape function during the no-choice condition (Carr and Durand, 1985). In contrast, George and Lori selected a particular reinforcer at a relatively high rate during the choice condition. This suggests that for these children, the reinforcers provided by engaging in the task competed with the reinforcers provided by engaging in problem behavior (Dyer, 1987; Lovaas and Newsom, 1976).

Right!

Unclear rationale.

It might be argued that similar results could be achieved by having the teachers deliver optimal proportions of preferred tasks and reinforcers rather than by providing choices. However, a number of studies (e.g., Dyer, 1987; Green et al., 1988; Parsons et al., 1990) have shown that teachers' selections are not as effective in identifying reinforcers as is a procedure of systematic assessment of preferred stimuli. Also, in the present study, Mary's teacher was naive with respect to the experimental hypothesis during all but the last session, and Lori's teacher was naive throughout the entire experiment. Further, during Lori's sessions in the no-choce conditions, the proportions of tasks and reinforcers were nearly equivalent. These controls reduce the potential for the beneficial effects of choice to be influenced by teacher selection of preferred tasks and reinforcers. Additional studies should addresss this issue by implementing a yoking procedure in which equivalent proportions of tasks and reinforcers are presented in the no-choice and choice conditions.

Good.

Rationale is unclear.

Another possible explanation for the results is that the opportunity to choose tasks as well as reinforcers may have been a reinforcer in itself. This hypothesis is supported by a study conducted by Brigham and Sherman (1973) in which children of normal development responded at higher rates during a condition in which they were allowed to choose their reinforcers, as opposed to a condition in which the experimenter selected the reinforcers. Because the reinforcers were the same in both conditions, the authors suggested that the opportunity to choose may have been as important as the reinforcers provided. Along these lines, Monty, Geller, Savage, and Perlmuter (1979) found that college students exhibited improved performance in a learning task when they were offered an attractive choice compared to a condition in which they were offered an unattractive choice. These authors suggested that the positive effects of choice-making opportunities may be attributed to the extent to which a subject perceives control in the situation.

Good control of sequence.

To control for possible sequence effects in this investigation, the order of choice and no-choice conditions was counterbalanced across children. However, it is noteworthy that George's aggression increased in the second no-choice condition. This effect was also reported anecdotally by teachers from classrooms in which choice-making opportunites were introduced and then taken away (Dyer, Williams, Santarcangelo, and Luce, 1987). Given these observations, it is important to investigate the potentially deleterious effects of withholding opportunities for control (i.e., choice) after a period in which choice-making opportunities are provided.

Good point.

Alternative explanation of result.

The children who participated in this study appeared to have preference for specific tangible reinforcers (George and Lori) or tasks (Mary). It is important to determine whether similar results would be found by students who were motivated primarily by social reinforcement. In addition, there is a need for controlled studies examining the effect of choice making on problem behavior in natural settings. In this regard, pilot data collected by the authors suggest that choice-making strategies can be integrated into a variety of everyday activities (Dunlap, Dunlap, Clarke, and Robbins, 1990; Garling, Carroll, Luce, and Dyer, 1987) and that these options can effectively reduce levels of problem behavior.

Good qualification of results.

In summary, this study suggests that choicemaking options provide a simple strategy that can be used to reduce serious problems exhibited by students with severe handicaps. The fact that these results contribute to a growing body of literature that stresses the importance of increasing personal autonomy for persons with severe handicaps indicates that this is an important area of future investigation.

Rather weak conclusion.

References

Bannerman, D. J., Sheldon, J. B., Sherman, J. A., and Harchik, A. E. (1990). Balancing the right to habilitation with the right to personal liberties: The rights of people with developmental disabilities to eat too many doughnuts and take a nap. *Journal of Applied Behavior Analysis, 23;*79–89.

Barlow, D. H., and Hersen, M. (1984). *Single-case experimental designs.* New York: Pergamon Press.

Brigham, T. A., and Sherman, J. A. (1973). Effects of choice and immediacy of reinforcement on single response and switching behavior of children. *Journal of the Experimental Analysis of Behavior, 19;*425–435.

Carr, E. G., and Durand, V. M. (1985). Reducing behavior problems through functional communication training. *Journal of Applied Behavior Analysis, 18;*111–126.

Cox, S. (1988, December). The effects of choice-making on the production rate of three tasks performed by four students with severe handicaps. In E. Siegel-Causey (Chair), *Choice-making as a means of empowerment session: The role of choice-making in the lives of persons with sever handicaps. Implications for teachers, researchers, and personnel preparation programs.* Paper presented at the meeting of the Association for Persons with Severe Handicaps, Washington, DC.

Dunlap, G. (1985). Review of *An educative approach to behavior problems. Journal of the Association for Persons with Severe Handicaps, 10;*237–238.

Dunlap, G., Dunlap, L. K., Clarke, M., and Robbins, F. R. (1990). *Functional assessment and curricular revision in solving the serious behavior challenges of a student with multiple disabilities.* Manuscript submitted for publication.

Dyer, K. (1987). The competition of autistic stereotypes behavior with usual and specially assessed reinforcers. *Research in Developmental Disabilities, 8;*607–626.

PURPOSE/JUSTIFICATION

The purpose is suggested in the abstract and made clear at the end of the introduction, though a clearer statement might have been made, such as: "The purpose is to investigate the efficacy of student choice of task and reinforcer in reducing problem behaviors of severely handicapped children." The study is justified as an extension of previous research and argument favoring this (and other) nonintrusive methods. Ways in which this study differs from prior research are made clear. There appear to be no problems regarding risk, confidentiality, or deception.

PRIOR RESEARCH

Several references support the authors' rationale. While little detail is provided, the outcomes of prior studies are given.

DEFINITIONS

No definitions are provided as such and would be helpful. In further descriptions, the essential terms do become clear (i.e., the particular problem behaviors of each child are described under "dependent variables"; "choice-making" is defined under "design and experimental conditions," and "students with severe handicaps" is defined under "subjects"). While these descriptions clarify the use of these terms in this study, the authors clearly intend them to apply more generally and therefore should ahve defined them accordingly (e.g., "choice" is defined as "providing the student the opportunity to decide what task to work on from a selection provided by the teacher and to choose among several reinforcers previously identified by the teacher," "problem behavior" is defined as "any behavior which is a major impediment to teaching"). Note that use of the term "such as" in clarifying "serious disruptive behavior" (under "Subjects") is not satisfactory, because it does not indicate what other behaviors (e.g., "object misuse" under "Dependent Variables") are included by the authors, in addition to aggression, self-injury, and tantrums.

HYPOTHESES

None are stated. However, a directional hypothesis is clearly implied (that all three children will demonstrate less problem behavior when given a choice of tasks and reinforcers than when these are determined by the teacher). It is unclear what the researchers expected with respect to the other dependent variable (task performance).

SAMPLE

Since this type of design requires the collection of extensive data on very few subjects, generalization is extremely tenuous, as the authors acknowledge indirectly in their suggestion of further studies with different students.* Since the study was, in effect, replicated across three different subjects differing in age, gender, and diagnostic descriptions as well as in the nature of their disruptive behavior, the authors could have made a somewhat stronger argument for generalization of their findings to other severely handicapped students exhibiting disruptive behavior. Limitations to ecological generalization *are* addressed in the authors' recommendation that studies be done in natural, as opposed to contrived, settings and on the acqusition of *new* skills.

INSTRUMENTATION

The basic instrumentation is observational tallying of specific, identified behaviors in 30-second intervals during each session of 10 to 20 minutes. For disruptive behavior, the score used in analysis was the percentage of intervals in which the behavior occurred during each session. For task performance, the score used was the rate of correct responses (presumably obtained by dividing correct responses by total responses) during each session.

The authors' discussion of reliability addresses only observer agreement for which the data are satisfactory. A sizable proportion of sessions were observed by two observers, and the overall agreement across sessions is above 90 percent, although as low as 75 percent for problem behavior in individual sessions.

As is common in this design, consistency across time and content is not specifically addressed. Considerable inconsistency across sessions is expected and shown in Figure 1. In this study, time is mixed in with differences in both task and reinforcer, though these could have been systematically compared to determine consistency across tasks and reinforcers. The important question is whether, despite the fluctuations from session to session, there is sufficient consistency within *conditions* to permit differences *between* conditions to emerge. Visual inspection of Figure 1 strongly indicates that this is the case. Again, as is customary in such studies, long-term reliability and content reliability are of minimal concern, since the focus of the research is on behaviors demonstrated within a highly specified context.

With regard to instrument validity, the absence of discussion reflects reliance on logical or face validity. It is customarily argued that the extent to which behaviors ar precisely described *and* the high degree of observer agreement is sufficient evidence that the variable being tallied is, indeed, the intended variable. While this argument is much more persuasive in studies of this type than in studies assessing more ambiguous variables, such as reading ability or assertiveness, one can question whether observation of "whining," "forceful" pressing of objects to the face, and "destroying" objects is entirely objective. That one observer's "whine" may be another's "complaint" is suggested by the occasional disagreement among observers. In total, however, we would agree that what was observed was, indeed, disruptive behavior.

PROCEDURES/INTERNAL VALIDITY

Procedures are described in considerable detail. It is implied that the experimental teachers were the students' regular teachers, but this should be made clear. This design is an A-B-A-B design (see p. 000), but it does not contain a baseline since the authors' purpose is to compare the effectiveness of two methods rather than to see if either is effective. Thus A and B represent different treatments. This design provides good control over several threats to internal validity (subject characteristics, mortality, testing, history, maturation, regression, location, and data collector characteristics) (see p. 000). Instrument decay and implementor effects are minimal problems in this study. While observers might become less accurate, the alternation of conditions makes it unlikely that one condition was affected more than the other. Each teacher implemented both

* As is customary in studies using this design, the authors do not indicate the basis for selecting these particular children. This is unfortunate since it raises the possibility that those selected were those most likely to provide data supportive of the hypothesis.

methods (see page 000), and, in addition, the finding of similar results for three different teachers is evidence that effectiveness of the "choice" method is not due to teacher characteristics. Data collector bias remains a possible threat but is reduced by using two observers in many sessions. The authors recognize a possible attitudinal threat in that disruptive behavior during "no-choice" may be due to resentment after having "choice" removed. Unfortunately, only one of the three subjects received the no-choice treatment first. This subject did not show greater overall disruptive behavior in the second no-choice condition, but did show an increase in aggressive behavior, an indication that this explanation of results may be important.

DATA ANALYSIS

Results for "disruptive behavior" are shown in the customary charts. In addition, tables present data on the proportions of usage of various tasks and reinforcers (Table 3) and on rate of correct response (Table 2). The altter are presumably averages, although this is unclear.

RESULTS

The study findings are clearly presented and justified in the data. Differences between choice and no-choice conditions consistently favor the choice condition in reducing disruptive behavior for all three children. The data show no consistent differences in task performance across conditions and few consistencies across task and reinforcer preferences. One peculiar result which is not discussed is the generally low rate of successful task performance on tasks identified as within the subjects' response capabilities.

DISCUSSION

The authors recognize limitations on ecological generalizability, as mentioned previously. They also suggest replication with different students and recognize an attitudinal threat to internal validity. They recognize correctly that their study cannot determine the relative importance of the two types of choice (task versus reinforcer). We find the discussion of this point (p. 000) confusing. While the points raised may be good ones, too little data and/or supporting argument is provided. Similarly we do not see why naiveté on the part of teachers is relevant: if teachers had assigned preferred tasks or reinforcers, the data should have been *less* supportive of the hypothesis and there seems to be no reason for teachers to assign less preferred ones.*

The major conclusion of the authors is that the treatment studied (choice-making) *can* produce reductions in specific problem behaviors and they indicate how it is more efficient than previous (daily preference) methods. We find this wording perplexing. When this method of research with severely handicapped students began, it was important to demonstrate that such teaching methods *could* influence behavior since many professionals were skeptical—and this provided a rationale for studying only one or two subjects. Today, however, it is expected that such treatments *will* affect behavior; the question remains as to which are more effective. Thus we would ahve concluded that the choice method was *more* effective than the more common teacher determination of task and reinforcer. This seems a significant finding provided subsequent studies control the attitudinal threat to internal validity and obtain similar results.

* The authors also discuss the possibility that the effectiveness of the choice method may be due to the provision of choice itself rather than the nature of what is chosen. Note that this is not a threat to internal validity because this interpretation is consistent with the hypothesis—it simply attempts to explain further the reason for the method's effectiveness.

APPENDIX G

Analysis of an Observational Study

From: Journal of Cross-Cultural Psychology, 20(3):244–262, 1989.

Pupil Occupancy Time in Classroom Settings Across Cultures

M. M. Scott
Indiana University

Abstract

Two primary purposes of this study were (1) to explore the conceptual and theoretical relationship between the concept of culture and that of behavior settings as described by Barker and (2) to demonstrate the applicability of ecological methods to the study of behavior cross-culturally. In this exploratory investigation, third-grade classes were studied from Apache, Papago, and Anglo groups varying along a dimension of cultural distinctiveness. Analysis of segment logs (natural habitat records of full days of classroom behavior) showed many more behavioral similarities at the molar level *among the three groups than differences. Several possible interpretations of these findings are explored. Cultural differences unquestionably influenced third-grade behavior, but at molecular and global levels. Comparisons with a study done 20 years ago showed substantial stability of thrid-grade classroom behavior, with some shifts in teacher leadership patterns. Methodological implications are also discussed.*

Two primary purposes of the work to be reported here were (1) to explore the conceptual and theoretical relationship between the concept of culture and that of behavior settings (Barker, 1968) and (2) to demonstrate the applicability of ecological methods to the study of behavior cross-culturally.

BACKGROUND

Ecological Studies

Barker (1968; Barker and Wright, 1955/1971) defined a behavior setting as a naturally occurring unit of the environment with specific influence on and control over behavior. A behavior setting is a combined set of (1) time, place, and object props *and* (2) an attached, standing pattern of behavior. *Both* clusters of attributes are necessary to a behavior setting. Examples of settings which cultural distinctiveness influenced daily classroom activities could then be tested. Third grades were selected for comparability to earlier work (Gump, 1967, 1969).

Entry to the schools was through a key person in the educational system—a principal on the Apache reservation and in the Anglo city and the director of education for the Papago tribe. Following approval of the research proposal by these officials, principals of schools meeting criteria stated above were interviewed to identify potential third-grade classes for observation. Classes were identified as potentials if they appeared to have a fairly regular program with fairly regular students for examples; not a special education class and if the teacher was a regular teacher that is; not a substitute or a temporary teacher. Nine teacher were approached, the study explained to them, and their participation solicited. Eight agreed to participate. Owing to time constraints, six of these classrooms were studied. All the teachers were Anglo. There are still very few Indian teachers.

Is this all of them?

How were they selected?

Observations

Orientation and adaptation preceded any data collection. When the observer first appeared in the classroom, the teacher usually made a brief announcement about her presence and asked the children to ignore her and go about their usual activities. The observer then remained in the classroom taking notes until it appeared that most of the children had stopped attending to her. Specific criteria for judging adaptation have been described by Scott (1980). Adaptation was accomplished in all cases in one or two sessions of several hours each. All data were collected by the same observer, who had been trained to criterion using procedures described by Scott (1976).

What criterion?

Data were collected in the form of full-day segment logs for each classroom day. Segment logs are a modification of chronicles, described by Gump (1967). The observer was in the room before any pupils arrived, began taking data with the arrival of the first pupil, and continued until the last pupil left for the day, with interruptions of the record when no pupils were in the classroom (e.g., lunch, recess). The focus of the segment log was the various activities taking place in the classroom, and the observer took sufficiently detailed notes to permit transcription immediately following the observation day of a full behavioral record at the molar level (Barker and Wright, 1955/1971; Scott, 1980). The focus was on the behavior, and interpretations or inferences were avoided. Numbers of children and adults in each activity were recorded, as were time notations. An excerpt from a segment log is presented in Figure 1. Two full-day segment logs were taken on each classroom. Days for the observations were described by the teachers as typical. Days when markedly different activities were planned, such as field trips or gymnastic days, were excluded. Otherwise, the classroom schedules were left free to vary naturally.

Good to include.
Small sample of days.

References would help here.

Background on American Indian Groups

No studies were identified on behavior settings in American Indian cultures. Two groups were selected for the present study, the White Mountain Apache, a branch of the Western Apache, in northern Arizona, and the Papago, or Desert People, in southern Arizona. Both of these groups are stable, with intact, complex cultures and fully functioning tribal governments. Both are located on their original home ranges. The two groups may vary in the amount of regular ongoing interaction with Anglo culture, groups, and institutions, perhaps for reasons of geography and history. Both groups have a number of productive working relationships between their cultures and those of Anglos; for example, tribal leaders regularly interact with government and social leaders elsewhere, and members of the tribe move back and forth as they wish. The Apache people, however, seem to have conducted a substantial number of their activities within their own group, whereas the Papago, over the years, have had more interaction with Anglo groups (Kelly, 1974; Underhill, 1969). Again, this difference may reflect historical and geographical factors. For example, the Apache reservation is in a mountainous and remote area of Arizona and there is frequent snow in winter, whereas the Papago reservation is only 50 miles from Tucson and the weather is more temperate.

At least three trends may be seen. First, the members of both the Apache and Papago tribes find themselves somewhat between worlds. The U.S. government's historical reservation policies encouraged separatism. In both tribes there has been a recent resurgence of interest and participation in cultural traditions. Apache children are learning ancient songs and rituals. Papago students in elementary school learn Papago language and history. Second, there is considerable variation among the members of each tribal group. For example, neither group is unanimous on the desirability of returning to ancient traditions and on the appropriateness of forging new relationships with Anglo culture. Third, Apaches and Papagos are subject to the constraints placed by the beautiful yet sometimes harsh mountain and desert regions.

METHOD

Participants

Participants were third-grade classes from three population subgroups: Anglo, Western Apache, and Papago, or Desert People. The two American Indian groups were selected as examples of distinct cultural groups with geography and cultural and governmental patterns separate from the dominant mainstream. In each group, however, there were a number of schools conducted under the aegis of the state department of public instruction, which helped to hold constant school organizational pattern. The degree to are Thompson's Drugstore, Tigers' basketball game, Mrs. Smith's third grade. Barker (1968) has described procedures for conducting a behavior setting survey. The K-21 Index is used to determine which settings are independent and which part of some larger setting.

Several studies have shown that the effect of these behavior settings is, in many cases, at least equal to that of individual difference variables and frequently more powerful in explaining behavior. For example, Gump (1964) showed that the amount of hostile behavior emitted by a boy at camp depended more on the setting than on the boy. This does not obscure the fact that hostility varied among boys. It simply shows that setting was a more powerful explanatory construct than individual differences. This setting effect has now been replicated across a range of situations and groups: large and small high schools (Barker and Gump, 1964), college students (Baird, 1969; Bowman, 1980), marginal and nonmarginal faculty (Lund, 1982), hyperactive children (Hatfield, 1983). The conclusion reached from this research is that the naturally occurring behavior of many kinds of human beings is heavily influenced by their settings.

Little detail provided.

Cross-Cultural Studies

Research in cross-cultural psychology on the present question has yielded limited results. No studies were identified that used behavior settings as a structural classroom variable in non-Anglo cultures. Other cross-cultural studies provide some information on related variables, such as perception (Jahoda and McGurk, 1982; Pick, 1975; Wagner and Stevenson, 1982; Werner, 1979; Whorf, 1956), language (Chomsky, 1968), and social behavior (Mails, 1974; Mead, 1978; Mead and Wolfenstein, 1955; Whiting and Whiting, 1960). The general conclusion reached from these studies is that culture is a major influence on human behavior at many levels.

Is this true?

Relationship between Culture and Behavior Settings

The relationship between the concept of culture and the concept of behavior settings is largely unexplored. Ecological theorists (Barker and Wright, 1955/1971; Barker and Schoggen, 1973) suggest that behavior settings are embedded in culture in that they represent the operating environments that cultures provide their members. Different cultures, then, should show different behavior settings, and similar cultures similar settings. At a minimum, cultures, through their social organziations, should mediate the relationship between the physical environment and behavior, as suggested by Ogbu (1981).

Purely theoretical justification.

Why should it be explored?

Why is this important?

Research Questions

Research questions addressed in this study were: (1) Does the structure of the molar units of behavior in third-grade classes vary as a function of cultural group membership? (2) If so, how?

Purely theoretical justification.

Why is this important?

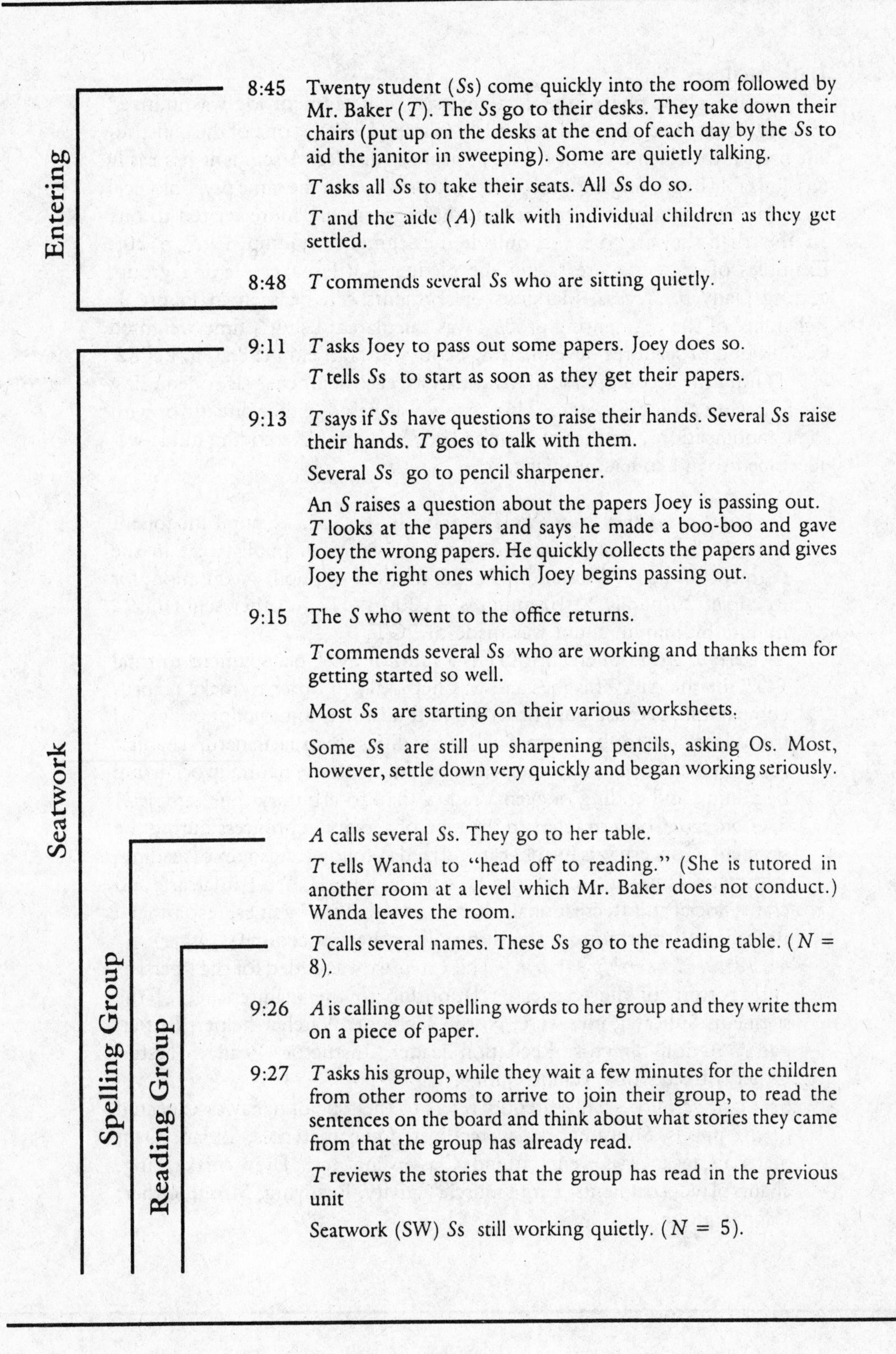

8:45 Twenty student (*Ss*) come quickly into the room followed by Mr. Baker (*T*). The *Ss* go to their desks. They take down their chairs (put up on the desks at the end of each day by the *Ss* to aid the janitor in sweeping). Some are quietly talking.

T asks all *Ss* to take their seats. All *Ss* do so.

T and the aide (*A*) talk with individual children as they get settled.

8:48 *T* commends several *Ss* who are sitting quietly.

9:11 *T* asks Joey to pass out some papers. Joey does so.

T tells *Ss* to start as soon as they get their papers.

9:13 *T* says if *Ss* have questions to raise their hands. Several *Ss* raise their hands. *T* goes to talk with them.

Several *Ss* go to pencil sharpener.

An *S* raises a question about the papers Joey is passing out. *T* looks at the papers and says he made a boo-boo and gave Joey the wrong papers. He quickly collects the papers and gives Joey the right ones which Joey begins passing out.

9:15 The *S* who went to the office returns.

T commends several *Ss* who are working and thanks them for getting started so well.

Most *Ss* are starting on their various worksheets.

Some *Ss* are still up sharpening pencils, asking Os. Most, however, settle down very quickly and began working seriously.

A calls several *Ss*. They go to her table.

T tells Wanda to "head off to reading." (She is tutored in another room at a level which Mr. Baker does not conduct.) Wanda leaves the room.

T calls several names. These *Ss* go to the reading table. (N = 8).

9:26 *A* is calling out spelling words to her group and they write them on a piece of paper.

9:27 *T* asks his group, while they wait a few minutes for the children from other rooms to arrive to join their group, to read the sentences on the board and think about what stories they came from that the group has already read.

T reviews the stories that the group has read in the previous unit

Seatwork (*SW*) *Ss* still working quietly. (N = 5).

Data Analyses

During phase one of the data analysis, each segment log was unitized into segments. A segment, as defined by Gump (1967), is one of the constituent parts into which a classroom day naturally divides. A segment has easily recognizable beginning and end points and proceeds in the same psychological direction throughout. "Events within the segment are more related to one another than they are to events outside the segment" (Gump, 1967, p. 20). Examples of segments are saying the pledge, Rattlesnakes reading group, getting ready for recess. Markings of segments can be seen in Figure 1. Reliability of the segmenting process was calculated, using a time-weighted formula and procedures developed by Scott and Hatfield (1985), to be .82.

Unclear, although referenced.

During the second phase of data analysis, each segment was coded using the following category system. This system was based, either directly or with some modifications, on that of Gump (1967). A complete coding guide was developed to aid coders in their task.

Good.

1. *Pupil occupancy time (POT).* This is the sum of pupil inhabitant minutes for each segment. In segments where all pupils were in the segment for its total duration, POT is number of pupils × duration; for example; 20 pupils × 10 minutes + 200 POT. In other segments, a minute-by-minute count was made of POT.
2. *Percent POT.* Percent POT is a ratio of POT per segment to total POT for the day. This measure was necessary in order to make records comparable, because both observation time and number of pupils varied from classroom to classroom. Such inequalities are usual in natural habitat research inasmuch as data collection conforms to the naturally occurring beginning and ending of events rather than to arbitrary time samples.)
3. *Concern.* Concern refers to the type of activity in progress during the segment. Concern was further categorized as follows: Academic (reading, arithmetic, language, social studies, science, mixed); Arts (ritual, arts and crafts; Social and Recreational (sharing, story, "fun" games, rest, other); Procedural (transition-in, transition-out, other procedural); Other.
4. *Teacher leadership pattern.* This category was coded for the "persistent" pattern of the teacher's relationship to the maintenance of the segment. Subcategories were: Not in segment; Watcher-helper; Participator; Action director; Recitation leader; Instuctor; Reader; Tester; Other; Mixed; Aide; Cannot judge.
5. *Pupil activity.* This category refers to the type of behavior expected of the pupils. Subcategories were: Rest; Own materials, attend; Own materials, task; Class events, attend; Class events, task; Draw/make; Sing, chant, play instruments; Large muscle activity; Readying; Mixed; Other; Cannot judge.

6. *Pacing.* This category refers to the signal source (Kounin and Gump, 1974) for the students' behaviors, or the cue for action. Subcategories were: No pace; Self-pace; External pace, teacher; External pace, aide; External pace, other individual child; External pace, other children; External pace, other (audiotape, movie, dog); Mixed (two or more of the above); Other; Cannot judge.
7. *Location.* This is the proportion of the room in which the activity took place. Subcategories were: All or most (75% to 100%) of the room; Half to three fourths of the room; One fourth to one half of the room; Small portion of the room.

Scoring agreement only.

Reliabilities for the coding were calculated, again using a time-weighted formula (Scott and Hatfield, 1985), to be .96 (location), .87 (concern), .73 (teacher leadership pattern), .79 (pupil activity), and .70 (pacing).

Good idea, but poor justification.

Variability between the two segment logs taken on each classroom was compared with variability across the whole sample. Within-classroom variability was judged to be substantially less than between-classroom variability; therefore, each segment log was treated as a separate unit.

RESULTS

Behavioral output. A total of 59 hours and 54 minutes of observational data was collected. Behavioral output data by class are presented in Table 1. Actual observational time per class averaged 4 hours, 58 minutes, but there

TABLE 1

Behavioral Output Data

Record	Obs. time	Segments	Total POT	Seg./Hr.
1	6'24"	18	10351	2.8
2	5'25"	19	7924	3.5
3	4'42"	30	5330	6.4
4	3'32"	25	3737	7.1
5	4'21"	25	5281	5.8
6	4'26"	24	4901	5.4
7	4'30"	16	3917	3.6
8	5'24"	21	5598	3.9
9	5'41"	33	6058	5.8
10	6'00"	29	6826	4.8
11	4'38"	25	5857	5.4
12	4'51"	21	4775	4.3
$\bar{X}$	4'58"	23.8	5852.7	4.9

was considerable variation among the classrooms (3′32″ to 6′24″), the longest record being nearly twice as long as the shortest.

Pupil occupancy time (POT) (Gump, 1967) is considered to be the best measure of the actual amount of behaving time available for study. As described earlier, POT is the actual number of pupil inhabitant minutes in any given activity. POT varied from 3,737 to 10,351 pupil minutes per day. Percent POT was used as the main dependent measure in this study, because it permitted comparability of records of varying durations and varying numbers of pupils. It also equated periods of time when more than one segment was in progress simultaneously—for examples; reading group, seatwork, and spelling test. POT and observation time are, of course, related (r + .84, p = .001).

There was an average of 23.8 segments per day in the classes studied, with a range of 16 to 33. This is somewhat lower than Gump's (1967) finding of 31 segments per day. A rather interesting inverse relationship obtained between number of segments per hour and observation time, r + −.64 (p = .012). The record with the longest observation time had the fewest segments per hour, and vice versa. Total POT was also inversely correlated with segments per hour (r = −.58, p = .023). The causative factor in this relationship is not clear and needs further study. Schedule differences may have affected this relationship.

Interpretation?

p values are meaningless.

Concern. Two things stand out in regard to the concern of class segments as presented in Table 2. The first is that there is substantially more similarity among the classes of population subgroups than there is difference. Far and away the majority of POT in all classes is spent on academic matters, and these POTs actually fall within a fairly narrow range (68% to 74%). To be sure, academic work is the primary objective of school classes, but there appears to be considerable agreement on the amount of academic work appropriate in this setting. There is also considerable similarity among the population subgroups. There is also considerable similarity among the population subgroups in the next most frequent category, procedural. Social/recreational activities and arts show variation by subgroup, and these are inversely related to each other. It should be remembered that this would be true by definition inasmuch as percent POT is an ipsative measure. These categories are also particularly vulnerable to scheduling differences.

The second impression apparent from Table 2 is the substantial similarity of all three groups of classes to those described by Gump (1967) in Kansas despite the interval of nearly 20 years. Apparently, American education is a fairly stable enterprise.

Teacher leadership pattern. Again, the similarity among the population subgroups is striking, as seen in Table 3. The patterns are also somewhat surprising; for example, the most frequent strategy employed by all teachers

Need standard deviations

TABLE 2

Mean Percent Pupil Occupancy Time in Segments of Various Concerns

Concern of segment	Anglo	Apache	Papago	Gump (1967)
Reading	5.60	11.16	13.91	10.3
Arithmetic	12.61	14.67	14.33	10.8
Language	13.71	16.56	12.87	12.4
Social Studies	10.24	2.00	9.94	7.1*
Science	3.75	1.78	3.29	
Mixed	22.87	21.72	19.24	31.2
All academic	68.78	67.89	73.58	71.8
Ritual	.71	.59	. . .	
Arts and Crafts	—	2.50	7.68	
All arts	—	3.09	7.68	6.7
Sharing	2.90	. . .	. . .	
Story	4.07	5.64	1.83	
Fun games	. . .	2.21	. . .	
Rest	. . .	.76	1.10	
Other	10.95	3.71	.56	
All social/recreational	17.92	12.32	3.49	9.4
Transition in	6.59	3.52	2.97	
Transition out	3.97	5.79	4.92	
Other	1.59	4.44	5.84	
All procedural	12.15	13.75	13.73	11.8
All other	1.20	2.97	1.52	

* Gump's 7.1 represents a composite of social studies and science scores.

Circled values appear to indicate that differences do exist, contrary to author's statement.

Cultural mixing

Good qualification.

is that of watcher-helper. This contrasts with the traditional view of a teacher as either a recitation leader or an action director, which was, indeed, the case in Gump's data. This difference between the current data and those of Gump may be due to a coding artifact. It appears that if the teacher was predominantly not in the segment, Gump coded not in segment, whereas if the teacher was in and out of the segment but intermittently attending to the children, in this study we coded watcher-helper. Inasmuch as this decision is particularly applicable to the seatwork segment, which is often a long segment, this may account for the differences in these two categories across the data bases. Finally, it appears that teachers are able to emit complex behaviors in order to keep their settings going: the second most frequent strategy employed by teachers from all groups was a mix of strategies.

Pupil activity. Pupils in all groups spent the greatest percent POT per-

TABLE 6

Mean Percent Pupil Occupancy Time in Segments in Various Locations

Location	Anglo	Apache	Papago
All or most of room	94.41	85.36	85.70
Half to $\frac{3}{4}$	—	. . .	. . .
One-fourth to $\frac{1}{2}$	. . .	.62	. . .
Small portion of room	5.60	14.02	14.29

remarkably similar. This was particularly true with respect to the dominant behaviors—that is, those ranked first or second in each category. There aer several possible interpretations of this finding.

First, the fact that all the teachers were Anglo may have been the controlling variable. It could be argued that teachers are the major initiators and controllers of the program of the behavior setting and that they simply imposed their cultural template for this setting on it. In order to determine whether the culture of the teacher is the controlling factor, Anglo, Apache, and Papago teachers would have to be compared. Because few Apache and Papago individuals have as yet completed teacher training, such a comparison is virtually impossible to conduct.

Schools from the Apache and Papago samples were selected from among those operated under the aegis of the state department of education (in contrast to schools operated by the Bureau of Indian Affairs, church groups, or independently contracted groups) in order to avoid a potential bias based on organizational structure. This variable, however, may have been sufficiently strong to override others.

It could be argued that public schooling in the United States is largely under the control of the Anglo culture, regardless of the participants. That *most* schools are Anglo in character would surprise no one, but that any, or even most, cultural differences are lacking in influence of the tribal councils was insufficient to permit the demonstration of cultural differences in these educational settings at this level of analysis.

Second, in the Apache and Papago cultures there is a systematic attempt to provide opportunities for children of the culture to learn both Apache or Papago culture and Anglo culture, and public school is one of the major clusters of settings for learning Anglo culture. Discussions with people from both Indian groups gave some support to this explanation.

Third, more similarities among groups than expected may have appeared as a function of the level of analysis. The unit of analysis for this study, the behavior setting (or segment), is a unit at the molar level. It may be that

TABLE 4

Mean Percent Pupil Occupancy Time in Segments with Various Types of Pupil Activity

Pupil Activity Types	Anglo	Apache	Papago	Gump (1967)
Rest	—	2.38	1.10	.8
Own materials, attend	—	—	3.43	.2
Own materials, task	37.47	37.15	29.06	35.6
Class events, attend	26.44	14.18	28.72	36.7
Class events, task	2.56	10.40	2.06	9.8
Draw/make	. . .	2.50	7.69	2.8
Sign, chart, play	. . .	.59	. . .	3.5
Large-muscle activity	. . .	3.71	.17	1.1
Readying	10.56	10.90	11.84	9.3
Mixed	23.00	13.43	11.81	
Other	. . .	4.77	.91	
CNJ	. . .	. . .	3.21	

And again, the circled values suggest differences do exist.

to be very contained, usually using only a small portion of the room. In fact, intermediate amounts of space were infrequently used.

DISCUSSION

Explaining the Similarities among Third-Grade Classrooms

Despite substantial differences in the cultures of the three population subgroups, the structures of the third-grade classroom day in each were

TABLE 5

Mean Percent Pupil Occupancy Time in Segments with Various Types of Pacing

Type of Pacing	Anglo	Apache	Papago
No pace	—	.76	1.10
Self pace	46.88	41.95	45.14
External pace, teacher	16.75	27.98	24.06
External pace, aide	2.90	3.91	9.68
External pace, child	.44	.91	. . .
External pace, children	1.16	2.49	. . .
External pace, other	13.04	.12	1.79
Mixed	18.85	21.69	18.22
Other	. . .	. . .	. . .
CNJ	. . .	.19	. . .

And again, the circled values suggest differences do exist.

TABLE 3

Mean Percent Pupil Occupancy Time in Segments with Various Teacher Leadership Patterns

Teacher leadership pattern	Anglo	Apache	Papago	Gump (1967)
Not in segment	7.48	5.15	3.12	22.5
Watcher-Helper	32.16	30.08	30.95	17.2
Participator	13.04	2.65	2.19	.2
Action Director	14.47	11.77	14.97	23.1
Recitation Leader	9.10	6.84	9.17	27.8
Instructor	.47	2.08	.76	3.2
Reader	4.07	5.05	1.83	3.1
Tester	—	1.69	.68	2.7
Other	. . .	. . .	1.03	
Mixed	19.25	29.85	25.62	
Aide	. . .	4.87	7.85	
CNJ*	. . .	. . .	1.83	

* Cannot judge.

Again, the circled values appear to indicate that differences do exist.

forming a task for which each person had her or his own materials, such as doing math worksheets, reading silently, or coloring (Table 4). The second-ranked percent POT for all groups was listening to the teacher explain how to multiply, chanting the multiplication tables, and so on. Either mixed or readying ranked third and readying or mixed fourth. A good amount of time does seem to be spent in classrooms in preparation for subsequent activities. Again, there are similarities to Gump's earlier data in the two top-ranked categories and similarity in readying but more dispersion after that.

Pacing. This category is similar to one used by Gump but with substantial modifications. Again, the dominant feature is the similarity among groups (Table 5). A somewhat surprising finding was the large percent POT paced by the children themselves, this category being ranked first in all classes. Apparently the traditional model of the teacher as the main source of direction in the classroom has given way to one of children being responsible for directing themselves. Activities paced by mixed sources ranked either second or third in all classes, as did activities paced by the teacher. After these categories, differences among groups appeared.

Location. As can be seen from Table 6, far and away the greatest percent POT in third-grade classes of all population subgroups is spent using all or most of the room. What the data may be reflecting is that when small-group instruction occurs, the number of children involved relative to the total number of children in class is sufficiently small to disporportionately affect the percent POT. Further, when small groups do work together, they appear cultural differences tend to appear at other levels—for example, molecular and global (Tolman, 1932; Scott, 1980). Some anecdotal evidence emerged during the study in support of this contention. For example, at the molecular level, in both Apache and Papago classes there was a fairly high incidence of drumming on desks in the pattern of the major percussion accompaniment to many Indian songs. While such activities might be seen occasionally in Anglo classrooms, they were a more frequent occurrence in the Indian classrooms. At the global level, one day several little Apache boys acted out the roles of various individuals in a ceremonial dance and later discussed which of them had special powers. In the Papago schools an educator told of a boy who had difficulty understanding that he was not to leave school of his own volition and go across the street to the store. A visit to his home in the desert revealed that he was expected to range several miles from home to gather firewood and to do this without either permission or supervision.

A final possibility is that third grades may be mostly under the control of a set of variables that are very similar across cultures—namely, the developmental characteristics of 8-year-olds. Learning, at least in literate societies, might be most efficiently accomplished by presentation of material—by either reading, listening to reading or discussion, or a combination—followed by practice, such as doing exercises of some kind.

Ecological Methods in the Cross-Cultural Study of Behavior

Methods from ecological psychology are considered to be appropriate for studying behavior across cultures. They permit the study of the environment and behavior in a single, integrated unit—that is, the behavior setting (Barker, 1968; Wicker, 1979, 1987). They also permit the investigator to focus intensively at the molar level on the behavior of groups (segment logs, as in this study, or chronicles; see Gump, 1967) or on the behavior of individuals (specimen records, Barker & Wright, 1955/1971; chronologs, Scott, 1980).

References

Baird, L. L. (1969). Big school, small school; A critical examination of the hypothesis. *Journal of Educational Pscyhology, 60;*253–260.

Barker, R. G. (1968). *Ecological psychology.* Stanford, CA: Stanford University Press.

Barker, R. G., and Gump, P. V. (1964). *Big school, small school.* Stanford, CA: Stanford University Press.

Barker, R. G., & Schoggen, P. (1973). *Qualities of community life.* San Francisco: Jossey-Bass.

Barker, R. G., & Wright, H. W. (1971). *Midwest and its children.* Hamden, CT: Archon Books. (Originally published 1955).

Bowman, R. W. (1980). The behavior of field-dependent and field-independent students as assessed by an ecological approach (Doctoral dissertation, Indiana University). *Dissertation Abstracts International, 41;*987A.

Chomsky, N. (1968). *Language and mind.* San Diego, CA: Harcourt Brace Jovanovich.
Gump, P. V. (1964). Environmental guidance of the classroom behavioral system. In B. J. Biddle & W. J. Ellena (Eds.), *Contemporary research on teacher effectiveness.* New York: Holt, Rinehart and Winston.
Gump, P. V. (1967). *The classroom behavior setting: Its nature and relation to student behavior* (Final Report on Project No. 2453, Bureau No. 5-0334, Grant No. OE-4-10-207). Washington, DC: U.S. Office of Education.
Gump, P. V. (1969). Intra-setting analysis: The third grade classroom as a special but instructive case. In E. P. Willems & H. L. Raush (Eds.), *Naturalistic viewpoints in psychological research.* New York: Holt, Rinehart & Winston.
Hatfield, J. (1983). The behavior of hyperactive childen and unlabeled peers across classroom subsettings: An ecological analysis (Doctoral dissertation, Indiana University, 1982). *Dissertation Abstracts International, 43;*260A.
Jahoda, G., and McGurk, H. (1982). The development of picture perception in children from different cultures. In D. A. Wagner and H. W. Stevenson (Eds.), *Cultural perspectives on child development.* New York: W. H. Freeman.
Kelly, W. H. (1974). The Papago Indians of Arizona. In D. A. Horr (Ed.), *American Indian ethnohistory: Indians of the southwest: Papago Indians III.* New York: Garland Press.

PURPOSE/JUSTIFICATION

The stated purposes are theoretical and methodological rather than practical; this is consistent with publication in a journal oriented toward psychology rather than education. The author's justification rests on previous work showing the importance of studying behavior settings such as classrooms and demonstrating the influence of culture on behavior in general. The author implies that studying cultural differences in behavioral settings is important but does not make the reasons explicit. Presumably, implications would include better resolutions of conflicts between cultural and classroom expectations. We believe a strong case could have been made in terms of implications for educational practice, but this was not done.

PRIOR RESEARCH

The author states that no studies were found which were directly related to this one. This appears to be a major oversight since there have been studies comparing classroom behaviors across cultures. The research cited is not directly related to the present study but does support the justification.

DEFINITIONS

A good definition of "behavior setting" is provided; the reader presumably would agree that a classroom fits this definition. Culture is not defined, and we believe it should be. Finally, much clarification would have been provided by a definition of"structure of molar units of behavior." The reader must infer meaning from the observation coding system—a kind of "operational" definition. Examination of the observation system shows that there are in fact five dependent variables: concern, teacher leadership pattern, pupil activity, pacing, and location, each of which is adequately defined though some subcategories are still ambiguous (e.g., "participator," "reader")